WAYS
OF
WRITING

WAYS

WILLIAM F. IRMSCHER
University of Washington

OF

WRITING

McGRAW-HILL BOOK COMPANY
New York   St. Louis   San Francisco
London   Sydney   Toronto   Mexico   Panama

WAYS OF WRITING

ACKNOWLEDGMENTS

Richard D. Altick, excerpt from *The Scholar Adventurers*, 1966, pp. 224–225. Published by The Free Press.

James Baldwin, excerpt from "The American Dream and the American Negro" by James Baldwin, March, 1965, from *The New York Times Magazine.* Copyright © 1965 by The New York Times Company. Reprinted by permission.

Jacques Barzun, excerpt from "Detection and the Literary Art" reprinted from *The Delights Of Detection,* edited by Jacques Barzun. By permission of Abelard-Schuman, Ltd. All rights reserved.

Ruth Benedict, excerpt from Chapter IV, in *Patterns of Culture,* 1934, by Ruth Benedict. Reprinted by permission of Houghton Mifflin Company, Publishers.

Arthur E. Bestor, excerpt from "Aimlessness in Education" by Arthur E. Bestor, *Science Monthly,* Vol. 75, pp. 109–116, 1952.

Walter Blair, excerpt from "Story of the Bad Little Boy," from *Selected Shorter Writings of Mark Twain,* edited by Walter Blair, 1962. Reprinted by permission of Houghton Mifflin Company, Publishers.

Rachel L. Carson, excerpt from *The Sea Around Us,* 1951, by Rachel L. Carson. By permission of Oxford University Press.

V. G. Childe, excerpt from *Society and Knowledge* by V. G. Childe, Harper & Row, 1956. By permission of Harper and Row, Publishers.

Morton Cronin, excerpt from "The American Intellectual," *AAUP Bulletin,* Summer, 1958. By permission of The American Association of University Professors.

E. E. Cummings, excerpt reprinted by permission of the publishers from *i: Six Nonlectures* by E. E. Cummings. Harvard University Press, Cambridge, Mass. Copyright 1953, by E. E. Cummings.

Wilson Follett, excerpt from "Sabotage in Springfield" by Wilson Follett. Appeared in *Atlantic Monthly,* Vol. 209, January, 1962. Copyright ©

1961 by the Atlantic Monthly Company, Boston, Mass. Reprinted by permission of Mrs. Margaret Follett and *Atlantic Monthly.*

Freedman Morris, excerpt from "Wonderful Town?" Appeared in *The New Republic,* Vol. 136, June 10, 1957, pp. 12–13.

Jean Giraudoux, excerpt from "Paris Impromptu." Appeared in *The Tulane Drama Review,* III, Summer, 1959, p. 119, tr. by Rima Drell Reck. Reprinted by permission of *The Drama Review* (NYU).

James Joyce, excerpt from *Finnegans Wake,* 1939, p. 3. Published by The Viking Press, New York.

Alfred Kazin, excerpt from *A Walker in the City,* 1951, by Alfred Kazin. Reprinted by permission of Harcourt, Brace and World.

Jack Kerouac, excerpt from *The Subterraneans* by Jack Kerouac. By permission of Grove Press, Inc. Copyright © 1958 by Jack Kerouac.

Joseph Wood Krutch, excerpt from *The Voice of the Desert,* by Joseph Wood Krutch. Reprinted by permission of William Morrow and Company, Inc. Copyright © 1954, 1955 by Joseph Wood Krutch.

D. H. Lawrence, excerpt from "Cocksure Women and Hensure Men" in *Phoenix II* by D. H. Lawrence, edited by Warren Roberts and Harry T. Moore. Copyright 1928 by the Forum Publishing Company, 1956 by Frieda Lawrence Ravagli. Reprinted by permission of The Viking Press, Inc.

Russell Lynes, excerpt from *A Surfeit of Honey* by Russell Lynes, 1957. By permission of Harper and Row, Publishers.

Marshall McLuhan, excerpt from *Understanding Media* by Marshall Mc-Luhan. Copyright 1964 by Marshall McLuhan. Reprinted by permission of McGraw-Hill Book Company.

H. L. Mencken, excerpt from *The American Language* by H. L. Mencken. Copyright 1936 by Alfred A. Knopf, Inc., and renewed 1964 by August Mencken and Mercantile Safe Deposit Trust Co. Reprinted by permission of the publisher.

Samuel Miller, excerpt from "The Evolution of Religion" by Samuel Miller. *Saturday Review,* November 14, 1959. Copyright Saturday Review, Inc., 1959.

Herbert J. Muller, excerpt from *Issues of Freedom* by Herbert J. Muller. Reprinted by permission of Harper and Row, Publishers.

George Jean Nathan, excerpt from Chapter XV in *Living Philosophies,* 1941. Published by the World Publishing Company.

NCTE, excerpt from *The Students' Right to Read,* 1962, by permission of the National Council of Teachers of English.

Sean O'Faolain, excerpt from *The Vanishing Hero.* Copyright © 1956, 1957 by Sean O'Faolain. Reprinted with permission of Atlantic-Little, Brown and Company, and Sean O'Faolain.

George Orwell, excerpt from "Politics and the English Language" in *Shooting an Elephant and Other Essays* by George Orwell. Reprinted by permission of Harcourt, Brace and World, Inc., Miss Sonia Brownell, and Secker and Warburg.

Luigi Pirandello, excerpt from *Naked Masks: Five Plays* by Luigi Pirandello. Edited by Eric Bentley. Copyright 1922, by E. P. Dutton and Co., Inc. Renewal 1950 in the names of Stefano, Fausto, and Lietta Pirandello. Reprinted by permission of the publishers.

Washington Platt and Ross Baker, excerpt from "The Relation of the Scientific 'Hunch' to Research." First appeared in the *Journal of Chemical Education,* 8, 1975, (1931). Reprinted by permission.

Max Rafferty, excerpt from the *Los Angeles Times,* June 25, 1967. Copyright 1968 by the Los Angeles Times. Reprinted with permission.

Herbert Read, excerpt reprinted by permission of the American publisher, Horizon Press, and Faber & Faber, Ltd. From *Selected Writings: Poetry and Criticism* by Herbert Read. Copyright 1964.

Theodore Roethke, excerpt from "How to Write Like Somebody Else," from *On the Poet and His Craft* edited by R. J. Mills, 1965. By permission of The University of Washington Press.

Bertrand Russell, excerpt from *Unpopular Essays* by Bertrand Russell. Copyright 1951. Reprinted by permission of Simon and Schuster and George Allen and Unwin Ltd.

George Santayana, excerpt from "The Sentimental Bandit" in *Dominations and Powers,* 1954, by George Santayana. Reprinted by permission of Charles Scribner's Sons.

Arthur M. Schlesinger, Jr., excerpt from *The Vital Center,* by Arthur M. Schlesinger, Jr. Reprinted by permission of Houghton Mifflin Company.

George Bernard Shaw, excerpt from *Androcles and the Lion* by George Bernard Shaw. Reprinted by permission of Penguin Books Ltd.

Gertrude Stein, excerpt from *Lectures in America* by Gertrude Stein. Copyright 1935 and renewed 1963 by Alice B. Toklas. Reprinted by permission of Random House, Inc.

Adlai E. Stevenson, excerpt from *What I Think* by Adlai E. Stevenson. Reprinted by permission of Harper and Row, Publishers.

Harvey Swados, excerpt from *A Radical's America.* Copyright © 1957 by Harvey Swados, with permission of Atlantic-Little, Brown and Company.

Time, excerpt from "Old Moderately." Appeared in *Time,* March 11, 1966. Courtesy of *Time.* Copyright Time Inc. 1966.

Arnold J. Toynbee, excerpt from "Militarism and The Military Virtues" in *War and Civilization,* 1950. Reprinted by permission of Oxford University Press.

Carl Van Vechten, excerpt from *Selected Writings of Gertrude Stein* edited by Carl Van Vechten. Copyright 1946 by Random House, Inc. Reprinted by permission.

E. B. White, excerpt from "Cold Weather" in *One Man's Meat,* 1944, by E. B. White. Copyright 1943 by E. B. White. Reprinted by permission of Harper and Row, Publishers.

Lynn White, Jr., excerpt from *Frontiers of Knowledge* by Lynn White, Jr. Reprinted by permission of Harper and Row, Publishers.

Colin Wilson, excerpt from "Where Do We Go from Here?" in *Zero Anthology of Literature and Art*, No. 8, edited by Themistocles Hoetis, 1956. Reprinted by permission of Harold Ober Associates.

Tom Wolfe, excerpts from *The Kandy-Kolored Tangerine Flake Streamline Baby* by Tom Wolfe. Reprinted by permission of Farrar, Strauss & Giroux, Inc.

It is a privilege to know and work with
some men. This book is dedicated to
one of them:

Robert B. Heilman

Preface

This text is essentially an informal, nontechnical book about writing—a rhetoric that doesn't use the word. The word *rhetorical* is used to describe what is strategically effective, but the word *rhetoric* itself does not appear. I have no aversion to the word, but it does mean many things to many people and little to some, particularly students. I have also made an honest attempt to stay away as much as possible from abstractions about writing. There is a theory behind this text —I think every instructor should have a theory that informs practice—but it is not the kind of theory that excludes all nonsubscribers. Above all, I have attempted to emphasize what I consider most basic to writing improvement: recognition of intuitive perceptions. In trying to be as practical as possible about a dimension of writing that obviously does not reduce itself easily to method, I hope, nevertheless, that I have been successful in directing students toward what to look for intuitively. At a time when we see clear evidence of a surge of neo-romanticism in education, when the value of feeling has risen immeasurably, it becomes urgent to appeal to the personal initiative and sensibilities of students, not to substitute the mechanical conformity and prohibitions that are characteristic of many approaches to writing.

It seems to me that many instructors have a common experience: after years of writing during their college experience, they are confronted with the problem of teaching someone else to write. What they very often do is to teach a practice of writing that is based upon an a priori theory —a theory of "shoulds" and "should nots"—a theory that does not correspond closely to practice. In writing this book, I have tried to take into account what successful writers have done and what students, both good ones and weak ones, characteristically do. I have drawn upon my experience with students in writing classes, my experience in training instructors who teach writing, my own experience as a writer, and my experience as an editor in reading what many other people have said about writing. I am indebted therefore to more people than I can acknowledge by name.

I have also tried to write a book that does not supplant the instructor, but only to say those things that he very often does not have time to explain in detail with appropriate illustrations. If an instructor does not agree with some of my views—for instance, my idea that the logic of composition is something essentially different from formal logic—I think this difference opens up possibilities for student discussion. We need more dialogue back and forth with students about the process of writing, not pronouncements in this book or from the lectern about what the indisputable truth is.

I have therefore tried not to say too much, not to exhaust every topic. In deciding upon the things I would include, I have made certain assumptions about the student who reads this book. I assume that he has done some writing and that he is familiar with sentences and paragraphs, whether he writes good ones or not. I also assume that he has a basic vocabulary of the writing terms that now commonly appear in secondary texts—*denotation* and *connotation,* for example. In short, I do not start at zero. I like to think that college composition courses can be a new experience for the incoming freshman, just as psychology and oceanography and engineering are. Unfortunately, many composition courses only review and then move one slow step forward. I have learned that students, even the less accomplished ones, can leap as well as step, and that they find excitement in leaping, particularly if we encourage them. I hope this book represents some kind of leap, not an impossible one, but one that requires more than a casual effort.

A few specific acknowledgments are in order. I am indebted to Mr. Charles Mohler for setting this book in motion. Once in motion, two books helped to shape it. *Factors in Judgments of Writing Ability,* a research study of Educational Testing Service by Paul Diederich, John French, and Sydell Carlton, suggested a structure; Jerome Bruner's *The Process of Education* strongly reinforced my own thinking about the importance of intuition in the learning process. The chapter on the paragraph owes much to the work of Professors Alton Becker, Francis Christensen, David Karrfalt, Leo Rockas, and Paul Rodgers, although they may not approve of my eclectic view of their work. I am grateful also to the *Oregon Council Newsletter* for permission to reprint in Chapter 1 major portions of my article entitled "The Four Freedoms of the Writer."

I also add my thanks to a number of professional readers, unknown to me, to Mrs. Jean Hundley, and to my wife Mildred for their valuable criticism of the manuscript; and to my secretary, Mrs. Shirley Hanson, for her invaluable assistance. I hope the final product in some way reflects the worthiness of their efforts.

William F. Irmscher

Contents

Introduction

A student once wrote to me: "I have worked so strenuously on my weaknesses that I no longer know my strengths." When I reread that comment, I am always moved by a certain sadness because I realize that hundreds of other students might have written the same sentence. I have therefore tried to write a book that talks more about strengths in writing than about weaknesses. I would like to encourage every student to realize that he has capacities within himself to do the job of writing well if he will discover what his abilities are and stop thinking that he could do much better if someone would only tell him exactly how to write. A three-year research study made at Wisconsin State University at Platteville revealed that "nearly 70 percent of student performance could be predicted by items measuring, for the most part, a student's attitudes and values." [1] Self-initiative and self-confidence are basic.

When students do not do well, however, they are tempted to blame the course or the instructor. One student complained, "I have never had a course that taught me how to write, only courses in which compositions were graded and criticized." What this student failed to realize was that in the correction and constructive criticism of his own writing he had possibly the best possible instruction, individualized and relevant. If a student seeks only prescriptions about writing, not the freedom to experiment, which includes the freedom to go wrong, then he is not likely to make much progress because prescriptions simply cannot anticipate all of the needs of the writer. Every writing assignment is a new situation. The key words in this book therefore are *discovery* and *awareness,* specifically self-discovery of ways to write and self-awareness of the resources every individual has and can develop.

To the perennial and most haunting question that instructors hear from students in a composition class, "What can I do to improve?"—to which the student sometimes expects an answer in a ten- or fifteen-minute conference—there is no brief reply. The answer is a book, like this one, that tries to explain what the writing process involves and what the student's involvement in that process is. Obviously, what is said here is not completely novel. But to study the structure of writing—as I would like to think this book does—does not necessarily demand learning a vast stock of new information, but organizing what knowledge we have. In its

[1] Don Eulert, "The Relationship of Personality Factors to Learning in College Composition," *CCC,* XVIII (May, 1967), 62.

approach therefore, this book will try to say what factors are involved in the process of writing, show the results that some people get, suggest how students can hope for comparable effects, and attempt to generalize about the qualities that have come to be identified with good writing of different varieties. These are intended to be guides for the writer. After they have been given, he must then look to himself. In the moment of composition, everyone is on his own.

William F. Irmscher

WAYS
OF
WRITING

The Nature of Composition

There is no formula by which a man can become a writer,
and there is no end to the number of ways in which a
man can be one.   *John Ciardi*

Writers should have their own basic freedoms: freedom to say what they think and feel, freedom to choose and err, freedom from interruption, and freedom from fear. Like all freedoms of the individual, these exist within the limits set up by the same freedoms of other people, who are also entitled to their full share of them. Freedom in any area, however, is a give-and-take proposition. Sometimes it boomerangs. A writer is free to criticize, for example, but speaking too bluntly may seriously injure someone else and bring on a flood of violent disapproval. The writer has to decide for himself what he wants to risk. If by reading and study he learns the objections, serious or mild, that can be registered against writers, he need not find himself an innocent in the world of words.

THE FREEDOM TO WRITE

But the writer can go too far in his caution. He can tyrannize himself. If he lets himself be inhibited by fears, chiefly the fear of offending anyone at all, he finally limits himself to the easiest and most ineffectual way of expressing himself—a narrow path with dangers all around. During World War II, soldiers who arrived in France early after the invasion, before the first port at Cherbourg had been captured, waded in to the beaches from small landing craft. Once ashore, they discovered that the engineers had been at work clearing mines and marking off narrow paths for access. These were the only safe places to go. Anyone wandering outside risked his life, and no one dared.

A good many people take a similar approach to writing. They are afraid of explorations and explosions. They move with trepidation. They want someone to mark off a safe path with all of the prohibitions printed in large letters. The fact is that an infinite number of such warnings exist for writers. But the only reasonable thing for a book of this kind to do is first to clear away the mines so that warnings are unnecessary and we have more free space in which to move around. We can do this simply by letting a collection of familiar taboos about writing comment upon themselves.

The tangle of taboos

For a moment, let's imagine a hypothetical student—a completely scrupulous one who wants to make absolutely certain that he doesn't

2

violate any of the taboos that have been established about writing. To this end, he goes to the trouble of collecting a list of things he shouldn't do—warnings he finds in books and restraints his teachers have imposed. He ends up with the following collection, although in some books he may find more discreet and sensible phrasing. Instead of "Avoid long words," he may find an explanation, "Do not use big words where little ones will do," or instead of "Avoid long sentences," he may find, "Do not use sentences that are so long that the reader loses his way in them." In other versions, however, qualifications get lost. To his own amazement, he accumulates these working rules, which he arranges in fairly arbitrary categories for convenience:

1. Taboos concerning words and usage:
   Avoid general and abstract words.
   Avoid slang.
   Avoid big words.
   Avoid colloquial English.
   Avoid foreign words and phrases.
   Avoid clichés.
   Avoid poetic expressions in prose.
   Avoid fancy words.
   Avoid using the first word that comes to mind.
   Avoid using nonce words.
   Avoid inventing words.
   Avoid use of *be*-verbs.
   Avoid *so*.
   Avoid *all* and its compounds.
   Avoid qualifiers like *very, just, little, seemingly*.
   Avoid *contact* as a verb.
   Avoid *factor*.
   Avoid using *in fact*.
   Avoid *I think* and in *my opinion*.
   Avoid nouns turned into verbs with *ize*.
   Avoid *I* in expository prose.
   Avoid *there is* and *there are*.
   Avoid the editorial *we*.
   Avoid the casual use of *we*.
   Avoid *you*.

Avoid *one.*

Avoid contractions.

2. Taboos concerning techniques:

Don't begin a sentence with a coordinating conjunction.

Don't begin a sentence with *however, therefore, moreover,* and similar expressions.

Don't begin a sentence with *I.*

Don't begin a sentence with a numeral.

Never begin more than two sentences with the same word (except *a, an,* and *the*).

Don't end a sentence with a preposition.

Avoid generalities.

Avoid repetition.

Avoid alliteration.

Avoid rhythm.

Avoid rhetorical questions.

Avoid irony.

Avoid long, involved sentences.

Don't use overly long or overly short paragraphs.

Don't discuss more than one idea in a paragraph.

Don't split an infinitive.

3. Taboos concerning grammar and mechanics:

Avoid sentence fragments.

Avoid putting into possessive case nouns denoting inanimate objects (*the roof's slant*).

Avoid the passive voice.

Avoid too much punctuation.

4. General:

Don't chew on your quill when writing.

Think again for just an instant of this hypothetical student, who in his conscientiousness is by no means a complete fabrication. How does he overcome his newly imposed timidity? How does he write anything without becoming the offender he doesn't want to be? From such a tangle of taboos, there is only one possible escape: to discard the notion that prescriptions have general application to all people and all kinds of writing. Ultimately, the only useful prescriptions are suggestions that are made about an individual's own writing, ones that he himself may be willing to accept as remedies for his shortcomings.

If one wished to pursue this collector's hobby further, he could assemble an even longer list of "do's," including much sound advice, to be sure, but phrased frequently like orders made by a sergeant to his platoon: limit the subject, list ideas, group related ideas, outline, write an introduction, main body, and conclusion, revise constantly.

The truth is that the concept of writing as a rigid discipline, one we are supposed to practice like calisthenics, creates a strong sense of guilt in a great many people, who find that what they do when they write is quite different from what they think they should do.

HOW PEOPLE WRITE

Within the past three years, I have asked about one hundred students to tell me how they write. I have asked them to record, not how they think they *should* write or, if they are teachers, how they teach other people to write, but how they customarily go about the job of producing a written composition. These writers fall loosely into four categories that attempt to take into account both their temperaments and working habits, although some writers fall into more than one classification or conceivably into none. For convenience, let's call them disciplinarians, impulsives, procrastinators, and strugglers.

Disciplinarians find an orderly, systematic method of writing compatible with their makeup. If they have not been taught a particular discipline, they have invented an efficient one of their own. They are likely to start at the beginning, well ahead of their deadline, and proceed step by step to the end. Their writing is carefully structured and strategically conceived. They tend to write tight, precise, deliberate prose which, in quality, may range from outstanding to pedestrian. As a group, they uniformly shy away from the flamboyant. As one very fine writer of this variety said, "When I achieve a brilliant phrase, I strike it out because it sounds insincere and uncharacteristic."

Impulsives are capable of flaunting a daring phrase. They represent the opposite of the disciplinarians in temperament and habit. For the assurance of method, they substitute the confidence of ego: "I always view my writings as gems of logic and wit, although I know the reader may not agree." These people seem to have a penchant for writing. Whether they have talent or not is another question. But writing is effortless for them; ideas come spontaneously. Impulsives accomplish such striking feats as writing the first and final draft on the typewriter at one sitting. They do not pretend, however, that such a production is done without forethought and preparation. In his essay "How I Write," Bertrand Russell tells how after months of intense concentration upon a topic that he had chosen for a series of lectures in Boston during 1914 and after prolonged frustration in getting his material to fall into shape, he resolved the entire problem in a single flash and, without hesitation, dictated an entire book to a secretary whom he had asked to come at a designated time. All impulsives, of course, are not Bertrand Russells. They may write unevenly and superficially. But almost all impulsives do admit to some pleasure in creating—either pleasure in the release writing brings or pleasure in the reflection of themselves on paper.

Procrastinators wait for the deadline to get as close as possible so that the pressure upon them is as great as possible. Once started, they may turn out as fine a product as anyone else, marred only by the rough spots which time does not permit them to smooth out. Before the plunge, they occupy themselves with all kinds of diverting tasks. One lady confessed that she never did as much housework as when she had an assignment due. Inevitably, procrastinators will be found working frantically late at night or still making last-minute changes as they submit their papers. The causes for delays are various—lack of discipline, reticence to make the commitment that writing demands, fear of criticism, a mental block about writing, an overloaded schedule. These are writers who finally must force themselves into the act of writing, although they may be wholly satisfied with what they finally produce. One of them says, "I can write easily and naturally when I take my subject seriously, not myself."

Strugglers seldom find satisfaction. They may not delay their task, but they begin without confidence and enthusiasm because they think they are undertaking something they do not know how to do well: "I have never written enough to acquire the craftsman's attitude toward his craft." Because they lack skill, they are anxiety-ridden. They seek gimmicks and gambits as their salvation. They look for solutions outside themselves, not inside. If pressed for an analysis of their problem, they are likely to use grammar as their scapegoat: "I never could understand grammar." Strugglers are conscientious. Yet in bleeding over the word, they lose the paragraph. They write and discard what they have written. They try too hard. Their nervousness defeats the perfection they seek. The final product is often forced, studied, and self-conscious.

These distinctions should not suggest that any one of these approaches necessarily provides the best possible results for its user. Some impulsives could, no doubt, profit by more discipline; some disciplinarians, by more flexibility. But writers ordinarily incline toward a method that they consider right for themselves. If the results are not completely satisfactory, then they need to resort to analysis and consider ways that may possibly lead to more effective prose.

The flexibility of writing

Unfortunately, some books about writing admit only a disciplinarian point of view, as if it were possible to shape all writers by one mold. Any book for *all* writers has to concede that writing is flexible, that learning to write better is not so much a matter of finding answers from an outside source as discovering one's own answers by one's own efforts. There is no single absolutely correct way to write. There are conventions and fashions and proprieties, but few foolproof prescriptions. There are past traditions of famous writers, but no obligations to follow. Creation is a continuing process, and every composition is a creative act, whether premature or mature.

THE WHOLENESS OF THE PROCESS

One prevalent, and rather naïve, belief likens the process of learning to write to the technique of building a brick house. An apprentice works a while at the wall of vocabulary, piling on words brick by brick. Then, to keep the construction balanced, he shifts to the wall of grammar, to the wall of logic, and to the wall of style. Finally, when the structure is complete, he enters, a master craftsman, and dwells in the house securely forever.

As analogies go, this one serves up to a point. But even though we may learn about composition in this brick-to-brick fashion, we don't actually write that way. We don't study grammar and logic before we are expected to compose. When a child in elementary school gets up before his class and makes a few remarks—his first oral presentation— he becomes immediately involved in all the factors of composition that ultimately concern the advanced writer: something to say, a starting point and an ending, words to use, feelings to express, a choice of tone, and, if his words are written down, spelling, capitals, and periods. These are simply elementary versions of content, structure, diction, feeling, style, and mechanics—all present from the earliest stages, ready to grow and develop.

Another analogy about the process of writing suits the facts much more closely. We learn to write the way plants grow. The seed holds the potential; the rest depends upon where it is planted and how well it is cultivated. The roots of language largely determine the growth process. Stunted roots produce inferior plants; inferior plants produce inferior fruit and flowers. From the first moment on, however, all is growth—organic growth. Some plants grow rapidly, some slowly; some strongly, some weakly; some regularly, some irregularly. The finest and strongest plants are pruned—properly, of course, so that they are not destroyed. Francis Bacon has commented: "Natural abilities are like natural plants that need pruning by study." Judicious criticism is also pruning. But growth for the writer, as for the plant, depends upon elements both outside and inside.

THE INTUITIVE DIMENSION OF WRITING

Paul Engle once wrote, "Writing is like making love—it is astonishing how far pure instinct (if it is really pure) will carry you." The quip is by no means an empty witticism. It becomes much more informative about expository writing, however, if one changes two of Engle's words: ". . . it is astonishing how far informed intuition (if it is really informed) will carry you."

Informed intuition, as it relates to ordinary writing, has nothing to do with philosophical intuitionism, a kind of suprarational or mystical faculty that gives the perceiver a very special and unexplainable insight—something close to vision or to Engle's original term *instinct*. A writer's intuitional perception permits him to operate without resorting to the whole analytical process—to write a sentence, for instance, without first analyzing its components, to write anything without reference to an exact procedure. Of course, intuition can mislead, but if it is an intuition informed by fact and study and actual writing experience, it is less likely to mislead.

The scientist depends no less than the humanist upon this kind of intuition. An explanation of its function is included in a study made by two chemists concerning the role of the hunch in scientific investigation:

> A scientific hunch is a unifying or clarifying idea which springs into consciousness suddenly as a solution to a problem in which we are intensely interested. In typical cases, it follows a long study but comes into consciousness at a time when we are not consciously working on the problem. A hunch springs from a wide knowledge of facts but is essentially a leap of the imagination, in that it goes beyond a mere necessary conclusion which any reasonable man must draw from the data at hand. It is a process of creative thought.
>
> Washington Platt and Ross A. Baker
> *Journal of Chemical Education,*
> Vol. 8, October, 1931

In these terms, intuition transcends analysis. It is the very source of discovery and invention. The scientist resorts to it; the writer depends upon it constantly.

Our culture has been remarkably successful in creating a mythology about analysis and intuition, chiefly in drawing sharp lines of distinction between the analytical approaches of science and the intuitive approaches of the humanities. The result has been to think of the one as operating on the basis of sure, verifiable data, the other as floundering whimsically in a sea of imprecision. A few humanists have aided this myth by undermining their own confidence in intuitive powers. They say that we do not know precisely how people write, that we cannot explain scientifically the disturbing variables that sometimes produce good writers, sometimes bad ones. We have no foolproof method of teaching composition. Envy of the scientist's good fortune in being able to explain precisely what happens in a given situation has now encouraged application of scientific methods of research to problems of writing. What we can learn scientifically about the intuitive dimension of writing, however, would seem comparable to discovering how we can test the taste of a macaroni and cheese casserole by measuring its heat.

THE IRREDUCIBLES

Computers now compose, even poetry of a kind. Yet no professional writer of my acquaintance is worried about the competition. Nevertheless, the computer will certainly be of value to the student of writing. Its use in stylistic analysis will make easily accessible much knowledge about word frequency, typical structures, and characteristic usages in a writer's work. All of these data represent a body of fact that can inform intuition. But even in an age of mechanical miracles, it is difficult to think that the machine will ever be able to codify the intuitive qualities of writing, because these are *irreducibles*—the perceptible but unteachable qualities of writing that cannot, like grammatical structures, be reduced to algebraic formulas.

By what formula, for instance, does one test when repetition is effective and when it is monotonous? We can demonstrate, but we cannot reduce the measure to a rule. Is emphasis an irreducible factor or a mechanical matter of learning a few techniques like saving the most important word in the sentence for the final position? Are proportion and balance wholly reducible to outlining procedures? How does one acquire a sense of distinction between the obvious and the subtle, between the sincere and the sentimental, between the imaginative and the farfetched, between humor and gaucherie?

We seem to have few precise names for the intuitive qualities in the vocabulary of writing. We grope to describe them when we use words like *grasp* (the writer's grasp of a subject), *ear* (his ear for words), *flow* (rhythmic flow), *sense* (of symmetry), *taste,* his *feel* for, his *balance,* his *touch,* his *insight*. All of these suggest sensory qualities, although they do not describe actual sense perceptions. They are analogies for inner senses—an inward eye or inward ear. These sensibilities are the source of our intuitive perceptions and understanding.

No one needs to write himself off at this point because he now concludes that he has none of these illusive faculties. Every writer brings to his task intuitive resources, perhaps little aware that they can and should direct the process. The chief difference between highly talented writers and almost everyone else is that talented writers need no conscious development of their natural resources. One cannot buy the staples of a writer: a respect for language, an ear for sound, a taste for phrase, and a sense of proportion. But one can acquire them and cultivate them over a period of time by reading and analyzing and evaluating other people's writing as well as his own—by informing his intuition. If anyone insists upon proof, he can refer to the testimony of recognized writers, who consistently say that their reading, more than anything else, has influenced their writing. If anyone insists upon knowing precisely how this influence occurs, perhaps he needs to reflect upon the speech made by a character in one of Giraudoux's plays:

> I knew a child who insisted on "understanding" a kaleidoscope. What was the result? He took it apart and ruined everything. His friends left theirs alone and "understood" the colors of the rainbow —blue, red, green—clouds, lightning, hell, passion and death. He understood nothing and broke his machine.
>
> *Paris Impromptu*
> tr. Rima Drell Reck

An unmysterious mystique

If emphasizing the irreducibles seems to suggest that I have taken refuge in a mystique, clouding the process of writing with a jargon that only the high priest and a few select initiates can grasp, I can only urge that my purpose is the opposite. Writing is completely open and accessible. Almost any literate person can try it and may do it extremely well. The only mystique about writing is the mystery of what goes on inside to make the act possible, and that mystery persists about almost any kind of creativity. Analysis explains up to a point, after which it must defer to intuition. To refuse to acknowledge the working of intuitive qualities, however unexplainable, is to close one's eyes to an essential part of the process and perhaps to one's best hopes.

EXPOSITORY AND IMAGINATIVE WRITING

Phrases like "creative writing" and "imaginative writing" to characterize verse, drama, and narrative create a misconception about expository writing. Good expository prose is neither uncreative nor unimaginative. All writing is creative in the sense that it produces something where nothing was and brings a degree of order out of chaos. All writing is imaginative to the extent that it makes readers see familiar things in a new way.

"Imaginative writing," nevertheless, is a serviceable phrase. It acts as a cover term for fiction, drama, and poetry. These follow their own conventions, which deviate at times from the conventions that operate in expository writing. The essay, no less a form of literature than the others, gets classified as expository writing. Forms and conventions, therefore, serve as one means of distinguishing between imaginative and expository writing. One other distinction is worth mentioning here: imaginative literature ordinarily appeals in a heightened degree to our intuitive senses, at times depending wholly upon these perceptions to convey the grotesquerie of the dream world, the illogic of the subconscious, or the subliminal aura of the visionary. When expository prose takes on the coloration of imaginative writing, we coin a label like "poetic prose" to explain its overlap.

DISCOVERY AND AWARENESS: PREPARATION FOR WRITING

Words alone do not convey a writer's intentions. Everything he does with them also speaks. If he knows how to create a special effect, he is a better writer for knowing the art. In order to gain confidence, however, and to become personally aware of what he can try in his own writing, every writer has to make firsthand discoveries about the effects of writing, no matter how obvious they are. Let's consider only one example here—we talk about the idea of discovery throughout the book, especially in Chapter 7.

One of the taboos listed above recommends that writers ought to avoid rhythm. The prescription as it stands in isolated form is, of course, ridiculous. No writer or speaker can avoid rhythm, even if he uses only a single word like *typewriter*. The rhythm of the English language is basically iambic, and anyone who writes will fall essentially into that pattern or flexible variations of it. What the prohibitionist undoubtedly had in mind was a rhythmic pattern that obtrudes, gets in the way of meaning, or makes a jingle out of words. I can do that easily by writing a sentence like the following one: The most I could make of the mess was a muddle of men and a mingling of women with them. In this sentence, sound takes over from sense. One cannot ignore the anapestic meter, accented by alliteration. Although the word order is completely normal and the tone colloquial, the sentence sounds affected and contrived.

But consider another example, John Paul Jones's famous statement, "I have not yet begun to fight." One adjustment—"I have not begun to fight yet"—indicates what the meter is doing for this sentence, whether one reads it as regular iambic or with heavy stresses on the first four syllables. The change destroys the flow and the ascending degree of emphasis that ends with *fight*. The rhythm, perhaps more than any other factor, accounts for the memorability of these seven simple, unalliterated words. We therefore have one sample which permits us to discover that regular rhythms may have an impact upon prose statement without being obtrusive and another which denies it.

No matter how insignificant that finding is or how obvious it is to anyone else, a writer has to come to a personal awareness of it if it is going to be meaningful to him. Not all decisions about rhythm are so obvious as these two examples. Whether metrics jeopardize communication or enhance the effect of communication will often be a matter of intuitive judgment, which needs to be informed by more examples than this brief illustration provides. Discovery is not learning by unconscious osmosis; it is an analysis of actual writing that forces an inference, which may or may not be altered by later experience. If a writer informs himself by discoveries of this kind, he does not need to appeal to anyone else for untrustworthy guidelines like "Avoid rhythm."

THE PREWRITING STAGE: THE WRITER

There is strong reason to accept the hypothesis that almost all the important things in writing occur during the prewriting stage: hitting upon a topic, getting a main idea, determining a purpose, absorbing materials, observing, preparing a plan, focusing, relating parts, developing more ideas, mentally verbalizing, sensing the moment to begin. Whether or not the writer makes notes, outlines, or jots down key phrases at this stage, these steps are part of a complex amalgamation that goes on inside before writing actually begins. By allowing plenty of time before his deadline, any writer is free to find out whether or not careful preparation during the prewriting stage will produce easier and better prose. Then he is also free to choose whether he will place his emphasis on prewriting at the beginning or on revision at the end.

The freedom to think, feel, and choose is actually the freedom to be oneself. The self—the writer, the producer—is more important than any other single part of writing. The makeup of the self, of course, is the writer's own business, but he has to realize it will be reflected in all but the most starkly impersonal prose, and even then indirectly in the choices he makes. Strategies he discovers will work only if he can adapt them to his own purposes.

Thus far I have resisted repeating the cliché that "the successful writer must first of all find himself." The phrase "find himself" is by no means clear. If it means that he must first determine his purpose, to know what he thinks and why—a kind of general commitment—then he must find himself. If it means he must size himself up to learn what his potentialities are (the limitations make themselves clear soon enough), then he must find himself. If it means that he must acquire enough self-esteem to think of himself as a confident spokesman, no matter how modest his voice, then he must find himself. Writing demands that the self break from its usual passive role and find release in expression. Given these terms, it is not too difficult to explain why many people are unwilling to write.

FUNCTION OF THE ASSIGNMENT

Readiness and willingness are two different kinds of problems, sometimes related, sometimes not; that is, readiness does not always lead
to willingness, but the unready are almost never willing. Fortunately,
the act of writing itself is a means of self-discovery, so that, once begun,
one writer discovers he was ready all along and needed only to start;
another discovers that he was not ready but, once under way, can
find what he lacks. Both need the push that an assignment represents.

Although it is clearly simpler not to write than to write, to be able
to do so is still one of the marks of an educated man. The assignment—
whether it is a school assignment or a job assignment—is a demand as
well as a prod. This circumstance is not at all unusual. Most writing done
by ordinary people is done upon demand, and the expectation usually
is that they are able to express themselves literately and convincingly.

Apart from the test that an assignment represents—in school or
at work—it has certain salutary effects. By definition, composition is a
putting together or a putting in order. The assignment therefore compels
the writer first to focus upon a topic, whatever it is. The assignment
changes the circumstances of perception. It increases awareness and
acuteness. It forces the writer to see relationships and draw inferences.
He is required to assert himself and make judgments. In brief, he must
organize what he knows or learn what he yet needs to know in order
to go about the job of writing.

The extemporaneous assignment is a test of a special kind. It
does not offer the writer the opportunity to prepare. It tests what resources he has—both his knowledge and his skills—and his ability to
bring these to bear upon a topic within a limited time. Under such
circumstances, the writer also learns about himself, mainly how quickly
he can generate ideas and to what extent his skill in writing has
become as much second nature to him as driving a car.

THE WRITING STAGE: THE COMPOSITION

A major portion of this book is concerned with the composition, the
thing produced. But our concern is less with ways to produce the

composition than with ways for the writer to judge what he is producing. In short, the discussion of writing in this book is based upon the practice of writers as it shows in their prose, not upon a Procrustean, all-purpose theory of how it should be done. The methods under discussion are chiefly the means of learning more about writing in order to help a student discover on his own how he can become a better practitioner. Bertrand Russell tells how for a time, out of his respect for Logan Pearsall Smith, he tried to follow Smith's chief advice about writing, "Always revise." After a period of faithful subservience, Russell finally made a time-saving discovery: his first draft was always better than the second. Revision worked for Smith, not for Russell. Where procedures are concerned, a writer has to come to his own conclusions. To my knowledge, compositions are seldom judged on the procedures the writer uses. What he does is usually an unknown factor. All that stands is the written form, separated from the writer and substituting for him as an actual person.

Once the composition is complete, the writer is separate from it—he cannot fill in the gaps, clarify the obscurities, reaccommodate the thought, or smooth out the rough places. It must stand or fall on its own; it must be judged, not by the standard of what the writer might have done, but by what he actually did. The judge is the audience, the reader.

THE AFTERMATH: THE AUDIENCE

Writing is more like acting on the stage than it is like working a physics problem. It is performance for an audience that involves the total person—his thoughts, his feelings, and the conscious techniques he uses to influence. It is possible to conceive of a completely private, therapeutic kind of writing that might be as incoherent, as salacious, as vehement, or as vindictive as the writer wants it to be, scribbling as he supposedly is for an audience of one, himself. At the same time, we might ponder whether such writing is ever done completely without the subconscious hope that someone might see it and be either shocked or drawn to it sympathetically. That anyone ever writes solely for himself is highly questionable.

The moment that a writer composes for a known audience, even though he may be a student writing for his instructor, writing becomes a social act. Conventions impinge upon a writer. An audience places restrictions upon his unlicensed freedom if he intends to appeal to that audience. However, Sir Arthur Quiller-Couch reminds us that an author usually invites an audience. If he does, he has an obligation to accommodate himself to it.

All writing would be simplified if the audience were as well defined as it is when a student writes for his instructor or an employee for his peers, or when an author submits an article to *Esquire*. Whenever the audience can be characterized within bounds, the writer can adjust accordingly. He knows how casual he can be or how formal he must be. He knows what may appeal, what is sure to offend.

Despite the crucial effect of the audience upon the writer, the fact remains that the audience is often nebulous. The writer does not have the advantage of the speaker, who not only may have a fairly clear notion of his audience in advance but may, if he wishes, adjust the tone of his remarks to suit the response of his audience. They may not applaud or hiss, but they may very well nod approvingly, laugh, or yawn to indicate interest or boredom. The writer, like the actor behind the glare of footlights, may be able to discern nothing about his audience until he gets the final signs of approval or disapproval. A writer hopes for a warm, understanding, receptive audience, but he has no reason to expect that it will be indulgent. In many instances, he encounters readers who have predispositions: they may want to be entertained, they may want to be informed. If the writer's design is to be urbane and theirs is to be informed, then purposes cross and the audience is lost. But if a reader is uncommitted in his opinions and reading open-mindedly, then the writer has a unique opportunity. He can create his own audience. To do that, he must imagine what kind of readers he wants, how they are likely to respond, and what will please them about his writing. It is highly probable that the audience he imagines will be only an extension of himself. In such cases, the self is then the first and most important audience. The writer includes what convinces himself, what *he* finds delightful, what *he* approves of in the style of others, hoping that he will attract readers who discover these inclinations in themselves.

THE MEANING OF PERSUASION

No persuasion is necessary if a reader and a writer agree. No persuasion is possible if the reader does not for a time suspend the notions and predispositions that may separate him from the writer. He has to involve himself in a writer's opinions if he is going to consider them at all seriously. But the writer cannot depend upon a voluntary surrender. He has to create a context in which the reader can be involved and possibly won. That is the meaning of persuasion.

Of course, we readily associate argumentation and persuasion, although argumentation is only one kind of persuasion—the kind that depends mainly upon setting up premises, assembling evidence, refuting, and affirming in such a logical way that the conclusions are undeniable. This kind of formal argumentation originated in the law courts of early times. It still corresponds to winning a case. For instance, in arguing for capital punishment in an article that appeared in *The American Scholar,* Jacques Barzun sets down the familiar arguments of those who oppose capital punishment:

> The four main arguments advanced against the death penalty are: *1.* punishment for crime is a primitive idea rooted in revenge; *2.* capital punishment does not deter; *3.* judicial error being possible, taking life is an appalling risk; *4.* a civilized state, to deserve its name, must uphold, not violate, the sanctity of human life.
>
> "In Favor of Capital Punishment"

These are impressive arguments, and they are the ones that Barzun must either concede, refute, or answer satisfactorily before he can proceed to his own conclusions. During the course of the argument, he must either keep his reader in a "willing suspension of disbelief" or forgo the possibility of persuasion. But he has basically set up for himself a framework for rational argument.

Other writers may choose less methodical but no less deliberate means of persuasion. In order to win the case, they may choose to sway the reader, to appeal basically to feeling rather than to reason. It is a fallacy to assume that an appeal to emotion is an inferior mode of persuasion, because one might well argue that the appeal to feeling is upon occasion the necessary wedge that forces closed minds to open. Consider one paragraph written by James Baldwin:

Sheriff Clark in Selma, Ala., cannot be dismissed as a total monster; I am sure he loves his wife and children and likes to get drunk. One has to assume that he is a man like me. But he does not know what drives him to use the club, to menace with the gun and to use the cattle prod. Something awful must have happened to a human being to be able to put a cattle prod against a woman's breasts. What happens to the woman is ghastly. What happens to the man who does it is in some ways much, much worse. Their moral lives have been destroyed by the plague called color.

"The American Dream and
the American Negro"

This is persuasion that seeks involvement, that appeals to the reader to identify with the writer and to cooperate with his aims. This is persuasion that creates a climate for belief. This is persuasion that functions as fiction and drama do, creating scenes, introducing people, recording what these people say and think, suggesting motivation. This is writing that becomes "for the time the only present, and fills both the stage and the reader's mind completely"—words that Erich Auerbach wrote in praise of Homer. What Auerbach says about filling the reader's mind completely should not escape the writer who may wonder how persuasion is accomplished. The writer conditions his audience to approve when he fills their minds with detail, when he commands the page so that his own assertions seem wholly true for that moment and may possibly remain unforgettable in the reader's mind. The surest persuasion overwhelms the audience. The actor does it; so can the writer.

SUGGESTIONS FOR DISCUSSION

1. What are common student attitudes toward the job of writing? Is it difficult? Why? What are common attitudes toward the purpose of writing? Is writing necessary?
2. What other kinds of writers do not seem to be covered by the categories of disciplinarians, impulsives, procrastinators, and strugglers? Elaborate further upon the habits and attitudes of people in these particular groups.
3. One young lady explained that she wrote "from the inside out." Is there any other way? What are the implications of other ways?

4. Explore further the operation of the intuitive in the writing process. When do we depend upon it particularly? What is there in composing that corresponds to what the two chemists refer to as a "scientific hunch" (page 9)?
5. Can you cite specific ways in which knowledge of your audience affects the way you write? Do you write differently for different teachers and professors? for friends? for family? In what ways? Why?
6. A student ends a serious discussion of social manners with the following quotation:

> Hearts, like doors, will ope with ease
> To very, very little keys,
> And don't forget that two of these
> Are "I thank you" and "If you please."

What implication does this choice of quotation leave about the writer's attitude toward his audience?

ASSIGNMENTS

1. Jot down a list of taboos that you personally have accumulated from books and teachers. Attempt to explain why five or ten of these may have arisen. Have they been a help or a hindrance to you? To what extent would they seem to be applicable to all writers? Can you cite examples in which you think the practice forbidden by the taboo would serve a useful purpose?
2. Write a short paragraph in which you describe your characteristic way of writing. How and when do you start? Do you know precisely what you are going to say before you say it, or do you discover your thoughts as you go along? Do you revise and polish? When? Pose other questions for yourself.
3. Attempt to characterize the audience of one magazine you know well. Who is included by age? by education? by political philosophy? Who is specifically excluded? What proof can you offer for your conclusions?

2

Thinking Talking & Writing

The graces of writing and conversation are of different
kinds, and though he who excels in one might have been,
with opportunities and application, equally successful
in the other, yet as many please by extemporary talk,
though utterly unacquainted with the more accurate method
and more labored beauties which composition requires;
so it is very possible that men wholly accustomed to works
of study may be without that readiness of conception
and affluence of language always necessary to colloquial
entertainment.   *Samuel Johnson*

n this chapter thinking and talking are discussed, not within the specialized framework of psychology or speech, but within the general range of human experience, as anyone might discuss them if he stopped to reflect upon something he has been doing spontaneously for almost all of his life. No system, no experimental data are offered. The ideas here will be true only as they seem true to the reader's own experiences. In *The Mind in the Making,* James Harvey Robinson comments that he thinks poets and storywriters have made the most profound observations about intelligence because, as nonspecialists, they take the whole being of man into consideration, not mind alone, as if it could be excised and studied independent of all human problems. In a similar way, thinking and talking may in a nonspecialized way be seen as functions intricately bound up with the writing process. They cannot be isolated, but they can be disentangled enough by simplifying their procedures so that the reader should be able to compare how he writes with how he thinks and how he talks.

THINKING

If I look introspectively into my own mind and compare my observations with those of other writers who have tried to approximate what the thinking process is like, I find we have the same general impressions. We all try to suggest some kaleidoscopic effect, something continuous and constantly changing, something often erratic and dynamic, something not exclusively thinking but feeling also, at times nonverbal, at times often diffuse and dreamlike and then again incisive and cogent. Words in their orderly procession fail somehow to catch the will-o'-the-wispish quality of mind. Thus writers who try to suggest what the act of thought is like either resort to metaphor or abandon the structural regularity of words altogether.

The psychologist William James objected to common metaphors like "train of thought" and "chain of thought" because he disliked the image of thought chopped into segments. He preferred "stream of thought" because, like a stream, thought flows. Other writers use "current" and "flux" to suggest the same concept. Phrases like "crooked thinking," "straight thinking," and "make up our minds" are also metaphorical. A phrase like "straight thinking" is a deliberate attempt to reconcile the supple nature of thought with the nonelastic, linear form that writing assumes. Or "straight thinking" describes the kind of thinking that immediately precedes the expression of a thought, when the writer must finally decide upon the order of his words. At that point, the straighter the thinking, the better; otherwise, writing will record how convolute thinking is, as it turns around and in upon itself.

Novelists often try to catch the gyrating and rapid quality of thought by transcribing a free association of words and phrases. Note this brief passage from Kerouac's *The Subterraneans:*

> Me thinking *O grayscreen gangster cocktail rainyday roaring gunshot spectral immortality B movie tire pile black-in-the-mist Wildamerica but it's a crazy world!*

This is not communication in the usual sense of the word. Neither is James Joyce's *Finnegans Wake,* a sustained effort of this variety. Some critics say that it annihilates the language; others contend that it records more completely than any other work what the creative process of the human mind is like. Whatever one thinks of Joyce's work, one thing is clear: in its attempt to get at the inner mental processes, it deviates strongly from conventional prose, as this brief excerpt shows, commenting upon the fall and death of Finnegan the hod carrier:

> The fall (bababadalgharaghtakamminarronnkonnbronntonnerronntuonnthunntrovarrhounawnskawntoohoohoordenenthurnuk!) of a once wallstrait oldparr is retaled early in bed and later on life down through all christian minstrelsy. The great fall of the offwall entailed at such short notice the pftjschute of Finnegan, erse solid man, that the humptyhillhead of humself promptly sends an unquiring one well to the west in quest of his tumptytumtoes: and their upturnpikepointandplace is at the knock out in the park where oranges have been laid to rust upon the green since devlinsfirst loved livvy.

In *Tender Buttons,* Gertrude Stein also tries to escape discursive patterns we ordinarily associate with conventional prose. She communicates by intimation. The result is that her writing suggests the preverbal nature of thought, which paradoxically can be hinted at only in words. Almost any passage from *Tender Buttons* shows this effect:

COLORED HATS

Colored hats are necessary to show that curls are worn by an addition of blank spaces, this makes the difference between single lines and broad stomachs, the least thing is lightening, the least thing means a little flower and a big delay a big delay that makes more nurses than little women really little women. So clean is a light that nearly all of it shows pearls and little ways. A large hat is tall and me and all custard whole.

This is an extremely upsetting passage if we read it expecting to find a coherent statement about colored hats. The prose consists of a profusion of non sequiturs and meaningless repetitions. As an impression of the free association of the mind, however, it makes more sense; at least, in those terms, we find it more familiar, more akin to the kind of collage our thinking represents when its immediate concern is not verbalization for an audience.

Thinking has no vehicle of its own. Speaking and writing give it one, but in so doing they make their own demands upon the thinker. The ephemeral must be stayed, the flow of thought controlled, the profusion made selective, the disjunctive given order.

The relevance of this discussion to the writer, especially to the inexperienced one, should begin to be apparent. What stream-of-consciousness writers record only dramatizes the qualities of disconnectedness and fragmentariness that appear all too commonly in the writing of people who have not adequately disciplined thinking to the conventional demands of writing.

TALKING

Spontaneous talk—unprepared, unwritten, unrecorded—corresponds to the free thinking process more closely than almost any other kind of speaking or writing. Speeches that are formally delivered bear little resemblance to the unstudied, unedited comment that passes as conversation. They are closely related to written compositions; in fact, they are often written to be read. To consider the nature of informal talk is to glance at what the mind does when it has responded to an outside stimulus and focused actively on a topic. All we need to do is to think of a fairly typical situation in which someone gropes to explain an idea he has not worked out ahead of time. He begins; he explores. He overextends a sentence; it gets abandoned. He sees he is not being understood; he restates. A new thought occurs. He puts it in. Silence is his enemy. He fills it with any sound, meaningful or not. He pushes his thinking; he finds his point. He makes it. Like thinking, talking continues repetitiously, messily, wastefully—but productively. Any kind of speech that differs from this description is simply more orderly, more controlled.

WRITING

Writing is a different kind of verbalization from speaking, not necessarily superior to it because it is transcribed, but only superior in its own right if it meets the demands of writing. The same thing can be said of speaking, which has its own set of demands and standards of effectiveness, but the methods of speaking and writing cannot be automatically interchanged. An extremely effective conversationalist, for instance, may turn out to be a very poor writer if he simply tries to write as he speaks.

Writing and formal speaking make the greatest demands upon the individual for selection, orderliness, accuracy, and efficiency. They therefore represent the most cultivated forms of thinking and so have been developed as crafts, at their best demanding skill and artistry that go beyond mere communication.

CONTROL: GROUPING, SELECTING, AND ARRANGING

The thinking process of an individual cannot be duplicated. It is his own melange. To discipline thinking, however, means to control it sufficiently so that it can be communicated logically to other people. Control consists chiefly of grouping, selecting, and arranging. These are topics we will be concerned with throughout the remainder of the book; at this point, we are interested in controls that need to be exercised upon thinking during the prewriting stage.

First of all, the kind of thinking that we refer to as musing or reverie suggests that the mind is not a great respecter of time barriers.

The past, present, and future mingle indiscriminately. In one of his sermons, the seventeenth-century poet and preacher John Donne gives a vivid account of this phenomenon as he describes himself in the act of prayer:

> I neglect God and his angels for the noise of a fly, for the rattling of a coach, for the whining of a door; and I talk on in the same posture of praying, eyes lifted up, knees bowed down, as though I prayed to God; and if God or his angels should ask me when I thought last of God in that prayer, I cannot tell. Sometimes I find that I had forgot what I was about, but when I began to forget it I cannot tell. A memory of yesterday's pleasures, a fear of tomorrow's dangers, a straw under my knee, a noise in mine ear, a light in mine eye, an anything, a nothing, a fancy, a chimera in my brain troubles me in my prayer.
>
> Sermon lxxx, folio of 1640

Controlled thinking brings thoughts into a stable time relationship. The writer decides upon a time base—present tense, for instance—from which he may deviate, to be sure, but to which he tries to hold and may always return. Writing ordinarily demands a consistency of verb tenses, unless the writer gives a clear indication that he is leaving his base.

The Donne selection also illustrates the subservience of the mind to particulars and irrelevancies. Sometimes the irrelevancies may be associated with one another, or they may be completely erratic. Controlled thinking has two obligations: (1) to categorize related thoughts and details; (2) to sift out those that are clearly irrelevant.

An article by Roger W. Brown on "Language and Categories" refers to a fact published by the Optical Society of America that human beings are able to discriminate about seven and one-half million different colors, but that in referring to colors we ordinarily use only eight extremely common categories. What this observation reveals, of course, is that the mind frees itself from the infinite complexity of particulars in the environment by organizing them into categories and minimizing their fine differences. But the statement also sheds light upon the relationship between thinking and writing. Writing frequently demands a reversal of the categorizing process. It must return to particulars for preciseness of meaning. For example, a description of paintings in an art gallery that limited itself to eight color words would scarcely satisfy most readers accustomed to far more refined perceptions. An argument based upon the broadest generalizations without supporting details would hardly stand. Readers do not demand a recital of everything that goes on in the thinking process, but they do want a selection of relevant and precise detail.

Let's see in what way grouping and selecting lead to control of thinking. The following account is the kind of exploration that might go on in a rather diffuse stage of prewriting, never reaching paper as I record it here:

A thought crosses my mind that I might be able to write an essay about nudity. What it will say I don't know as yet. I may reject it after I think further. I first consider the possibilities—what I know and what other people say. A number of random thoughts occur to me, not as the orderly list that follows, but as a flood:

Nudity is symbolic.
Nudes are nudes.
Nudity is purity.
Children like to go nude.
So do people in nudist colonies.
Nudist colonies always attract voyeurs.
Nudity is lustful.
Nudity is freedom.
The law forbids nudity in public.
Adam and Eve were nude.
Many nude statues have fig leaves.
Artists who paint nudes usually have nude models.
Nudity is representational.
Nudity is unworldliness.
Nudity is indecent.
The figure of Christ in crucifixion paintings is nude.
Nudity is natural.
Postcards of nudes are pornographic.
The figure of Sacred Love in a painting by Titian
    is nude; Profane Love is clothed.
Goya painted a clothed version of his Maja nude.

In recording these thoughts, I have tried to be honest—to write down quickly the things that have come spontaneously into my mind. All I have excluded are those intrusions of the ever-present upon thinking: students talking outside my window, a bell ringing, doors slamming, cars whirring up a slight incline.

The first thing that occurs to me as I look over the list is that most of the thoughts are generalizations; only four of them are particular enough to refer to specific names: Adam and Eve, Christ, Titian, and Goya. The mind had done its categorizing, or at least it has borrowed the categories and generalizations made by other people. As I look again at the list, I am also reminded that if I were going to write on a topic growing out of these thoughts, I would have to have many more particulars.

As I proceed further to categorize these first thoughts, I sense that they fall into two general divisions: concepts of nudity that imply it is wholesome and concepts of nudity that imply it is indecent. Most of the statements fall into one category or the other, although one like "Artists who paint nudes usually have nude models" is neutral, unless one wants to assume that anyone who makes the remark intends it as an innuendo.

As a further possibility, the list of thoughts suggests a division between nudity as it is represented in art and nudity as it is represented in experience. A statement like "Nudity is representational" then serves as a transition between them—art recording life.

These categories are broad, perhaps too broad for any short paper. I therefore look for other ones:

Prevailing attitudes toward nudity
Nudity as a moral issue
Function of nudity in art

Or:

Nudity as purity (Titian example)
Nudity as naturalness (Adam and Eve example; children)
Nudity as lust (pornography)
Nudity as freedom (nudist colonies)

Notice that in the first division of three I have statements that closely resemble familiar topics for writing. In the second, I have categories that closely resemble an outline for actual writing. The more control one exercises upon thinking, the closer one moves toward an actual plan for writing. If I were to choose only one of these categories as a topic, I would then have to select statements from the original list, because all of the thoughts do not serve all of the categories. Expository writing demands a high degree of control if the writer wants a logical effect, not a purely impressionistic one. Expository writing at its best is a commitment to order.

WRITING IN RELATION TO TALKING

If we think about the control that good writing demands, we have an almost immediate indication of why talking is easier than writing. Its demands for structure are fewer. Talking is not formless, to be sure, but the form is loose and plastic. Sermons and orations are often better read than heard because they are highly structured and tightly reasoned. But in their exercise of control, comparable to that demanded by writing, they lose the qualities that give talking its distinctiveness.

First of all, speaking involves a lively sense of communication. The speaker is constantly aware of his divided interest—interest in what he is saying and interest in the response of the person listening. These two interact. The speaker draws encouragement from a favorable response or resets his course if he thinks he is not being understood. He has the advantage of immediate feedback. The writer, on the other hand, has to overcome the barrier of an absent audience. He also has one, but he is less constantly aware of it. He has to sustain a lonely soliloquy and anticipate in advance as many misunderstandings as possible.

In the second place, speaking, as opposed to writing, is animated, whether the subject matter is dull or interesting. All too frequently, written prose seems to be a corpse wholly abandoned by its author's spirit. But a speaker and his material are inseparably linked, and the hearer cannot ignore the effect of the speaker's person, if he is seen, or of the speaker's voice, if he is not visible. A speaker may hold an audience's attention by his appearance alone—his posture, his movement, his gestures, his ability to look people in the eye. He may influence by his voice—his pitch, his tone, his volume, his accent, his timing. These are dynamics for which the writer attempts to compensate in a silent medium. He, as it were, has to write what Keats called "ditties of no tone." Nevertheless, he does have resources on paper to counterbalance the sounds of speech. These we discuss in Chapters 7 and 8 as stylistic features of writing.

In the third place, speaking is more flexible than writing in its strategies and language. The units of speech are the word, the phrase, and the clause. In informal talking, the fragment may be as common as the sentence. Essentially, the paragraph is nonexistent and unrecognizable, even in formal speech, unless the writer makes a deliberate pause to shift his topic or emphasis. Like thinking, speaking is unconcerned with mechanics—no spelling, no semicolons, no quotation marks. Inflections and pauses are periods, commas, and exclamation points.

The writer finds himself easily influenced by habits of speech. Incoherent and undeveloped paragraphs sometimes correspond to the kind of skipping from one thing to another that goes on in talk. The dependence of inexperienced writers upon *etc.* is either a carry-over into prose of the· speaker's tendency not to want to leave gaps of silence or a translation of "You know what I mean," a filler remark that dumps the responsibility of completing a thought upon the hearer. The use of the dash as a substitute for all other marks is also an indication that the writer, in trying to record speech patterns, finds the dash the only mark of punctuation flexible enough to meet all of the departures from customary word order that occur in talking.

A good writer, nevertheless, adapts the best speaking techniques to his own uses. Posing a question and answering it is a clear attempt to catch the spirit of dialogue. Rhetorical questions are also borrowed from occasions of formal speaking, when the speaker does not intend his audience to ˜answer. Further, a writer knows the effectiveness of repetition from speaking, although he has to adapt it to his own medium. For instance, a writer cannot repeat an entire sentence verbatim for special emphasis, as a speaker sometimes does.

Because a speaker has a sense of freedom from the firm commitment that writing involves, his language is also highly flexible. He may say openly what he would never dare to write. If he falls into a monstrous malapropism and realizes his mistake, he can laugh it off. A writer unaware of his blunder is stuck with it and may be memorialized by a professor who collects such oddities for his amusement.

The compulsion of a speaker to keep going, in contrast to the writer who may dawdle over a phrase as long as he likes, dooms his speech to a heavier dependence upon clichés, trite expressions, familiar jargon, and other varieties of hackneyed English. The conversationalist has little time to invent. If he repeatedly hits upon brilliant phrases, one begins to suspect that he regularly prepares his *bon mots* in advance —phrases that in written prose would not seem pretentious at all.

Even though a speaker ordinarily limits himself to a smaller vocabulary than a writer, he customarily draws from a larger repertory of popular speech—slang, profanity, shoptalk, localisms—that the writer has to consider risky. Despite the breakdown of rigid stratifications in the varieties of English, a strong sense of language etiquette still prevails among most people. They do not consider all words appropriate for all occasions. A conversationalist is free to adjust his level of speech to different people as he meets them; a writer, trying to anticipate an appropriate level for an audience he does not see, has less flexibility. The spoken word, however, has strongly influenced changes in language, particularly through the media of radio and television, and noticeably relaxed highly rigid proprieties that formerly prevailed for written prose.

Further, we may observe that the language of informal speech is often far less exact than that of writing. Oral communication is at times only a rough equivalent of the kind of statement that a writer has to make in order to be understood. For a short period of time during former President Eisenhower's administration, the *New York Times* printed verbatim transcriptions of the President's press conferences. In print, these appeared chaotic. Yet some members of the press who heard him speak protested that Eisenhower's remarks were not only intelligible but sometimes effective. If they were, we can only conclude that oral delivery was responsible. But the example of President Eisenhower is not unique. A transcribed version of anyone's extemporary remarks is likely to be highly convincing proof that acceptable speaking habits do not pass for acceptable writing.

At times, in speech, meaning becomes so completely lost that only the sound of the speaking voice serves as a bond of communication. As spoken, the words may have little denotative value, or they may not signify at all what they say. Much chitchat falls into this category. It doesn't say much, but it does something to join speakers together. Formal greetings are also of this order. They serve as recognition, even as expressions of regard and friendliness, even though they may not mean literally what they say. A perfunctory "How are you?" may convey a warm greeting, although it does not invite anyone to rehearse his ailments. Writing cannot duplicate this kind of communication by sound waves. When it is designed to communicate, it depends upon exact word values. When it tries more subtle forms of communication, such as irony, it fails easily, because most readers do not expect words to mean the opposite of what they seem to say.

The capacity of the speaker to interpret his words by sound and gesture gives him another advantage over the writer. A speaker who says, "I too recently broke my leg," has no problem with communication. His intonation interprets what he says, and everyone who hears him understands. No ambiguity arises. Written without punctuation, however, the sentence invites two readings, although a larger context might also reduce the possibility of ambiguity. But the writer has problems to contend with that do not greatly concern the speaker. He has to be aware not only of his intentional effects but of the unintentional ones that the visual context of words on paper creates.

Finally, talking is marked by far greater dispatch than writing. One can say in ten minutes what it takes hours to write. In fact, the entire communication system of speaking is different. Conversation is broken up into segments. Anyone who filibusters does so at the risk of being a bore because everybody expects to take his turn. In writing, the author delivers a monologue, but the reader's expectation is different. His interruptions are the intermissions he takes from the printed page. He can always return, but it is the easiest thing in the world for a reader to skip out on a boring writer.

Fundamentally, the circumstances and techniques of talking and writing are so very different that a writer cannot risk talking his prose.

Sense of naturalness

The most desirable quality of talking that a writer needs to acquire is its naturalness, the quality of unaffected ease, which we perceive intuitively. Essentially, naturalness is a lack of self-consciousness. Writing, even though it may be eccentric, may still be natural if it is uncontrived and unforced. Naturalness also relates directly to an author's attitude toward his audience. The tone of the prose may be stiff or snobbish or curt or crude; we consider each of these an unnatural quality, even though it may reflect exactly what is natural to the writer's personality and attitude. Naturalness by normative standards implies flexibility, tolerance, and considerateness.

A FINAL ESTIMATE

If, for purposes of comparison, we line up side by side qualities of thinking and talking and writing, with the realization, of course, that each of these lists represents a simplified version of many complex variants, we may see clearly how writing consistently places the greatest demand for control upon the individual and so, as a skill, requires study and evaluation beyond one's own natural abilities to think and talk. Table 1 may suggest how some ailments in writing may be remedied by a more scrupulous observation of the differences between talking and writing.

SUGGESTIONS FOR DISCUSSION

1. Which of your speech habits would you consider inappropriate to your writing?
2. Some writers claim that they write chiefly "by ear," that is, that they test what they write by ear rather than by eye. What are the advantages? Are there possible limitations?
3. Examine the quotation from *Finnegans Wake* on page 23. What story in Joyce's mind affects the prose as he writes about Finnegan's fall? Examine the puns, the strange words, the strange spellings. Can you

Table 1

UNDIRECTED THINKING	CONVERSATIONAL TALKING	EXPOSITORY WRITING
Kaleidoscopic, unselected, erratic	Selective, but simultaneously exploratory	High selection of relevant detail
Unstructured, convolute	Partially structured, often loosely; roundabout, sometimes ungrammatical	More highly structured; loose or tight structure; straightened, orderly, and grammatical
Fragmentary, disjunctive, repetitious, overlapping	Less fragmentary; because thought may be more rapid than speech, production sometimes incoherent	Least fragmentary; ordered; transcribed
Free association, stream of consciousness; free of mechanical devices	Frequent irrelevant details; digressions; aided by its own resources: voice, gesture, tone, stress, pitch, juncture, and rhetorical devices of language (e.g., repetition)	Test of relevance more rigidly applied; aided by its own variety of mechanical and visual devices to compensate for absence of oral aids; rhetorical devices varied from speech techniques
Nonverbal, impressionistic, intuitive; seeking direction and articulation; fuzzy; verbal when communication imminent	Verbalized; defined, but not all problems of clarity resolved; broad range of language and usage	Verbalized; defined; no immediate recourse if statement is unclear; appropriateness of language and usage under scrutiny
Profusion of concepts, impressions, emotions	Often more productive of ideas than writing within a designated period of time; more words per minute than writing, but greater waste of words	Maximum economy and efficiency in use of words

Ephemeral, but subject to recollection	Transitory (unless recorded); subject to immediate qualification, retraction, and revision	Recorded, edited, revised; unretractable unless withdrawn or revoked by subsequent statement
Spontaneous, active, fluid	Also spontaneous, but words must be set down in linear fashion; prolix	Also linear; a cultivated function, less natural than speech; jelled, deliberative, reflective, strategic, most carefully planned
Frequently an undefined purpose; volitional or nonvolitional	Purposive; response to stimulus	Purposive; often assigned
Noncommunicative; no audience; no commitment	Communicative; immediate audience; feedback; oral commitment	Communicative; audience factor often vague; serious commitment because of transcription
Private, intimate	Private or public; subject to criticism	Private or public; subject to criticism
Uncensored, unrestrained	Often strongly emotive, but subject to social and linguistic conventions and taboos	More filtered, controlled; more conscious of social, linguistic and literary conventions

see what associations are taking place in the words and sounds? From a passage of this kind, what conclusions might be drawn about private and public associations in writing?

ASSIGNMENTS

1. Take a single word and, following the method of free association illustrated on pages 27 to 29, jot down in five minutes all the thoughts that come to your mind. How many are personal observations, facts from books, or hearsay lore? Did you exclude many things extremely private? Begin to group them into categories, striking out irrelevant ones that do not group with others. If you were going to write on a topic growing out of these thoughts, how much reading and study would you need to do? Suggested words: *sea, hair, night, heat, island, concrete, music, the past, poetry, law, experimentation, money.*

2. Examine your own writing (or samples of student writing provided by your instructor) for clear indications of the habits of talk. In what instances do these seem appropriate or inappropriate?

3. Examine the dialogue in a short story, novel, or drama. What conclusions can you draw about recording speech? To what extent is dialogue representational or conventionalized?

4. If a tape recorder is available, tape five minutes of extemporaneous speaking. Then type the playback. What adjustments would you make in the copy if the transcript were to be printed?

3 | Content

There is an important distinction between thoughts and ideas. Men possess thoughts but ideas possess men.

Max Lerner

hapter 2 discussed thinking with almost no reference to the things people think about. This chapter comments more specifically on ways to make thinking productive and ways to judge what thinking produces. In other words, this chapter discusses how the writer can generate and judge ideas—the very substance of writing.

IDEAS: THE SUBSTANCE OF WRITING

What is an idea in writing? Is it any different from any other idea—an idea in religion, an idea in philosophy, an idea in psychology? In one sense, no, because all of these disciplines supply ideas for writing. But in each field the interpretation of the term *idea* differs widely. If we consider that to some philosophers and men of religion ideas are absolute, eternal essences, to other philosophers and some psychologists they are mental images of sense impressions, to some men of science they are only facts and hypotheses about observable data, and to the general populace they are almost anything that goes on in the mind—perceptions, notions, dreams, inklings, fancies—we then begin to realize that the word *idea* carries a variety of meanings and implications. The nature of ideas is an enormously complex topic, and it would hardly be profitable here to explore the intricacies further. Suffice it to say that philosophers, psychologists, and educationists—those who concern themselves chiefly with discussing the nature of ideas—make fine distinctions between some terms that may, at times, be used synonymously in this discussion.

Ideas as the content of writing are chiefly the things we say about our perceptions, that is, our tentative or conclusive statements about actual or imagined phenomena. Therefore, our definition includes facts, opinions, propositions, and observations—assertions about things, whether they are made by real or fictional people.

The practical implication of this definition for the writer is simply this: any individual who, for instance, says he is going to write about war and calls this single word the idea of his essay has not stated an idea; he has only announced a topic. As a controlling thesis, he might choose to establish the essentially factual premise that wars have been almost continuous in the last hundred years. If so, what are the occurrences and dates to support the thesis? He might choose an opinion as a topic: War stimulates man to be his best self. If so, in what way? He might choose a proposition: War acts as a solution to economic and social problems we have not been able to solve in other ways. If so, what is the evidence? He might make an observation: More and more, modern warfare involves the civilian population as well as the military. Since this observation is so, what are the implications? All of these particular ideas are capable of being expanded. In fact, some demand development to be meaningful. One or two also require considerable knowledge; one or two stand as fairly self-evident assertions.

Two observations, however, may be made at this point. First, once an idea has been stated, the negative—the denial of it—also stands as a possible idea. There are almost no exceptions. What to some of us are closed, incontrovertible facts may be denied and argued by special minority groups or individuals.

Second, once an idea has been stated, it may be made more general or more particular. If the starting concept is a detail—for instance, the sound of the closing door at the end of Ibsen's *A Doll's House*—the writer's main idea may then be stated: the slam of the door signifies not only Nora's final departure from Torvald but woman's departure from her social and intellectual dependence upon man. Thus the detail of the slamming door may be developed in terms of its broader implications. If, on the other hand, the starting idea is a generalization—for instance, many of Ibsen's female characters epitomize the new "unwomanly woman" who asserts herself in the nineteenth century—then the particulars must follow to develop and support the idea. Once the writer has determined his direction, he has to proceed with the hard task of generating support for his lead idea.

GENERATING IDEAS

This section might have been called "Getting Ideas"—the phrase is more direct and natural—but it is misleading. We can get ideas anywhere. There is certainly no dearth of them. We hear them; we read them. We can parrot, borrow, or steal them. Getting ideas is quite different from begetting them. *Generating* carries the notion of producing or creating from the inside out.

Writing undoubtedly involves both getting and generating ideas. We constantly need to draw upon outside resources. Simple facts we learn are actually other people's ideas. They become a part of us only if we translate them out of their context into our own, not simply the context of our writing but the context of our thinking and experience. Ideas of our own must be generated from within, as any source of birth—the seed, the egg, the embryo—clearly suggests.

Conditions for generating ideas

Without taking into account an array of private factors that thwart individuals in their thinking, like limited intelligence and personality problems, we can establish two main conditions for generating new ideas: an active mind and an open mind.

Many people have few ideas of their own because they don't involve themselves in anything. Not that they fail to participate in activities, rather that they fail to attach themselves rationally or emotionally to them. They do things, but they never seem to discover an interest in ideas about the things they do. They miss the excitement of intellectual stimulation. Involvement, in this sense, refers to a general feeling, as opposed to distinct emotions such as love, hate, or sorrow. Feeling, then, suggests alertness and liveliness, as the antidote of sullen indifference. The shrug-of-the-shoulder attitude is, of course, recognizably human. Thinking about anything may be difficult and troublesome. It is simpler to defer to specialists and authorities; they know more and have thought more about the issues than we possibly could. We are willing to be influenced because it takes strenuous effort to be influential. However, if we protect ourselves from almost everything and involve ourselves in those things that concern only our most personal affairs, gratifying as that might be, the passive state in which we find ourselves is not likely to generate many ideas.

Ideas emerge from an active mind, a purposefully active mind. This is not to suggest that ideas come to us only when we deliberately try to summon them up, for once the mind has been actively engaged they are likely to pop up at any time or place, in fact so erratically that some people, anxious not to lose a single good idea, go to bed with a pad of paper and pencil at their bedside. Ideas have a way of coming involuntarily when we relax our anxieties about them.

In most instances, an active mind will also be an open mind, one that does not begin with a few presuppositions and attempt to adjust all learning and all experience to a closed system of living and thinking. An open mind entertains new ideas, tests them, adjusts them, discards or accepts them. An open mind changes. It does not worry about inconsistencies over a period of time. Everyone has a right to alter his position for good reason.

Many students have not yet opened themselves to a wide range of ideas; they are not fully conscious of their own lack of involvement. Others, however, are widely read and serious-minded, not even willing to be limited to theoretical discussions of the problems of society and participation in perfunctory substitutes like student government; they want to be actively engaged in the real issues. People with alert and responsive minds find not only that they can generate things to say but that they cannot restrain themselves from saying them. Such people do not need to read about the preconditions for writing.

But every writer needs to add to his resources and to have a few workable methods he can depend upon, occasionally or routinely, to stimulate his thinking.

Asking questions

When we recall that young children at one stage depend almost completely upon questions to probe new objects of their curiosity, we have a clue to a method that can be varied for adults. The variation consists of self-questioning—self-prodding in order to generate ideas. Some ideas of course will prove to be unproductive; some questions we pose cannot be answered or, once answered, are not worth pursuing. A worthwhile idea, however, yields results.

Let's take an example that would perhaps not seem very productive to anyone born after 1940. In 1947, Boulder Dam was officially named Hoover Dam in honor of the thirty-first President of the United States. If we ask why, the answer seems to be fairly obvious (Presidents are often honored in such ways), unless this dam was chosen to honor Hoover because he was particularly instrumental in initiating the vast Colorado project. He wasn't, however. Interest in the project predated Hoover's administration twenty-five or thirty years, and congressional authorization for the dam was made a year before Hoover reached office. The idea, therefore, would still seem to be unproductive.

But if we add to the statement given above three additional facts, then the question "Why?" takes on new meaning and generates a new series of questions. Fact 1: At the time of its construction, the dam, actually in Black Canyon, was called Boulder Dam because it was a part of the vast Boulder Dam project. Fact 2: In 1931, it was unofficially called Hoover Dam after President Hoover (1929–1933). Fact 3: In 1933, the name was again changed to Boulder Dam. Then, to return to our original statement: In 1947, Boulder Dam was officially named Hoover Dam in honor of the thirty-first President of the United States. Writing about this topic would clearly require research by anyone who had not lived through the Hoover era, but anyone sufficiently interested would have to ask key questions in order to generate his ideas: What was Hoover's reputation as President? What reevaluation took place between 1933 and 1947? Once into the topic, more specific questions would suggest themselves: Were particular individuals responsible? What was Hoover's reaction? We begin to see that the ideas generated by the first few facts are vast enough for a book-length project. We see here the difference between a single fact and a set of circumstances. An idea for writing often grows out of seeing relationships between several facts and drawing the implications that the total context suggests.

The purpose in asking questions is not only to discover what we don't know and need to know but also to remind ourselves of what we already know and have forgotten. Quizzing ourselves serves to focus on a topic. Just as we try to respond to questions asked of us by other people, so we have to try to respond to questions we ask of ourselves.

Reading: generating by contradiction

The importance of reading as a source of getting ideas is almost too obvious to mention, but to omit it would be to lose an opportunity to stress the truism that one idea frequently generates another. The extent to which reading generates new ideas, however, will always depend upon the response that goes on within the reader and to a great extent upon the nature of the reading itself.

We need to remind ourselves of our tendency to read the things we like, and the things we like all too frequently mean those books and articles that support our own pet ideas. When we encounter the friction of contraries, we inevitably find that our generating processes quicken. We either confirm our own ideas by defending them against contradiction or discover that our ideas are open to question.

Here the degree of openmindedness is crucial—the extent to which an individual will test himself by opposites. In this connection, required reading serves a very special purpose of forcing students temporarily out of their own orbits to gain a new perspective upon the things closest to them. John Stuart Mill claimed that anyone who didn't know enough about his antagonist's position to refute the arguments of the opposition wasn't rationally entitled to hold an opinion of his own. (See page 129 for exact quotation.) A mind that shies away from negative argument even in reading limits its capacity to produce new ideas, although, we must admit, it may be no less fertile in inventing variations upon old ones.

Observing and relating

Walking on campus recently, I suddenly became aware of a scene that might have inspired Aesop to write a new fable. Four other people also stopped to watch. We were caught by the sight of two dogs standing rigidly about twenty feet apart, tied together by a stare that fixed them as firmly as a rope. The small dog was a fluffy, buff-colored cocker; the other, a gaunt, meager-coated shepherd puppy that looked more like a coyote than a house pet.

After long moments of intense scrutiny, the shepherd edged forward, stalking, holding the cocker by his eye, for it was now apparent that he was the hypnotist. The cocker stayed, quivering. The watchers looked worried. After all, one dog was helpless; the other, ready to devour—or so I saw it.

The suspense ended suddenly, disappointingly. At the moment for attack, the two, with a signal that a human eye could not perceive, capered off together in high spirits.

Two dogs on the lawn, fifty seagulls on the roof, squirrels eating peanuts that students give them—these are common sights on one campus or another throughout the country, ordinarily too common to notice. But the scene of the shepherd and the cocker was a melodrama. I was not out to observe, but I was drawn. Once watching the scene, I found myself making a human drama out of the confrontation. I was disappointed in the sentimental happy ending because I was thinking of people, not dogs: usually, human dramas don't end that way. But for all of my allegorizing, I was impressed enough to write down the details without comment.

Robert Frost once said that an idea is a "feat of association." It is natural that the remark should come from a poet, who characteristically sees what everyone else looks at and doesn't see, who is drawn by less than melodrama. The poet proves to all writers that impressive moments are not necessarily the big events going on around us, that the truth of simple detail is more penetrating than great pronouncements.

Meaningful observation, however, is not limited exclusively to sense perception. It is also a matter of attentiveness to significant detail in reading and listening. I once asked a student who had come to me for a special examination to write an interpretation of Thomas Hardy's "The Darkling Thrush." The copy of the poem included the date— December 31, 1900. The student did a weak job of interpreting, primarily because he wandered off into a vague discussion of resurrection and hope without giving sufficient attention to the details of the poem. The one fact he had been provided as a possible aid—the date—might have helped him generate an idea he needed. He either ignored the date or saw no connection between it and lines like

> The land's sharp features seemed to be
> The Century's corpse outleant. . . .

Keeping notes

Writing down observations and keeping a daily journal are simple, practical ways of remembering the things we might otherwise forget. They are also ways of keeping the mind actively engaged. Something goes on inside at the same time that something goes down on paper. An experience triggers an immediate reaction; a notation on paper is a gamble on a delayed-action response.

Of various methods of recording, a daily journal is particularly helpful for self-observation. The thoughts on paper permit us at a later time to go back for an impersonal look at ourselves. We may not like what we see. We may see artiness. We may see superficiality. But these things we seldom perceive at the moment of writing. Getting a perspective is a means of generating new ideas.

Adopting a new point of view

Emerson observed that it would be a good idea if every once in a while we took a look at the world through our legs. We know what he was talking about. Everyone has done it, and it is not as silly as it sounds. If we really want to see familiar territory with fresh eyes, we need a new angle of vision.

One of the best examples in literature of the effects of changing perspective is found in the first two books of *Gulliver's Travels.* What Gulliver observes as a giant figure among the Lilliputians is decidedly different from what he observes as a minute figure among the huge Brobdingnagians. In the first book, his superior view leads him constantly to see triviality among men. In the second, he is moved by their grossness.

Any writer can generate new ideas by deliberately contriving a new point of view. It is a standard device among satirists, who find that in order to comment upon men and institutions, they must permit readers to detach themselves from the object being satirized. Thus Orwell's *Animal Farm* creates a world of animals that only thinly disguises the world of men. No true deception really exists, but Orwell knows that we will laugh at, and pass judgment upon, animals. Instinctively, we will come to the defense of people.

The following bit of light satire was written in response to an assignment asking students to write about a human foible from a novel point of view. A young lady submitted this essay:

LITTLE BROWN PICKET

Everyone knows what a peacock is, but how many people have heard of a peahen? This is the question asked by passers-by who notice a little brown picket in front of the NBC employment office, and this is the question the peahen asked herself when she decided to demonstrate to protest the employment discrimination practiced against the fair sex of the peafowl species.

"For too long," she screeches, her glassy, fixed eyes glittering with defiance, "peahens have built their nests in the deserted ruins of buildings and raised their wee peafowl in obscurity, submitting to the selfishness of the peacocks who insist on being the only sex to distinguish the species in the outside world." Her brown speckled feathers ruffle and stand out from her body as she struts up and down demanding that as NBC increases its color telecasts, the company must hire as many peahens as peacocks to introduce "living color."

The feathered suffragette did not begin her battle for recognition with the protest against inequalities in employment opportunities. Last year she struck her nest, refusing to hatch eggs until the peacock agreed to abandon his harem of four peahens and be faithful to her. The peahen does not claim that NBC was the first to relegate her to a position of obscurity. Even before Juno selected the peacock as her favorite bird and India recognized him as a sacred creature, people inferred that there was only one sex among peafowl. Of course the misconception has occurred because his colorful fan of tail feathers attracts admiration. As the peahen presents herself in front of the office— mud-colored, slim, tapered—the question arises: "Has the simple, dignified beauty of the pioneer women who established equality for their sex become less valuable than the gaudy display which glitters on Broadway?"

There is another question plaguing the producers, however. How will she look on colored television when they have to give in and allow her to take her horny, pavement-weary feet into the studio so that she and her peacock, like two peas in a pod, can enjoy equal employment opportunities?

The shock of recognition that comes with a shift in perspective occurs often when we move beyond our most immediate interests. We recognize home ground in far places, even strange places. For instance, we can certainly learn much about expository writing from sources that are not devoted exclusively to it—about logic and diction from poetry, about organization from painting, about style from music. To be sure, the applications are not direct, but the principles are often the same and the same irreducibles are involved. An awareness of factors that operate in other processes creates an awareness of factors that operate in writing. The perspective we gain from an outside source is often the stimulus we need for generating new ideas about our most immediate preoccupations.

JUDGING IDEAS

It is said that Winston Churchill generated ideas profusely, but he couldn't discriminate very well between the good ones and the bad ones. He depended upon his associates for advice. We have a tendency to categorize people by their strengths. Some are best as originators, some as testers, some as critics, and others as practitioners. But we cannot escape the fact that at some time or another everyone passes judgments upon ideas, his own and other people's. Sound judgment often depends upon the degree to which an individual can detach himself from his own views, that is, the extent of his objectivity. It is not unusual, therefore, that we are consistently better judges of other people's ideas than we are of our own. But it is difficult to offset the prevailing belief, particularly among students, that the evaluation of ideas is limited to agreeing or disagreeing with them. Doubtlessly, intuitive judgment operates strongly in the criticism of ideas, but that is not to say that criticism of this kind is insubstantial or uninformed.

The following sections represent an attempt to isolate considerations that enter into the judgment of ideas. These are not designed, as it might appear, for graders of compositions, but for writers, who in order to become better writers must try to make judgments about their own ideas. Self-criticism is the best insurance against adverse criticism from others.

Number and range of ideas

Some individuals obviously have more fertile minds than others. One might account for the difference by stating dogmatically that some people are smarter than others. But it is also true that some highly intelligent people are unproductive. It would be more to the point to observe that some people read more widely than others, and some people work more methodically at generating ideas—both matters of personal initiative. The student who protests that he has nothing to say confesses his inadequacy, his inhibitions, or his indifference.

Relevance of ideas

As we read an essay, we like to have the feeling that the writer knows what he is doing—that he has a purpose in the first place and that what he tells us relates to his own design and satisfies our motive in reading him. An idea, therefore, needs to meet three conditions of relevance: relevance to the writer's controlling theme (the *concept of unity*); relevance to other ideas surrounding it (the *concept of coherence and logicality*); and relevance to experience (the *concept of reality*).

The first two concepts are referred to throughout this book, particularly in Chapter 4. The third probably needs a brief explanation here. The concept of reality may be considered a dangerous test because our views of reality are individual and relative. But the concept of reality, as referred to here, has nothing to do with statements like "All men are inherently good" or "All men are inherently depraved." These are metaphysical assertions, not empirical statements. When a student writes, however, that "all men have the same chance in life," either he is also making a metaphysical assertion (all men are subject to chance), or he is not writing about the same world of daily experience that we know. Thus we apply the criterion of reality. Because we are aware of overwhelming evidence that refutes his idea, we are willing to dismiss it as unrealistic and unsound.

Or consider a corollary of the concept of reality—call it the probability factor. A young lady writes, "Every woman in her heart dreams of the day she will find the man she loves and be fulfilled in sharing a family and future with him." What she writes, of course, is what she feels individually and what many other women like herself undoubtedly feel. The statement is probably representative enough to be phrased "Most women in their hearts dream . . . ," but the probability of this young lady's feelings representing *every* woman is extremely low.

Soundness and reasonableness of ideas

We judge an idea as unsound if we think it cannot be supported by fact or reason, and often we cannot avoid making such a judgment, as this sentence from a student theme illustrates: "The Christian religion is the superior religion of the world, and the white race is the superior race." It is one thing to respond to this claim emotionally; it is another to judge it rationally. How can it be supported or verified? What are the criteria for judgment? To what extent can the criteria stand the test of contradiction on rational grounds? Under this kind of examination, we learn quickly that racism and religious bigotry are emotional positions, not rational ones. They are unsound, not because they are improbable, but because they are untenable.

An idea may also be unsound because it is logically inconsistent within itself; that is, it may be true, but, as stated, one cannot see the necessary connection in the reasoning. Here are several examples:

If people only had the foresight to handle their personal affairs deftly, it would be much easier to get along in the world.

Through his thoughtlessness, the student who cheats on a test puts the welfare of his business associates of later life into jeopardy.

All human beings must possess bad qualities because it is these individual negative traits that breed the problems of society and create the need for organized living.

All three of these statements are characterized by an immense gap between the cause that is stated and the effect that is anticipated. It is not clear how the consequences would necessarily follow from the starting principle because the steps in between are too numerous. These statements represent leaps of thought that a reader cannot easily make because he has not been helped along by the particular facts and illustrations that might support sweeping generalizations such as these.

Soundness, by analogy with medicine, also suggests strength and vitality. The strength of an idea may depend upon its accuracy, its authenticity, its indisputability, or its concreteness. Its vitality is related to its capacity to be developed and to influence. A dead idea is incapable of growth. It points in no direction. A dead idea is end-stop.

The possible influence of an idea has no relation to its size. "Big ideas" may be only inflated notions that are not really going to change anything or persuade anybody. To be sure, not many of us will formulate compelling ideas like Hegel's dialectic theory of progression, but a writer doesn't write great ideas. They become great. He has to start where he is and attempt to hit upon ideas that are open-ended and viable.

Maturity and universality of ideas

The maturity of an idea is easier to judge in some cases than in others, simply because maturity has a close relationship with age and experience. Up until some vague point in time that we call adulthood, maturity is relative. An eight-year-old who thinks like a fifteen-year-old is judged mature. As the years pile up, however, the relative standard diminishes. Adult ideas tend to be only mature or immature, not something in between.

Maturity involves the wise perspective of years. Saying that an idea is immature usually means that it might be more appropriately expressed by a child than by an adult. If an essentially mature idea is underdeveloped in writing, we use words like *premature* or *cursory* to describe it, not *immature* in the sense of not fully mature.

Not many objects that we perceive and think about are totally insignificant. Triviality is a way of looking at them. Even small things take on significance when we realize their implications. If they seem to have none, they remain unimportant—light and entertaining or usable, perhaps, but of no consequence. Note this example written by an adult for an adult:

> A house is a place which I use as a shelter. It shades me from the brightest sunshine and also the windy storms. When the snow starts to fall, I am glad I can get into the house, which can be called home.

These lines have an appealing simplicity, and they express a certain naïve joy. If we did not know their source, we would suspect that they had been written by a child or by an adult for children. But as writing for adults, the ideas are thin and the view trivial. Furthermore, nothing in the entire essay from which it was taken did more to develop the implications that might have grown out of the topic.

Compare a few sentences by Alfred Kazin on a similar theme. He describes his boyhood sense of warmth and shelter in the kitchen of his home and then adds these lines:

> The kitchen gave a special character to our lives, my mother's character. All my memories of that kitchen are dominated by the nearness of my mother sitting all day long at her sewing machine, by the clacking of the treadle against the linoleum floor, by the patient twist of her right shoulder as she automatically pushed at the wheel with one hand or lifted the foot to free the needle where it had got stuck in a thick piece of material. The kitchen was her life. Year by year, as I began to take in her fantastic capacity for labor and her anxious zeal, I realized it was ourselves she kept stitched together.
>
> "The Kitchen" from *A Walker in the City*

Although Kazin's description, like the other, is simple and homely, its maturity grows out of the expansion of the idea. The details are particular; the implication is universal.

Again, like greatness, universality is a judgment made by readers, not an ingredient that the writer throws in. It is a response by those who recognize in the ideas an expression of human experience that transcends time and place. Eugène Ionesco explains quite simply: "I am what I am, take it or leave it. Genuine self-examination is most successful when it helps you to be yourself. And it is by being completely oneself that one has the best chance of being other people too."

Originality of ideas

Originality is more closely related to uniqueness than to novelty. We may be totally incapable of inventiveness, but we all have the capacity, as Ionesco says, to be ourselves. E. E. Cummings says the same thing in his unique way: "To be nobody-but-yourself—in a world which is doing its best, night and day, to make you everybody else—means to fight the hardest battle which any human being can fight; and never stop fighting." In a sentence, he explains why originality is rare. It is easier to think like other people, speak like other people, and write like other people than to be original. Prejudices and clichéd thoughts win us over easily because we fail to resist by thinking our own thoughts and choosing our own words.

Long before the present day, the writer of Ecclesiastes concluded what we may daily conclude: there is no new thing under the sun. Perhaps true, but there is no idea that cannot be freshly rethought by a new mind in a new age. Millions of words have been written about *Hamlet* by millions of people, but a young person of a new generation has the opportunity to assume a unique stance that no one before him could. The hard way is to try to discover what that uniqueness is; the easy way is to rehash what has been said over and over again. The hard way is looking from the inside out; the other is looking around on the outside. Original insights may be all around us, but they are not ours unless we have gone through the business of first assimilating, then relating, then generating.

In the process of writing, we all employ a vast stock of general ideas that are everyone's common property—the source may not even be known—most easily identified as encyclopedic knowledge. These ideas form the broad base of all of our thinking, and our use of them is recognized, without censure, as derivative. But other ideas come to be distinctly identified as someone's personal property, like Buffon's statement that style is the man. If a writer has made a personal investment in an idea—an investment of his time or his insight—it is his, and he deserves to be given credit for it, whether it is quoted directly or paraphrased. The individual who passes off other people's ideas as his own is guilty of plagiarism—and, one might add, of ingratitude. John Ruskin reminds us that we should be more than willing to admit our indebtedness to the past by expressing our thanks, for all of our present knowledge is based upon it. We need to be both honest and grateful.

Clarity of ideas

We commonly refer to "fuzzy thoughts" and "vague notions." Such phrases refer to foggy thinking, not to obscure wording. In section I of his *Enquiry concerning Human Understanding,* David Hume complains about the abstruseness of metaphysics. He believed that the vagueness of the metaphysicians was a "shelter to superstition, and a cover to absurdity and error." Because Hume also believed that any idea, especially an abstract one, was less vivid than a sense impression, he vowed that in his writing about philosophy he would aim to reconcile "profound enquiry with clearness, and truth with novelty." He accomplished that aim especially in a famous passage explaining the idea of necessary connection in terms of playing billiards. The passage demonstrates not only that analogy is a concrete means of dealing with an abstract idea but that the idea was perfectly clear to Hume in the first place. Clear ideas are communicable ideas. A writer who has to struggle to express an idea may have a clue that he himself doesn't know precisely what he wants to say. Recourse to generalities is often a writer's way of pawning off his own uncertainties upon the reader.

Persuasiveness of ideas

Persuasiveness in writing is ordinarily associated with the writer's force—the way in which he can project his material to influence the reader. But there is also the possibility that ideas have a built-in persuasiveness. I refer to ideas that have almost a charismatic effect upon their readers simply because they are interested in anything that pertains to their mania—baseball coverage, even batting averages, to baseball fans; opera news, even cast listings, to opera fanatics; ballet gossip to balletomanes; how-to-do-its to do-it-yourselfers. Any writer who writes on the favorite topic of an enthusiastic audience has something working for him in advance.

On the other hand, there are ideas that carry no persuasiveness at all. Because they are completely self-evident, readers do not react in any way. In this category, we can include platitudes, maxims, bromides, and truisms, which by repetition have long ago worn out their capacity to comment meaningfully. Such statements in writing merely fill up space or try to suggest that anything that has been repeated often enough is bound to be true. In the nonpersuasive category, also, are ideas that are too obvious to bear repetition. Among such statements, I would include the following ones from student papers:

The world has survived for thousands of years and so has the human race.

All minds are different. It takes a while for some to learn, and it takes a relatively short time for others. Some people want to know as much as they can and are very eager to learn. Others don't understand readily and let nature take its course.

Peace is a funny thing, which has different meanings to different people, groups of people, and sections of people.

Statements of this kind neither inform nor persuade. They are truisms that we assume. The theoretical difference between the self-evident and the universal may be as fine a distinction to some people as that between foreknowledge and predestination, but, in practice, the difference grows sharper. One student writes:

A common characteristic of all men is eventual death.

Another:

Later came the misery, the time for burial.

I submit that there is a difference.

THE WHAT AND THE HOW

Favorable court decisions in the long struggle against censorship now permit published writing to contain almost anything. The manner in which it is said, however, is crucial. In our concern for freedom to write what we wish, we often blur the distinction between content and strategy and concentrate almost exclusively upon content. But form, language, and style are not appendages that the writer can cut off if he wishes. They are integral parts of what he is doing; and content, whether it is superb or superficial, depends upon all the parts of writing for its expression. Notwithstanding, we still tend to make separate judgments about the way a writer handles his material and what he says, even going so far as to qualify that a writer's ideas are good, but his presentation is poor. At this point, therefore, we turn more specifically to matters of presentation—to the *how* as well as the *what* of writing.

SUGGESTIONS FOR DISCUSSION

1. Below are a series of facts.
   A. In 1760, James Macpherson published a translation of poetry by the third-century Gaelic bard Ossian: *Fragments of Ancient Poetry, Collected in the Highlands of Scotland, and Translated from the Gaelic or Erse Language.*
   B. He published *Fingal, an Ancient Epic Poem in Six Books* in 1762 and *Temora, an Epic Poem in Eight Books* in 1763.
   C. The poems were greatly admired throughout Europe, particularly by Goethe.
   D. The poems were later proved to be forgeries.
   With these skeletal circumstances, what kinds of questions would you ask as a means of focusing upon a possible topic for writing?
2. Attempt to make correspondences between writing and other art forms. For instance, what does harmony in music correspond to in writing? What does chiaroscuro in painting correspond to? Do these analogies serve any useful purpose in understanding principles about writing?
3. Name several things that seem to you completely trivial, that seem to hold no potential implications for expansion in writing. Do other members of your class agree with you?
4. Examine some specimen writings of other students for statements that seem to have little relevance to the concept of reality as you have experienced it (see page 48).
5. Are there other criteria besides those mentioned in this chapter that should enter into the evaluation of ideas?

ASSIGNMENTS

1. As a test of observation, jot down as many things as you remember seeing at a certain place at some past time. Evaluate your list. How many items are big or small? How many observations are general or particular (a car or 1965 blue Corvair)? How many details can you make more specific if you prod your memory? Does your list comment upon observation or upon your memory of these observations?
2. Write down observations and ideas for a period of one week so that

you have a total of at least twenty-five. See how many of these serve as possible source material for themes during the quarter.

3. Someone once wrote, "Sometimes I look at the people and I think of the chickens." Choose a perspective that will permit you to write about something familiar in a novel way. To establish a perspective, use the formula, "When I look at _____, I think of _____." Then consider whether the analogy you have chosen is capable of expansion.

4

The Shape of Content

Form is formulation—the turning of content into a material entity, rendering a content accessible to others, giving it permanence, willing it to the race.   *Ben Shahn*

Ben Shahn's phrase "The Shape of Content" that is used for this chapter title condenses a great deal about form and structure in very few words. Basically, the phrase states that content comes first. Then form assumes the shape that is determined by that content.

THE NATURE OF FORM

To begin with an exact model or a prescribed form (an organizational pattern provided by an instructor, for instance) is to change the creative act of composition into a writing exercise—going through the motions to build up strength. As useful as exercises may be to learn about writing—and there are some in this book—they are not substitutes for the invention that composition demands. An exercise may provide a prescribed outline to follow, but I am unaware of any other set forms in nonfiction writing comparable to the sonnet, the villanelle, or the heroic couplet in verse. All prose forms are open-structured and flexible. The writer is free to choose his own pattern, just as a poet writing an ode improvises his own form.

I am all too aware that beginning writers sometimes look upon form as a restraint upon spontaneity, in fact as a paralyzing force upon the free expression of ideas. In their rebellion against form, they consider formlessness as the desirable alternative. They see only the extremes of fixed form and formlessness, ignoring flexible form that covers the vast middle ground. Flexible form grows freely and organically out of content. Accepting it as a principle, one writer can produce tight, highly disciplined writing; another one, loose, freely associative prose.

But the starting point, as Shahn suggests, is the thought. In a lecture he delivered at Harvard during his visit there in 1956–1957 and later published as *The Shape of Content,* Shahn speaks of six demands that form makes upon the artist. Although his remarks have particular reference to painting and sculpture, they seem so completely applicable to the task of the writer that they may be adopted here as the conditions for finding form in writing:

1. Determining a theme
2. Gathering material together
3. Setting limits, what Shahn calls an "outer shape"

4. Relating the inner parts to the outside limits
5. Eliminating material that does not fall within the bounds
6. Ordering the whole to meet the needs of content

In these steps, we have an orderly statement of the manner in which form disciplines content, or the way in which writing orders thinking. No one can say categorically to what extent form must be developed steadily or to what extent it emerges spontaneously. The difference will no doubt depend upon individual temperament. One writer will collect his material and harbor his ideas for a long period of time, suddenly to discover that everything falls into shape. Another writer will need to forge a shape first in order to mold the remainder of his thoughts. First or last, effortlessly or laboriously, the writer cannot ignore form. Weakness in structure may indicate an indifference to the discipline of orderly thinking or may result simply from the inadequacy of the materials to be formed.

Most of the six steps listed above are self-explanatory in terms of writing. What may not be readily apparent is the difference between outer shape and inward shape, suggested by points 3 and 4.

EXTERNAL AND INTERNAL STRUCTURE

Several years ago I heard a lecture by the American poet Howard Nemerov. One particular thing he said stuck with me—an extremely simple but revealing statement. He reminded us of the obvious but absolutely basic fact that form may be considered as either *the inside of the outside* or *the outside of the inside*. Think of an actual building— the outer walls and the inner structure. Think of the human body—the skeletal frame and the connective tissues. Finally, think of a piece of writing—not only the outside limits of the topic and the skeletal organization of the whole but also the cohesiveness that needs to exist within and between words, sentences, and paragraphs. One more important than the other? Surely not. Without doubt, the teaching of writing has weighed in favor of external form because it is the most easily perceived and most easily taught. Yet the truth remains that a student who may be able to construct a beautifully symmetrical outline and even follow it as the plan of his writing may end up with a poorly structured essay simply because he is careless about internal construction of sentences and paragraphs. To create an awareness of internal structure, we need a device that will show the *inside* of writing as graphically as the formal outline shows the outside shape. Here we encounter a handicap in trying to reveal what goes on in the mind of an individual writer because we are limited to showing the way he characteristically structures his thoughts on paper. But the transcription of thoughts is a clue. We can analyze the written structure of other writers in order to gain an intuitive sense of how to structure our own thoughts.

STRUCTURAL DIAGRAMMING: LEVELS OF GENERALITY

Structural diagramming demands first of all a careful reading of a paragraph to see if there is a perceptible structure. It is based upon the assumption that any thought that follows another is either more particular than the previous thought, more general than the previous thought, or an extension of the previous thought and therefore coordinate with it on the same level of generality. Thoughts that follow one another in sequence with almost no variation in the level of generality, like the most simple narratives, tend to move along quickly. But the careful speaker or writer cannot depend upon general statements alone if he wants to be fully understood. He needs to explain, to support, to illustrate, to describe; and in doing these things he constantly makes the thought more particular. He stops the forward movement of discourse, as it were, to linger over a particular point in depth.

Thus in speaking of levels of generality, we are probing the directions that thinking takes as it occurs. If we become aware of characteristic patterns of thinking, we can use them ourselves when our own thoughts need direction.

A simple diagram can indicate the movement of thought. Sentences that are coordinate can be placed under one another, indicating that the level of generality stays the same. Parallel phrasing, repetition, and balanced structure help to identify coordinate thoughts, although these devices are not absolutely necessary. A sentence that introduces a more particular thought is indented to the right. If the thought of the next sentence is clearly more general, the indentation moves out again to the left. The indentation is only a means to suggest which ideas are more general than others and which accordingly are more particular. The result should be a diagram that shows related thoughts and shifting levels of generality.

This brief illustration diagrams only the beginning of a paragraph by Robert Louis Stevenson:

> I overheard the other day a scrap of conversation, which I take the liberty to reproduce.
>
> "What I advance is true," said one.
>
> "But not the whole truth," answered the other.
>
> "Sir," returned the first (and it seemed to me there was a smack of Dr. Johnson in the speech), "Sir, there is no such thing as the whole truth!"
>
> Indeed, there is nothing so evident in life as that there are two sides to a question.
>
> "Crabbed Age and Youth"

This diagram attempts to illustrate that these five sentences contain three levels of generality. Stevenson begins with a fairly general remark to the effect that he recently overheard a conversation. In the next three sentences, diagrammed as parallel with one another, he records the dialogue. These are exact details. One is not more particular than the other; each merely adds to the previous thought. Stevenson then draws from this entire anecdote a generalization, which the diagram suggests is the highest level of generality in the paragraph. Thus the right and left movement in the diagram reflects changing levels of generality, while the unchanging indentation signifies coordinate thoughts of the same level.

Framed structure

Let's now look at an entire paragraph to see how a structural diagram reflects additional elements of structure:

Education, first of all, is the opposite of ignorance. Jefferson makes this clear.

The phrases he uses elsewhere as synonyms of education indicate the positive meaning he attaches to the concept.

The kind of schooling that is vital to a democratic society is

the kind that results in the "spread of information" and the "diffusion of knowledge;"

the kind that regards "science . . . [as] more important in a republican than in any other government;"

the kind that recognizes that "the general mind must be strengthened by education;"

the kind that aims to make the people "enlightened" and to "inform their discretion."

These are the ends that the schools must serve if a free people are to remain free.

These, be it noted, are intellectual ends.

General education, in short, is intellectual training.

Arthur E. Bestor, Jr.
"Aimlessness in Education"

Once the paragraph has been set down in this form, we begin to perceive its development and the strategies the writer uses to brace it internally. First, we have a general statement, phrased in the negative. ("Education . . . is the opposite of ignorance.") We then have a sentence that is so closely coordinate with the first that it is diagrammed as if it were a continuation of the first sentence. It affirms the opening statement and adds the authority of Jefferson to the author's own. Separated as the sentence is by a period (it could be joined to the first by a semicolon), it operates also as a kind of transition, for the clarification that the sentence promises is given in what follows by means of quotations from Jefferson. These phrases are catalogued, exactly parallel in structure. Although they are all contained in one sentence, I have emphasized the author's dependence upon parallelism as a structural device by placing the parallel phrases under one another. The author then draws two inferences from these phrases, returning us to the second statement and preparing for a reassertion of the original generalization of sentence 1, this time phrased positively ("General education . . . is intellectual training").

What we learn from this analysis and diagram is that Professor Bestor has written a precisely organized and tightly structured paragraph. Although in reading it we may think the thought advances, the diagram would suggest by its levels that it would be more appropriate to say that the thought has deepened, not moved forward to any significant degree. The final sentence brings us full circle. We come back to the beginning, ready to go on to the next paragraph once this thought has been established. The paragraph is a fine illustration of framed structure, in which the opening and closing statements frame the thought of the entire paragraph.

Free structures

All paragraphs by no means reflect such a balanced pattern. Nor should they. Paragraphs with different purposes and content will reveal different contours. Note how this paragraph poses a question, to be answered in the same paragraph:

The object of our scrutiny pleads for definition.

What is an intellectual?

I shall define him as *properly* an individual who has elected as his primary duty and pleasure in life the activity of thinking in a Socratic way about moral problems, whether these be social or individual.

He explores such problems consciously, articulately, and candidly, first by asking factual questions, then by asking moral questions, finally by suggesting action which seems appropriate in the light of the factual and moral information which he has elicited.

His function is analogous to that of a judge, who must first ascertain the facts, then the law, and in the end must accept the obligation of revealing in as obvious a manner as possible the course of reasoning which led him to his decision.

Morton Cronin, "The American Intellectual"

The first sentence of this paragraph is not an integral part of the thought. The writer might have omitted it except that it is transitional and attempts to explain briefly why a definition is necessary. Since the second sentence is the exact question and "the object of our scrutiny," it is indented. Because the answers give us particulars about an intellectual, those sentences are indented further: two statements are made about the preoccupations of the intellectual; the analogy in the final sentence merely extends those functions. But one should not ignore the considerable piling up of detail within sentences. The internal structure also operates to deepen the movement by giving even more particulars.

A paragraph by Rachel Carson shows a pattern like that of the Cronin example, but the effect is quite different. The appearance of the sentences also suggests that difference:

> On land and sea the stream of life poured on.
>
>> New forms evolved;
>> some old ones declined and disappeared.
>
>>> On land the mosses and the ferns and the seed plants developed.
>>>
>>> The reptiles for a time dominated the earth, gigantic, grotesque, and terrifying.
>>>
>>> Birds learned to live and move in the ocean of air.
>>>
>>> The first small mammals lurked inconspicuously in hidden crannies of the earth as though in fear of the reptiles.

> Rachel Carson, from *The Sea Around Us*

Note that in this essentially narrative paragraph the thought moves forward rapidly. The limited number of particulars, briefly stated, contributes to a fast pace. It would be difficult to insist that the second sentence moves to a lower level of generality, but phrases like "new forms" and "some old ones" are more particular than "stream of life." The last four sentences are illustrations and therefore indented further.

One last example illustrates another pattern, although it should now be apparent that every paragraph embodies a shape of its own determined by its own purpose and content and the author's conscious awareness of strategy. This paragraph is the opening one of a Freshman analysis of Theodore Roethke's "The Meadow Mouse":

> The question raised by Roethke in this poem is not *"Where* has he gone, my meadow mouse . . .?" but *why* has he gone, my meadow mouse?

> This is a bewildered emotional protest against the inevitable subjection of frail innocence to the laws of nature.

> > I think that it was not the "beastie" the man sought to shelter but the "sleekit, cow'rin, tim'rousness" within it.

> Innocence is good.

> > Because the meadow mouse possessed this quality, the speaker sought to shelter it, to rub shoulders with it, to be reassured of his own good—or innocence—by association.

> > This need to be recognized by the mouse is, indeed, so great that the poet is blinded to all else except acceptance and trust:

> > > "Do I imagine he no longer trembles
> > > "When I come close to him?
> > > "He seems no longer to tremble."

> The trembling never stops.

> The mouse is gone in the morning.

> Man is ultimately and completely rejected—by a mouse.

> > Better to tremble at the terrible hands of nature than to die in the alien hands of man.

> > Man's imperfections, his "out of tuneness" with nature, prohibit the presence of innocence.

> > > The crude, cradling hand would but crush the nestling thumb of the child.

> > > The silk stocking would but smother.

> > > The shoebox—a prison.

> It is better that this nestling should fall back into nature.

> The mouse, and all creatures, should live at the courtesy of nature's laws or not at all.

> This, to me, is why.

In diagram form, this paragraph appears less symmetrical than the others we have analyzed, but that is not to say that it is a bad paragraph, only that it is more loosely structured than the other samples. Yet at the end the writer makes it a framed paragraph; the last sentence takes us back to the opening. In between, the writer moves back and forth from particular details of the poem to reflections and generalizations that occur to him as he analyzes. Although the discourse flows freely, the writer seems to be in control of his material. He is not simply putting down the next thought that pops into his mind. His allusions to Burns's "To a Mouse" (sentence 3) and Wordsworth's "The World Is Too Much with Us" ("Man's imperfections, his 'out of tuneness' with nature . . .") are suggested intrinsically by the material.

Obviously, long paragraphs tend to shift levels of generality more frequently than short ones. The diagrammer's task is simply to see each sentence in relation to its immediate neighbor and to the neighborhood of the paragraph as a whole. One is free to make as many subdivisions of particularity as he wishes, but if he makes too many fine distinctions, he will lose the sense of contour that the diagram is able to portray.

Even though the structure of some paragraphs is more complex than that of others, it would be a mistake to associate simple structure with immature paragraphs and complex structure with mature ones. The quality of maturity or the lack of it depends much more upon the level of the thought, the texture of the sentences, and the sophistication of the language than upon the structure itself. The following student paragraph may illustrate:

> We all have faults and make mistakes.
> I think there are general weaknesses in men and women.
>
> > Men tend to be vain and fall into the female's trap of insincere flattery.
> >
> > Men tend to forget the little things in life that are important to women.
> >
> > Sometimes they get so involved in their job of breadwinning that their only thought is to earn money.
> >
> > On the other hand, women are domineering, conniving, and try to boss the whole family.

> Many times they forget their appearance and let them-
> selves go and actually become repulsive to their hus-
> bands.
>
> Today we have forgotten the old roles the man and woman
> used to play.
> It seems the father is to his family only chairman of
> entertainment.
> All the wife can see is her single role of mother.
>
> But we can't be perfect.

The arrangement of this paragraph is hardly responsible for the
impression of immaturity it gives. The writer is orderly; he is aware of
levels of generality and balance; he even consciously frames the
thought. But the content is platitudinous, the sentences are underdeveloped, the generalizations sweeping, and the language dull.

Doubtlessly, some paragraphs will resist diagramming altogether.
Although it would be futile to claim that a structural diagram infallibly
tests good writing, a struggle to diagram may suggest strongly that a
paragraph is faulty or, at least, that its structure might be strengthened
by closer attention to the kinds of structural connections that bind
sentences and paragraphs closely together, namely, mechanical, rhetorical, grammatical, lexical, and semantic links.

MECHANICAL CONNECTIONS

The most perfunctory kind of structural link is mechanical, mainly the
use of punctuation to do the job that words and meanings and strategies do
more subtly and effectively. However, even when a writer has composed
a coherent paragraph, he may still choose to bind his prose more
closely together by a mechanical device. Note this paragraph by Thomas
Huxley:

> For I hold very strongly by two convictions—The first is, that
> neither the discipline nor the subject-matter of classical education
> is of such direct value to the student of physical science as to
> justify the expenditure of valuable time upon either; and the second
> is, that for the purpose of attaining real culture, an exclusively

scientific education is at least as effectual as an exclusively literary education.

"Science and Culture"

Huxley's choice of punctuation, of course, raises the question how much he really gains by combining three separate sentences as he does. Each reader needs to answer that question for himself, just as he does if he chooses to do something comparable when he writes his own prose.

Writers of fiction commonly try to create special effects of continuity by punctuation, particularly when they want to suggest an uninterruptedness in speech or reverie. The stream-of-consciousness technique of *Tristram Shandy* relies heavily upon Sterne's mechanics:

> My father had scarce read the letter, when taking the thing by the right end, he instantly began to plague and puzzle his head how to lay it out mostly to the honour of his family—A hundred and fifty odd projects took possession of his brains by turns—he would do this, and that, and t'other—He would go to *Rome*—he would go to law—he would buy stock—he would buy *John Hobson's* farm—he would new forefront his house, and add a new wing to make it even—There was a fine water-mill on this side, and he would build a wind-mill on the other side of the river in full view to answer it—But above all things in the world, he would enclose the great *Oxmoor,* and send out my brother *Bobby* immediately upon his travels.

Bk. IV, Chap. 31

Many writers, like Sterne, favor the dash for this purpose. A few others use the colon.

RHETORICAL CONNECTIONS

Rhetorical connections operate to bind sentences in a paragraph together by structural resemblances. Or they may operate on a larger scale to join paragraphs together into larger units of discourse. The framing device we have already discussed qualifies as a rhetorical strategy of this kind. Writers also depend heavily upon exact repetition, parallelism, and balance, all of which may occur simultaneously, as the following paragraph illustrates:

On the other hand, we could compete with the Russians by imitating them.

We could force students to go into science and engineering whether they wish it or not.

We could draft scientists for governmental research.

We could arbitrarily restrict the production of consumer goods while we develop new scientific weapons.

We could pour unlimited money into special projects without regard to other needs.

We could reserve our universities for only those whose talents we seek.

We could impose upon our students a workload injurious to their health and personality.

We could remove all elements of choice in our high schools and colleges, all influence of public opinion, all vestiges of academic freedom.

> John F. Kennedy, Speech delivered at
> Loyola College, February 18, 1958

There is no question that the seven sentences following the first sentence and patterned after it were designed to fit together. Figuratively speaking, they are piled on top of one another, and they almost coincide because the subject and auxiliary verb of each are the same, the length is almost equal, and the basic sentence pattern is unvaried. The repetition and parallelism set up a regular rhythm that favors no one statement. Each is emphasized in turn.

Whereas Kennedy's material lends itself to repetition and parallelism, the content of Russell's paragraph quoted below invites extensive use of balance:

There is another important difference, and that is that Moscow orthodoxy is much more all-pervasive than that of Washington.

In America, if you are a geneticist, you may hold whatever view of Mendelism the evidence makes you regard as the most probable;
in Russia, if you are a geneticist who disagrees with Lysenko, you are liable to disappear mysteriously.

In America, you may write a book debunking Lincoln if you feel so disposed;
in Russia, if you write a book debunking Lenin, it would not be published and you would be liquidated.

If you are an American economist, you may hold, or not hold, that America is heading for a slump;
in Russia, no economist dare question that an American slump is imminent.

In America, if you are a professor of philosophy, you may be an idealist, a materialist, a pragmatist, a logical positivist, or whatever else may take your fancy; at congresses you can argue with men whose opinions differ from yours, and listeners can form a judgment as to who has the best of it.
In Russia, you must be a dialectical materialist, but at one time the element of materialism outweighs the element of dialectic, and at other times, it is the other way round.

If you fail to follow the developments of official metaphysics with sufficient nimbleness, it will be the worse for you.

Stalin at all times knows the truth about metaphysics, but you must not suppose that the truth this year is the same as it was last year.

Bertrand Russell, "The Future of Mankind"

Repeated words and phrases throughout the paragraph add to the strong sense of coherence that grows out of the balance. In fact, the failure of the last two sentences to follow the pattern breaks the cumulative sense of climax, and the paragraph sags at the end. But not without purpose. Russell adds the punch in a strategic, single-sentence paragraph:

In such a world intellect must stagnate, and even technological progress must soon come to an end.

GRAMMATICAL CONNECTIONS

We of course recognize syntactic features that tie the parts of a sentence together: verbs agree with subjects, pronouns agree with their antecedents, words modify other words. These relationships also establish dependencies. We concern ourselves with such things when we analyze a sentence. Similar kinds of grammatical interactions help to fuse the sentences of a paragraph. Note in what way pronouns and verbs serve as links in this paragraph by Russell Lynes:

> The newspapers, which in those days devoted a great deal of space to describing in loving detail the parties, costumes, guest lists and menus of Society, had a field day with Mrs. Bradley Martin's ball. The first five pages of the New York *Journal* were devoted entirely to **it** on the day after the party. Even the London *Daily Mail* regaled its readers with a full, if somewhat wryly amused, account of the ball. But it was the publicity that gave the Bradley Martins their comeuppance. The moralists got after **them**. In *The Saga of American Society,* where the story of the party is recounted in great detail (and from which I have borrowed), Dixon Wecter writes: "Newspaper editors, clergymen, and college debating societies discussed the heartless extravagance of wealth, and even more effectively the New York authorities more than doubled the city tax assessment of the Bradley Martins." As a result **they** gave up **their** home in New York and went to live permanently in London.
>
> Russell Lynes, *A Surfeit of Honey*

All the pronouns in boldface have antecedents in a previous sentence. Their form, as well as their meaning, therefore depends upon another sentence, and the grammatical interaction ties the paragraph together.

Likewise, the tenses of the verbs are set by the context. Consistency of tense unifies a paragraph grammatically. Although the Lynes paragraph begins in past tense and continues in the past for five sentences, the sixth sentence changes to present tense because conventionally quotations are given in the historical present. But once the quotation is ended, note that the last sentence resumes past tense, completing the grammatical pattern of the paragraph as a whole.

LEXICAL CONNECTIONS

Somewhat more obviously working toward connections between sentences are a large group of words and phrases that we ordinarily classify as *transitional.* Their chief reason for being is simply to cue the reader to relationships within sentences and between sentences. Here we are concerned with them as signals between sentences within a paragraph or between paragraphs in a larger unit of discourse.

One need only browse through a typical anthology of essays to observe that some writers depend more heavily upon these conjunctives than others, but that none can do without them altogether. These words operate not only as structural connectives but as logical guides. A classification of the most common ones in terms of their logical implications will suggest their usefulness to the writer, particularly to the inexperienced writer who may be uncertain where he's going once he has written his opening sentence:

1. Words signaling a sentence closely resembling the previous sentence, an elaboration of it (and thus a narrowing of the thought because it becomes more specific), a reinforcement or emphasis of it, or a summary: *also, too, and, or, nor, for, once again, in addition, furthermore, likewise, moreover, besides, that is to say, namely, in fact, of course, to be sure, indeed, finally, in conclusion.*

> Examples: The three plays are remarkably similar in form. The language is uncomplicated, simple, common to the point of vulgarity, and very much like actual conversation. The action, also, is uncomplicated and easy to follow.
>
> Anatol's problem is that he himself cannot love wholeheartedly, and he knows it. Indeed, he knows it, because he sees too clearly behind the illusions that people live by, even his own illusion of trying to find true love.

2. Words signaling a specific illustration or comparison: *that is, likewise, namely, for example, for instance, by way of illustration.*

> Example: Odets often attempts to equate the problems and prognostications of Communism with conditions existing in the United States during the post-depression decade. *Waiting for Lefty,* for example, deals with the unification of exploited New York cab drivers who want to raise

their economic status. [Moving the connective out of first position often produces a more satisfying rhythmic effect.]

3. Words signaling a contrast, discrimination, or qualification of a point that has already been conceded: *but, however, on the contrary, on the other hand, still, nevertheless, yet, notwithstanding, anyway, anyhow, in any event.*

> Examples: These three plays by Eugène Ionesco now enjoy a a lively present. But do they have a future?
>
> *The Lesson* is a farce. Yet every belly laugh is tempered with an awareness that behind the humor is the hint of impending tragedy.

4. Words signaling a time relationship or space order: *first, second, at the beginning, then, later, finally, at the same time, in front, to the side, at the top, a bit further on.*

> Example: As Gorky matured, his association with the under-privileged masses created in him a disgust for their plight. At the same time, he rebelled against the weakened intelligentsia who were losing their direction in the shifting social and political movements.

5. Words signaling conclusions, responses, results, or consequences: *so, hence, consequently, accordingly, therefore, then, thus, as a result.*

> Example: The characters discover that blame lies nowhere, that there is no basic inherent reason for their existence. Life, therefore, is what they see it to be; life is what they make it.

SEMANTIC CONNECTIONS

Despite the necessity of structural connectives and the familiarity of all writers with them, they do not appear in prose with the frequency that we might expect. They may be used only once in every five or ten sentences, perhaps less frequently. The coherence of most sentences, therefore, depends solidly upon close congruity of meaning. Note the thematic and verbal associations in this paragraph by Joseph Wood Krutch:

> The eighteenth century invented a useful distinction which we have almost lost, the distinction between the beautiful and the sublime.
>
> The first, even when it escapes being merely the pretty, is easy and reassuring.
>
> The sublime, on the other hand, is touched with something which inspires awe.
>
> It is large and powerful;
> it carries with it the suggestion that it might overwhelm us if it would.
>
> By these definitions there is no doubt which is the right word for the desert.
>
> In intimate details, as when its floor is covered after a spring rain with the delicate little ephemeral plants, it is pretty.
>
> But such embodiments of prettiness seem to be only tolerated with affectionate contempt by the region as a whole.
>
> As a whole the desert is, in the original sense of the word, "awful."
>
> Perhaps one feels a certain boldness in undertaking to live with it and a certain pride when one discovers that one can.
>
> Joseph Wood Krutch, *The Voice of the Desert*

The first sentence of this paragraph introduces two themes, the idea of the beautiful and the idea of the sublime. Because Krutch thinks we in the twentieth century have lost the distinction between the two, he undertakes to define. Sentence 2 therefore comments upon the beautiful. We are reminded of an equivalent phrase (*the pretty*) and provided with two adjectives that characterize the beautiful (*easy* and *reassuring*). The third sentence comments upon the sublime, associating *awe* with it. Sentences 2 and 3 are also connected by a lexical marker (*on the other hand*) that emphasizes their difference, the distinction we have lost. Sentence 4 elaborates further upon the sublime by associating additional words with it: *large, powerful, overwhelm.*

At this point, we have a transitional sentence, which first gathers up what has been said (*by these definitions*) and then anticipates what is yet to come (*the right word for the desert*). The next two sentences return to *pretty* and *prettiness,* conceding some prettiness in the desert but no enduring tolerance for it. The right word is *awful.* Krutch adds the qualifying phrase, *in the original sense of the word,* which takes us back to the eighteenth-century distinction he refers to in the first sentence. The final sentence is a philosophical reflection upon the adventure of living with the awful. But it is not left to dangle; it is tied grammatically to the previous sentence by the use of *it.* The entire paragraph thus plays variations upon a double theme, one finally emerging dominant. Nothing is irrelevant. Every sentence is doing work in establishing and connecting the meaning.

Contrast the semantic tightness of Krutch's paragraph with the following student paragraph:

We are considered to be products of our culture.

Each succeeding generation adds something to the culture.

Technology is constantly changing.

By comparing the mode of transportation and communication that is used today with that used a few decades ago, one can see major changes taking place within our short lives.

Cultures are subdivided into institutions.

These institutions vary a grèat deal between cultures.

A glaring example is the religious institution.

Some cultures hinge their very existence upon religion; other cultures have a haphazard approach to religion, or it may be non-existent.

Each culture must have a means to communicate within itself.

In earlier days when each group of people was isolated from each other, each developed its own language.

The individualism that developed from isolated cultures is one of the main problems of the world today.

As the diagram indicates, this paragraph is not without structure, not without rhetorical parallelism and balance, not without grammatical connectives, not without verbal ties and recurrent themes. But it lacks completely a controlling idea and thereby lacks unity of meaning. The thesis announced in the first sentence is altered in the second. From that point on, the writer skips and hops without control from one topic to another. The result is incoherence and illogicality.

INFORMAL LOGIC

What we customarily refer to as illogicality in composition is the very kind of disconnectedness noted in the student paragraph above. The logic of composition depends primarily upon relatedness, that is, internal consistency. The preoccupation of formal logic with external form is not binding upon the writer. We have to recognize that the formal logician does something quite different from the writer who produces logical prose. The logician is a master of his system, a refined but closed system. He makes categorical statements about formal errors in reasoning. He may at times concern himself less with the truth of his premises than with the validity of their form. He does not generate ideas; he tests them.

Although formal logic may be an aid to the writer by disciplining his thinking—making him aware of orderliness and fallacy—it may also deter him from inventing and freely exploring an argument. A writer is a dialectician, not a formal logician. If he starts with a syllogism—that is, a set model—he is likely to produce a stereotyped or sterile argument. He is subject to the danger that any writer risks who fails to start with content and let the shape suit the material.

CONTROLLING THESIS: COMMON REFERENT

Illogicality in composition, then, commonly results from an unbridged gap between sentences or a failure to arrange them appropriately. Observe this incredible opening paragraph of a student theme:

> Woman has become less feminine. The reason for her decline can be traced to the gradual decay of the moral fiber in mankind.

> Man has rejected his role as guardian; a delinquent womankind has been the result. We must realize that woman is not a completely rational creature and therefore cannot be held responsible for the predicament she is in.

Even though this paragraph may not seem to justify analysis, we sometimes learn more from egregiously bad examples than from exemplary ones. As we begin to read, we stumble almost immediately upon the non sequitur between the first two sentences. The writer presumably wants to say that the status of women has declined (from what point?) *because* women are now less feminine than they used to be; that is, he apparently wants to express a reciprocal relationship between sentence 1 and sentence 2 that he does not define verbally for the reader. One might dwell further upon the lack of coherence in this paragraph, but it soon becomes apparent that the logical problem originates from an absence of pattern. The three words *decline, delinquent,* and *predicament,* spaced throughout the paragraph, relate to one another. They characterize in a vague way woman's present predicament, the state of moral decline in which she finds herself. If the writer had established the idea of moral decline as his controlling thesis, he would then have seen that the remainder of his material included three reasons for that decline: (1) woman's flight from femininity, (2) man's flight from woman (his role as guardian), and (3) woman's inability to flee from her own irrational nature. If the writer had hit upon a controlling idea, he might have been able to give order to his otherwise nonsensical remarks. Simply stated, a writer needs an organizing principle—a controlling thesis.

A controlling thesis, however, should not be confused with what is often referred to as a topic sentence. A topic sentence in some cases may be the controlling thesis of a single paragraph. But if a paragraph is a part of a larger unit of discourse, consisting of three paragraphs, for instance, the controlling thesis might be stated in a topic sentence at the end of the first paragraph and be left implicit in the remaining ones. Either stated or unstated, the controlling thesis functions as a common referent—the hook on which other ideas have to hang. Logicality depends upon a unified theme, because as soon as we cannot determine the common denominator—as soon as we lose sight of the referent—a logical gap occurs. At that point, when the reader is left to his own resources to supply relationships and meanings, the writer has jeopardized his chances of communicating logically and effectively.

PATTERNS OF THOUGHT

Rather consistently I have avoided speaking of form as something set, something static. Form is actually a paradox. It both deactivates and activates content. It deactivates by giving a permanent written arrangement to thoughts. But when the prose is read, form again operates and functions for the reader as it did originally for the writer. Form is not inert; it does something to the reader. We might think of it as an elaborate mechanism set up by the writer that goes into motion when the reader turns it on. However, the analogy between writing and a machine cannot be pressed too far. One of the chief differences is that writing cannot be assembled by a layout and directions contained in a book. Form has to be invented, and it has to be adjusted to every situation. If this is true, several questions arise immediately. Does it necessarily follow that no patterns exist? that chaos reigns? that every writer is completely on his own?

To a certain degree, he is. But we should also remember that, individual though thinking is, we are all susceptible to conventional patterns of thought. Even though differences may exist, patterns of writing clearly resemble one another just as surely as big rectangles and little squares are more like each other than they are like circles. We know from our own experience and from the ways other people speak and write that we approach problems in a limited number of ways. We may first seek principles and then make applications, or we may begin with details and come to conclusions. In one instance, we have started with the general and proceeded to the particular; in the other, we have reversed the procedure.

We can think in serial fashion—first, second, third, finally; here, there, further on; least important, more important, most important. These are simply chronological, spatial, and rhetorical arrangements, and the human mind does not limit itself to an unvarying order. We find an arrangement of middle-beginning-end (*in medias res*) as logically satisfying as an order of beginning-middle-end.

In the course of thinking, we also make associations in terms of likenesses and differences, or we trace interactions, perhaps from causes to effects or from effects to causes. The mind finds direction in these general patterns. In such ways, the writer also proceeds.

Let's see the details of each of these patterns worked out in terms of single paragraphs of different purposes. I do not mean to suggest that the purpose determines the form or limits it, but only to show that these writers have worked out forms appropriate to their purpose. The marginal notations attempt to describe the pattern in general terms.

GENERAL TO PARTICULAR: DEFINITION AND COMPARISON

Definition 1	Poetry, when it is really such, is truth;
Definition 2	and fiction also, if it is good for anything, is truth: but they are different truths.
Differences	The truth of poetry is to paint the human soul truly: the truth of fiction is to give a true picture of *life*.
	The two kinds of knowledge are different, and come by different ways, come mostly to different persons.
Elaboration upon definition 1	Great poets are often proverbially ignorant of life.
	What they know has come by observation of themselves; they have found *there* one highly delicate, and sensitive, and refined specimen of human nature, on which the laws of emotion are written in large characters, such as can be read off without much study: and other knowledge of mankind, such as comes to men of the world by outward experience, is not indispensable to them as poets:
Elaboration upon definition 2	but to the novelist such knowledge is all in all; he has to describe outward things, not the inward man; actions and events, not feelings; and it will not do

for him to be numbered among those
who, as Madame Roland said of Bris-
sot, know man but not *men.*

John Stuart Mill, "What is Poetry?"

It should be apparent that Mill's exploration of a definition of poetry
in terms of two topics instead of one shapes the pattern of this paragraph.

PARTICULAR TO GENERAL: INDUCTIVE ARGUMENT

Five facts
Korematsu was born on our soil, of parents
born in Japan.

The Constitution makes him a citizen of the
United States by nativity and a citizen of
California by residence.

No claim is made that he is not loyal to this
country.

There is no suggestion that apart from the
matter involved here he is not law-abiding
and well disposed.

Korematsu, however, has been convicted of
an act not commonly a crime.

Conclusion
It consists merely of being present in the state
whereof he is a citizen, near the place where he was
born, and where all his life he has lived.

Justice Robert H. Jackson, *Korematsu v. United States*

This is the first paragraph of Justice Jackson's minority report in
the Korematsu case. It may be noted that the conclusion is highly ironic
on the basis of the selected evidence he gives in the first five sentences.

GENERAL TO PARTICULAR: DEDUCTIVE ARGUMENT

Context of the argument: a
man's guilt must be per-
sonal and not inheritable.
Now, if any fundamental assumption
underlies our system, it is that guilt is
personal and not inheritable.

Even if all of one's antecedents had been convicted of
treason, the Constitution forbids its penalties to be visited

upon him, for it provides that "no attainder of treason shall work corruption of blood, or forfeiture except during the life of the person attainted."

Assumed: Korematsu's guilt is inherited.

But here is an attempt to make an otherwise innocent act a crime merely because this prisoner is the son of parents as to whom he had no choice, and belongs to a race from which there is no way to resign.

Hence: Under peacetime legislation, Korematsu would be innocent.

If Congress in peace-time legislation should enact such a criminal law, I should suppose this Court would refuse to enforce it.

Justice Robert H. Jackson, *Korematsu v. United States*

This is the fourth paragraph in Justice Jackson's argument in the Korematsu case. He has shifted his approach from inductive to deductive. Accordingly, the form adjusts to suit the material.

SERIAL: DESCRIPTION, NARRATION, PROCESS

Action-location

I write these pages in a room which has a bay window of four sections.

Hypothetical action

If I rise from my desk and look out through the left-hand section, I may record in my mind that "I see the quadrangle."

Location

I do not, in fact, see the quadrangle.

I see only a portion of it.

Details

What I see, furthermore, is a portion of the quad isolated within the frame of this section of my window.

This frame encloses a form of picture—the tower, a tree, some grass, some stone, some windows, a student who has paused and is reading a letter, a segment of the sky and some clouds.

> Since all these things are artificially re-
> lated to one another by being framed, I
> not only see those various things but am
> aware of their pictorial relationship, which
> changes them from facts to forms, eloquent
> now through their relationship.

Sean O'Faolain, "Virginia Woolf and James Joyce"

This quotation is only one-half of O'Faolain's paragraph. In this portion, he describes how he writes description by a process of selection. Both narration and description are involved. The arrangement is serial.

GENERAL TO PARTICULAR IN SERIAL: CLASSIFICATION AND ANALYSIS

The whole, consisting of five parts	Ideally, the short detective story is a sequence of five parts, for which it is a pity that Greek names cannot at this late date be invented.
The first part	First comes the preamble, philosophic in tone, and if possible paradoxical or otherwise arresting.
	It sets the mood by providing a sample of what Poe called ratiocination.
	However you pronounce it, ratiocination is a heart-warming prospect.
	The detective theorizes upon some aspect of life which the story will bear out, though he himself does not as yet know this.
The second part	Next comes the predicament—mysterious, horrible, grotesque, or merely puzzling—the variation from the norm which invites inquiry.
	The commonplace mind, represented by the client or by some other embodiment of the *ewig-Watsonisches,* tries to assimilate the unusual and fails.

But the superior mind, the detective intellect, seen through a cloud of smoke, discerns the true question and feels immortal inklings upon him—as may be gathered from the irritating silence which follows his voluble beginning.

Jacques Barzun
"Detection and the Literary Art"

The missing three parts are discussed in Barzun's next paragraph, indicating that when the two paragraphs are combined, they represent a single unit of discourse.

SERIAL–GENERAL TO PARTICULAR: EXPLANATION

Assertion 1	The relationship between the male and female timber wolf is unique among lower and some higher forms of animal life.
Support	These animals mate for life, and if one dies the other will not take another mate.
	However, the survivor may join and assist another family.
Assertion 2	The undisputed head of the family is the male, which is generally larger and much stronger than the female.
	He is held in reverence by the females and will tolerate no nonsense from them.
Illustration	While a family is being raised, the male will do most of the hunting, returning each evening and disgorging a good part of the day's catch for the female.
	After the pups have been weaned, he will from time to time relieve her of her responsibilities, allowing her to hunt and assist in providing for the pups.
Assertion 3	The relationship between these two is generally cordial, provided that the head of

the house is treated with admiration and respect.

Qualifying statement   If he isn't, a good nip or two usually brings the female back into line.

Student Paragraph

This paragraph consists of three general facts, serially arranged. The movement from general to particular occurs after each one as the writer supplies evidence, illustrates, and qualifies.

Adaptability of patterns

If one convinces himself—and he does so best by practice—that patterns of this general order are applicable to all writing requirements, then he has acquired an all-purpose tool. One might complain that the patterns are too general to be useful. On the other hand, any writer who seeks a prescriptive method for every type of writing is certainly doomed to frustration. For instance, we speak of character analysis, operation analysis, structure analysis, stylistic analysis, critical analysis, and maybe a half dozen others. Added to these are terms like *classification* and *process,* which are just different words for *analysis.* Proliferation of terms of this kind creates the illusion that each of these is something different. In these particular examples, only the emphasis changes. What is common to all of them is the analytical method that can be described loosely as a piecemealing process—breaking down the whole into parts and seeing how they explain and impinge upon one another. All that remains to learn is how writers ordinarily go about this process. Until one has read analyses, tried to write them, and had his efforts criticized, he is not likely to have a very clear grasp of what *analysis* means. A writer must get a general idea how to proceed, but from that point on he still has the job of making applications. No one can shape his own thoughts as well as he can himself.

WHAT ARE PARAGRAPHS?

Up to this point, we have observed how paragraphs are internally structured and how they operate as logical and rhetorical units of discourse. I have purposely avoided asking what a paragraph is, not only because the answer is infinitely complex but because any definition that tries to cover all paragraphs must be extremely general. Nevertheless, here is a test definition: a paragraph is a unit of discourse, consisting of one or more sentences, set off by indentation or special typography, for rhetorical and logical purposes. I am not at all sure how much we learn from such a statement.

This definition undoubtedly raises more questions than it answers. For instance, how long should a paragraph be? If I say that paragraphs are usually 150 or 200 words in length, I am being evasive. I fail to say that wholly satisfactory paragraphs may run to 600 or 700 words in length (not too difficult to find in nineteenth-century prose) or that a three-word paragraph like "That's what's wrong" (used by Eric Sevareid), set off to comment upon all of the preceding discourse, may be extremely emphatic.

If I answer the question by saying a paragraph should be as long as it needs to be, I come closer to the truth of practice, but I have given a relative answer that leaves the writer dependent upon his own intuitive judgment.

Perilous, to be sure.

But any writer who has paragraph sense, as well as sentence sense, knows that intuitive judgment is both practical and efficient. Knowing the bounds of a paragraph—knowing how far it will stretch—is not as vague as it might at first seem. We have no trouble recognizing incompleteness in other arts—an unresolved chord, an unfinished sculpture, an abortive sketch. A paragraph serving its proper function leaves the reader satisfied that some step in the thinking process, whether long or short, has been completed. The division is usually "right" if the author has made it for a purpose. The reader who doubts this heresy will need to read many more paragraphs before he is ready for belief.

To return to questions which the test definition raises: if a paragraph is a unit set off by indentation or special typography, do we have to accept as a paragraph any group of words that an author indents? We usually do. Newspapers and many periodicals use spacing and indentation almost exclusively for visual purposes—to make reading simpler. Further our use of the verb *to paragraph* means nothing more than *to indent.* Thus we support the idea that a paragraph is a paragraph if it is written as one.

But if in a more precise way we hold to the notion that a paragraph serves a logical and rhetorical function, as well as a visual one, then we can pass judgments upon paragraphing. Or to put the matter differently: although we may be forced to call any division that a writer arbitrarily makes a paragraph, we are not bound to accept his paragraph as a *good* paragraph.

What are good paragraphs?

To set up normative standards for judging paragraphs, varied as they are in structure and purpose, is only to invite a mass of exceptions. The ultimate test of a good paragraph is a pragmatic one: a paragraph is good only insofar as it does well what the author intends it to do in a particular context. Paragraphs do not simply exist; they do something.

The pragmatic test proposed here is based upon several assumptions: (1) that the writer has a motive in paragraphing; (2) that he attempts to comment upon the material by breaking it at crucial points; and (3) that his purpose is accomplished only if the reader perceives the writer's intentions. All of this is summarized in a succinct statement by Professor Paul C. Rodgers: "To compose is to create; to indent is to interpret."

What do paragraphs do?

What, then, are paragraphs, singly or in combination, capable of doing? Some paragraphs, not all. Sometimes, not always.

1. Paragraphs clarify meaning by purposefully marking off steps in the movement of the prose.
2. They permit the reader to reflect and absorb.
3. They enclose a fully developed, self-contained topic.
4. They mark the end of a striking passage as much as the beginning of a new thought.
5. They shift the focus to a new topic by providing transitional material.

6. They preface or conclude.
7. They emphasize by separating material for special attention.
8. They identify speakers in dialogue.
9. They vary the pace and rhythm of the whole selection by alternating long paragraphs with short ones.

In all these instances, paragraphs function logically and rhetorically. To the extent that they function effectively, they are good.

EXTENDED DISCOURSE

Discussions of this kind tend to distort the true nature of discourse because the use of paragraphs as examples unavoidably overemphasizes a segmented view of the process, whereas actual writing is likely to be a much more continuous and fluid affair. A writer, having collected his material, often chooses a general destination and a few key stopping-off places and then ventures forth. Along the way, he sets out markers for the benefit of any reader who may want to follow him. If he is able to map out the exact route in advance and anticipate all of the detours, he is indeed an extraordinary writer.

Let's see in what way writers think in units of discourse more extended than the paragraph. We can pick quite at random an example from Orwell's well-known essay "Politics and the English Language":

> Each of these passages has faults of its own, but quite apart from avoidable ugliness, two qualities are common to all of them. The first is staleness of imagery; the other is lack of precision. The writer either has a meaning and cannot express it, or he inadvertently says something else, or he is almost indifferent as to whether his words mean anything or not. This mixture of vagueness and sheer incompetence is the most marked characteristic of modern English prose, and especially of any kind of political writing. As soon as certain topics are raised, the concrete melts into the abstract and no one seems able to think of turns of speech that are not hackneyed: prose consists less and less of *words* chosen for the sake of their meaning, and more and more of *phrases* tacked together like the sections of a prefabricated hen-house. I list below, with notes and examples, various of the tricks by means of which the work of prose-construction is habitually dogged:

From the first sentence of this isolated paragraph, we know immediately that this paragraph depends upon the quoted passages which precede it—five in all. We also know that Orwell intends to speak of two qualities common to all of them. He covers these in four sentences, after which the final sentence of the paragraph ends with a colon, leaving no doubt that the material that follows—four paragraphs in all—is a further development of this point.

In this single paragraph, therefore, two larger units of discourse are linked, at the same time that the paragraph develops a topic of its own.

Note another paragraph, which, unlike the Orwell example, has no transitional guidelines:

> Now that the Christian vision no longer reverberates in the life of the contemporary man, how will the minister find the insight or the courage to proclaim "good news"? Can he offer the Bible to a people disabused of its validity? Can he recall heaven and hell to a people who have laughed them out of existence? Can he talk to them of God, when they find God quite unimaginable in such a world, scientifically structured in iron law? Can he explain faith, redemption, grace, while they wonder what such things have to do with the defense mechanisms of the Ego or the libidinous expressions of the Id? Can he continue to conduct the rites of the church, and speak of "holy" things when life itself has been naturalized and even the church transfers its own significance to statistical categories and popular prestige?
>
> Samuel Miller, "The Evolution of Religion"

Here we have only a series of six questions, which when isolated stand without a referent. We know that this paragraph is clearly a part of a larger unit because the context is defined by the last sentence of the previous paragraph: "Thus the minister stands for a whole congery of notions which have become mere words, the realities seemingly no longer a part of modern existence, and he must deal with a turbulent age doing its best to create a new order of intelligible meaning."

In Truman Capote's essay "Brooklyn Heights: A Personal Memoir," we recognize three paragraphs as a single unit by his use of structural parallelism. The first paragraph of this unit begins, "Father is a world traveler"; the second, "Then Father comes home to Brooklyn"; the third,

"Father has a partner, his wife Florence." The three paragraphs, as we learn, characterize "Mr. George Knapp, known to his friends as Father."

These few examples of extended discourse suggest that composition is a constant combining process—words into sentences, sentences into paragraphs, paragraphs into nameless larger units of discourse—and the combination continues until the writer has reached the outer limits of his topic. If the process sometimes seems infinitely complex, one needs to remind himself that the skill of putting things together is not unique to composition. A good bit of the strategy in writing is simply doing naturally what one would be inclined to do in any job demanding orderliness. Customarily, one learns to do something on a small scale before he attempts a large one. In writing, we hold out the same hope—that proficiency in arranging sentences into paragraphs will lead to proficiency in arranging paragraphs into larger units.

EXTERNAL FORM: THE OUTLINE

Even though the organization of an entire essay may very well evolve from an accumulation of the parts—and thus from within—the writer usually has in mind, if not on paper, the outside limits of his topic and a skeletal framework of the whole. The most common blueprint of this kind is the outline.

An outline has two functions: it may serve as a planning device before the essay has been written or as a testing device after it has been written. In either case, it is most useful if it states a controlling thesis, which defines the limits of the topic, and then separates the major units of discourse. Whatever further subdivisions a writer makes will depend upon the accessibility of his material, if he is planning, or upon his concern for including all the subparts, if he is testing.

Working outlines no doubt come in all sizes and shapes, and they are useful whether they are scribbled or labored over. But the particular advantage of conventional outline form (see Appendix A for models) is its demand for disciplined phrasing and balanced structure. One always hopes that the writer who constructs a symmetrical outline will be conscious of symmetry and balance and parallelism when he writes. But this carry-over is not inevitable. Nevertheless, an outline has a salutary effect upon writing by forcing the writer to think about total structure and demanding of him some visual proof of orderly arrangement.

THE SENSE OF STRUCTURE

This chapter has attempted to *show* form, because in writing about structure one has no other useful recourse. Many writers, however, feel intuitively what is demonstrated here. They are not constantly thinking about form as they write sentence by sentence and paragraph by paragraph. As ideas arise, they fall into shape, and logical associations take over to keep them coherent and orderly. This kind of writing is not unmethodical; it is simply not conscious of method. Method does not tyrannize the writer; the writer controls it.

All reading and all practice in writing should help the individual to acquire a sense of structure and a sense of logical continuity. Without these, he will always be looking for props; with them, he will have resources adaptable enough to cover every demand of form.

SUGGESTIONS FOR DISCUSSION

1. Review what present concepts you have about paragraphs. To what extent do these ideas apply to some paragraphs, not all? To what kinds of paragraphs do they apply?
2. Read the following student paragraph:

> I would like to direct my comments toward the old saying that one who cheats hurts only himself. I do not completely agree, as it is quite possible this could be affecting the citizens of this nation as a whole. This must certainly be very true considering the rapid pace of living we must face today—what with fast development of spacecraft, nuclear-topped missiles and atomic submarines dotting our outer atmosphere and ocean depths. It seems this would indicate much advancement in the technical aspects of many varied fields. These men over the design boards, and those laboring in the laboratories more than likely had true ambition and sincere interest in education. These feats of progress could not come from the mind of a student who had slid through his college

days without a true and proper competitive motive. In the future the trend toward higher and even more technical educational background will surely rise even more. If the young people of our country fail to foresee the outcome of a nation that is being lifted by present-day scholars with no one following, then in future decades regression may be this country's final product.

Trace the line of logical association in this paragraph. Indicate at what point the writer forgot his referent. Does he make a jump in reasoning? What is the logical connection between the first and the last sentences? In what other ways might this paragraph be considered a substandard one?

3. Consider the following single paragraph of almost 500 words from *The Constitution of Man Considered in Relation to External Objects* (3d ed., 1835) by George Combe. Since contemporary prose seldom contains paragraphs of this length, first indicate all the possible places Combe might have indented. To what extent do members of the class agree upon new divisions? What markers in the prose indicate possible divisions? What purpose would be served by making indentations at particular points? Attempt to explain what new paragraphing would *do* for the prose:

In the American war Britain desired to gratify her Acquisitiveness and Self-Esteem, in opposition to Benevolence and Justice, at the expense of her transatlantic colonies. This roused the animal resentment of the latter, and the propensities of the two nations came into collision; that is to say, they made war on each other— Britain, to support a dominion in direct hostility to the principles which regulate the moral government of the world, in the expectation of becoming rich and powerful by success in that enterprise; the Americans, to assert the supremacy of the higher sentiments and to become free and independent. According to the principles which I am now unfolding, the greatest misfortune that could have befallen Britain would have been success, and the greatest advantage, failure in her attempt; and the result is now acknowledged to be in exact accordance with this view. If Britain had subdued the colonies in the American war, every one must see to what an extent her Self-Esteem, Acquisitiveness, and Destructiveness, would have been let loose upon them. This, in the first place, would have roused the animal faculties of the conquered party, and led them to give her all the annoyance in their power; and the expense of the fleets and armies requisite to repress this spirit, would have far counterbalanced all the profits she could have wrung out of the colonists by extortion and oppression. In the second place, the very exercise of these animal faculties by herself, in opposition to the moral sentiments, would have rendered her government at home an exact parallel of that of the carter in his own family [reference to a previous illustration]. The same malevolent principles would have overflowed on her own subjects: the government would have felt uneasy, and the people rebellious, discontented, and unhappy; and the moral law would have been amply vindicated by the suffering which would have every where abounded. The consequences of her failure have been the reverse. America has sprung up into a great and moral nation, and actually contributes ten times more to the wealth of Britain, standing as she now does in her natural relation to this country, than she ever could have done as a discontented and oppressed colony. This advantage is reaped without any loss, anxiety, or expense; it flows from the divine institutions, and both nations profit by and rejoice under it. The moral and intellectual rivalry of America, instead of prolonging the ascendency of the propensities in Britain, tends strongly to excite the moral sentiments in her people and government, and every day that we live, we are reaping the benefits of this improvement in wiser institutions, deliverance from endless abuses, and a higher and purer spirit pervading every department of the executive administration of the country. Britain, however, did not escape the penalty of her attempt at the infringement of the moral laws. The pages of her history, during the American war, are dark with suffering and gloom, and at this day we groan under the debt and difficulties then partly incurred.

ASSIGNMENTS

1. Make structural diagrams of the three following selections; then indicate what the pattern of development is in each one.

    A.   Much of William Blake's poetry, especially his *Songs of Innocence,* demonstrates his preoccupation with childhood as a thematic symbol. The "Introduction" to Blake's *Songs of Innocence* introduces his symbolic child, who in this poem, after listening from his cloud to the poet's joyful piping and singing, tells the poet to sit down and write "songs of happy chear"—songs that "Every child may joy to hear." Here the child assumes poetic roles of author, subject, and audience: the child-like mind of the creator (Blake), the symbol he creates, which leads to understanding, and the intellect capable of understanding. Blake's child thus represents those virtues he deemed necessary for one to enter his poetic world, a world of lamb-like innocence, faith, and joy. In this sense, the state of childhood has less to do with age than with the capacity to envision (and believe in) Blake's mystical world, which can be explained only through a comprehension of his child symbol. Blake himself thought and wrote as one of these children, a child of God, and a child of life.

Student Paper

B.   Man is the only animal that can communicate knowledge acquired by experience to other members of the species. A man, having found the way out of a maze by trial and error, could not only himself remember how to proceed if he found himself in the centre again; he could also tell his children and anyone, quite unrelated to him by blood, how to proceed, and that before they entered the maze at all. His knowledge, though derived from personal experiences and personally memorized, is communicable and, if communicated, public. That is an observable peculiarity of human behavior and may serve as an empirical criterion to distinguish human knowledge from other kinds of knowledge or awareness. Strictly speaking the term knowledge should be confined to information that is thus communicable.

V. G. Childe, *Society and Knowledge*

C.   In the long run nothing will meet the needs of the people of our nation or of the world short of abolishing the very institution of war as an arbiter of disputes or a tool of annihilation.

We must, of course, continue to preserve and to build our alliances, to help free nations gain strength to preserve their freedom, to develop our own armed strength—indeed, until the aggressors come to tolerable terms we must even continue building our own nuclear power.

But this is not enough. To stop here is to dwell still in the house of the past, with a bomb ticking in the basement. We can no longer rest contentedly on the framework of the old diplomacy and the old strategy of preponderant or balanced power. We must move beyond to that brighter day envisioned just ten years ago when the Nazi nightmare died and the United Nations came to birth in San Francisco amid great rejoicing. We must resume the attack on the institution of war itself.

Adlai E. Stevenson, *What I Think*

2. Analyze Example A in terms of its semantic connectives.
3. Analyze Example B in terms of its grammatical and lexical connectives.
4. Analyze Example C in terms of its rhetorical connectives. What effect does Stevenson gain by paragraphing at the points he does?
5. Choose one of your own paragraphs to diagram. Can you come to any conclusions about its structure and development? Does the diagram indicate how the paragraph might be developed more fully?
6. In an article or essay, find a series of paragraphs that are not self-contained, but together represent a longer unit of discourse. What signals does the author give to indicate that the paragraphs form a unit larger than a single paragraph?

5. Diction

But don't you see that the whole trouble lies here in words,
words. Each one of us has within him a whole world of
things, each man of us his own special world. And how can
we ever come to an understanding if I put in the words
I utter the sense and value of things as I see them; while
you who listen to me must inevitably translate them
according to the conception of things each one of you has
within himself. We think we understand each other,
but we never really do.   *Luigi Pirandello*

ne of the professors in Swift's Academy at Lagado (in *Gulliver's Travels*) solved the dilemma of language in this way: since words, he said, were only names of things, it would be simpler to save breath and communicate by showing the things themselves. There were two major disadvantages to his new universal language: the sacks that the learned had to carry were extremely weighty, and all the common people, particularly the women, objected that they wanted to speak in their original tongue. Another professor at Lagado, acting on the assumption that most things were nouns anyway, proposed to shorten discourse by eliminating all verbs and participles and reducing all polysyllables to one.

CHOICE OF WORDS: UTILITARIAN CONSIDERATIONS

As much as we appreciate Swift's satire, we still have the problem of coping with communication by means of more than 450,000 words listed in *Webster's Third New International Dictionary* and numerous other words not listed there, polysyllables and participles alike. The recognition vocabulary of a college student may be approximately one-third of the immense total in the dictionary, and his active writing vocabulary considerably smaller. Even though Swift's professors assume that communication would be simpler if we had fewer words to use, a writer knows that his task is eased if he has a large stock of words from which to draw. The first considerations in the use of words, therefore, are purely utilitarian: how many words a writer has at his disposal and how precisely he knows their meanings and implications.

Selection of words

As soon as we contemplate the thousands of words that are available, we wonder whether they are all actually usable. First, we can assume that those listed in the dictionary have been used and are likely to be used again. Even though some of them are extremely technical and rare, they may be the only words that satisfy a special context precisely.

At times, taboos against particular words are dictated by a sense of delicacy or decency, but, more often than not, they are prohibitions invented to enforce a general principle about writing. For instance, words like *aspect, field, factor, area,* and *element* are indispensable words of the language. To prohibit their use in writing, as some teachers do, is their attempt to get students to use more concrete terms and to avoid their superfluous use, as in this sentence: "I grew through Uris's novel *Exodus* in the field of toleration and understanding for people and ways of life strange to my own." Or to avoid the pomposity of this sentence: "The opportunities in the chemical field are still as unlimited for the advancement of oneself as they were when I was in high school." Yet the word *field* is not bad; in this sentence, it is simply a symbol of a common malady among inexperienced writers. Ultimately, a writer has to know that his selection of words must be determined by his own context and the capacity of the words to blend with others in creating the overall effect he wants. The writer's initial decision about language, then, may be compared to the artist's choice of colors. His job is a matter of choosing the words that fit together for a purpose.

Accuracy of words

Despite varying shades of meaning that individual words assume— consider *liberal,* for instance—almost all words have a hard core of meaning that makes communication possible. A writer's first responsibility is to be sure what that hard center is. What further significations a word has may determine whether or not it is appropriate to a particular context.

Some inaccuracies are careless errors, possibly misspellings, that do not actually confuse the meaning of a sentence, but they do create an impression of illiteracy, for instance, the substitution of *to* for *too,* *there* for *their, then* for *than, principle* for *principal,* and *effect* for *affect.* The list of homonyms in the language that need to be separated is a long one. Some of these we may confuse simply because we are aware of one word and not of its counterpart or not aware that two meanings of the same sound are spelled differently, for instance, *compliment* and *complement* or *discreet* and *discrete.*

Finally, other inaccuracies of this kind may simply embarrass the writer. If he doesn't know the difference between *sensual* and *sensuous, illicit* and *elicit,* or *scatology* and *eschatology,* he can blunder very badly. Or if he confuses words like *eminent, imminent,* and *immanent,* he may say something he does not mean to say at all. Other kinds of distinctions are necessary in differentiating between words like *envied* and *enviable, visual* and *visible,* or *onto* and *on to.* The list might be extended indefinitely. Everyone has his own special list of confusions and particular definitions he never seems to get quite straight in his mind. Because of this all too human failing, no writer should attempt to write anything of serious intention without a dictionary nearby.

Overtones of words

What the dictionary cannot consistently indicate is the extended meaning of words, the connotations that personal experiences attach to them. Linguists differ in their views whether isolated words carry a kind of built-in emotional stimulus or whether the words derive their emotional effect from context only. Whatever the source of the effect in theory, it is clear that readers will respond differently to the same word in a variety of contexts. For instance, we can test our own reactions to sentences like these:

Seventeenth-century writers were preoccupied with the theme of death.

The death of Mahatma Gandhi in 1948 moved masses of the Indian people to grief.

There is no doubt that your father's death will come in a matter of hours.

In these instances, the fact conditions the degree of emotion, not the word.

On the other hand, we can assess our responses to single words and phrases out of context, as we frequently see them on the covers of books: *Society and Knowledge, Indigo, The Affair, Man Alone, No Exit.* These may or may not arouse feelings depending upon our personal experiences and the associations we are free to make.

What the writer can never fully anticipate is the extent to which the personal reactions of the reader will intrude upon the writer's job of communicating with him. What he can be sensitive to, however, is the potential that certain words of the language have to appeal to feelings. At one extreme are loaded words, frequently slangy, like *prig, guts, sleazy,* and *slob.* These words are capable of offending and insulting, and any writer who deliberately uses them ought to know what response he will get. At the other extreme are relatively neutral words, *most, few,* and *three,* for instance, which in isolation seem barren of feeling but become words of emphasis when they modify other words: *most objections, few volunteers, three pythons.* Other neutral structure words like *to, from,* and *because* also begin to take on associations when they connect and introduce other words: *to the moon, from the ghetto, because they were indifferent.*

In between the clear-cut extremes on this hypothetical emotional scale are innumerable words that stand midrange, words that can be shoved in either direction by the context; it may either charge them or sober them. A word like *food* in a sentence such as "We stopped to eat our food" is almost completely neutral; it is not even specific enough to cause us to react, as we might to *snails* or *okra.* But in a sentence like "To a man with an empty stomach food is God," attributed to Gandhi, the word *food* derives from the context a special emotional impact. I. A. Richards calls this dependence of words upon one another in context an "interinanimation of words." They interact and are actually capable of transferring a kind of liveliness to one another.

No word, however, can transfer a liveliness it does not have. Some words are unspirited, like *nice;* some words are tired, like *great.* The result has been that some writers try to recover the lost force of words by practicing inflation. Thus the syndrome of superlativism—of the *superdivine* and *supermarvelous*—that characterizes American speech and finds its prime expression in advertisements has clearly jaded the sensibilities of the reading public. They are no longer able to sustain the heightened intensity that the inflation of words now demands. *Giant* may signify medium-sized; *supreme* may describe a commonplace taste experience. The trivial is magnified; the ordinary is glorified. What overtones strong words once had are now mainly lost. Understatement has become the safest recourse for the writer trying to express high praise and genuine enthusiasm. A pleasant switch of typical advertising hard sell may be seen in a sentence that reads, "We may be the only telephone company in town, but we try not to act like it."

General and particular

Advertising has also had remarkable success in popularizing verbal legerdemain—the kind of statement that tosses in magic phrases like "laboratory scientists," "after years of research," "millions of dollars expended," "carefully tested," and "the modern trend"—all impressive generalities that never supply the particulars to support vague claims about a product. Generalities can be stated in a few words in an incontestable tone. Hard facts—details of explanations—are time-consuming. Furthermore, generalities tend to be safe; we often agree with one another in principle, but not in details. One of the prevalent weaknesses among Freshman students is the tendency to write in unsupported generalities. One substandard theme will serve to illustrate.

SHAKESPEARE'S CHARACTERS IN THE TAMING OF THE SHREW

The characters William Shakespeare has introduced into *The Taming of the Shrew* are individual but well representative of most people. He has somewhat stereotyped each player, but has succeeded in giving this stereotype a switch, as in the case of Katherine the shrew. He has shown her selfishness, stubbornness, and unreasonableness up until the end of the play, when she is tamed. Her final speech exemplifies a great sensitivity toward marriage and life.

Petruchio, the tamer of Katherine, is stereotyped from the beginning and plays his role throughout the play as the strong, purposeful tamer. Bianca, Katherine's sister, is a deceptive person. She plays a role she is not and for some time carries the sympathy of the audience. She cannot be immediately stereotyped because she carries her deception well. The father is typical, wishing happiness for his children, but he is not as forceful as he might have been with Katherine. He obviously dotes on Bianca, thus unconsciously causing jealousy and dissension between the sisters. The servants are definitely stereotyped as ignorant help. The author seems to feel the character of each player and realize the humanness of each, giving each a definite personality. Christopher Sly, the drunken bum, for whom and around whom the inner play is developed, is human and a good illustration of human nature. Shakespeare is obviously sympathetic with his characters, or he would not have been able to give them the humor and individual life that he did.

In such a theme, we have only an illusion of particulars. We need not be misled by the proper names of the characters. The ultimate question is what details we learn about them. In what way is Katherine selfish, Petruchio purposeful, Bianca deceptive? The writer screens the particulars almost in the same way that a letter of recommendation says nothing about a candidate when it describes him, like a good boy scout, as honest, kind, helpful, clean, and reverent. As we have said before, the general words of the language are category words. A successful writer depends heavily upon the particular and concrete.

Abstract and concrete

Concrete words, like precise and particular ones, are strong words. They are vigorous because they have their roots in experience. They are strong because they derive vigor from the basic elements, like the giant Antaeus in ancient myth. The invincible Antaeus challenged men to wrestle with him on condition that he would slay them if he won. In his struggle with Hercules, he constantly gained the advantage because when Hercules threw him to the ground, Antaeus always arose refreshed. When Hercules realized that Antaeus revived his strength each time he touched his mother, the Earth, he strangled Antaeus by holding him high above his head. Separated from the primal source of strength, Antaeus was powerless.

Like Antaeus, words also lose their force in the rarefied atmosphere of abstraction. Concrete words touch the solid ground of specific fact. Note how H. L. Mencken writes specifically and concretely in a passage that would lend itself easily to abstract treatment:

> In 1924 the *Realtor's Bulletin* of Baltimore reported that certain enemies of realtric science were trying to show that *realtor* was derived from the English word *real* and the Spanish word *toro,* a bull, and to argue that it thus meant *real bull*. But this obscenity apparently did not go far; probably a hint from the alert general counsel was enough to stop it. During the same year I was informed by Herbert U. Nelson, executive secretary of the National Association, that "the real-estate men of London, through the Institute of Estate Agents and Auctioneers, after studying our experience in this respect, are planning to coin the word *estator* and to

protect it by legal steps." This plan, I believe, came to fruition, but *estator* never caught on, and I can't find it in the Supplement to the Oxford Dictionary. *Realtor,* however, is there—and the first illustrative quotation is from "Babbitt"!

The American Language

This is lively prose because it is packed with specific detail. There is nothing vague, nothing fuzzy. The setting is concrete.

Slang

Slang is a vigorous form of speech, not necessarily because it is specific, but because it is current, inventive, and frequently raw. There is an earthiness about it—nothing remote—the kind of plain words that ordinary people say in everyday talk, many of which never gain sufficient recognition to be listed in a dictionary. In terms of current use, we might wonder why collegiate dictionaries include *kookaburra* and not *kook,* but the difference, of course, is that *kookaburra* has passed the test of time (earliest citation in the *Oxford English Dictionary:* 1890); *kook* has not.

Slang has youthful appeal because the words are quick to be born and quick to die before anyone can be bored with them, although a few words survive to old age. J. Louis Kuethe tells us that *brass* (impudence) and *duds* have survived as slang since the sixteenth century. Other slang terms, however, gain enough respectability over a period of time to move from their customary colloquial status into the accepted ranks of standard written English. *Jazz* has clearly made the grade, although some of its implications still mark it clearly as slang. The vulgar origins of *jukebox* are completely forgotten.

If slang were as precise in all instances as it is alive, it would serve standard usage well. Slang terms that survive and acculturate seem to fill a specific need in the language, like *rubberneck, jerk, loony,* and *highbrow.* But consider words like *cool* and *neat,* which by their ubiquitous use come to mean little more than a vague approval of almost anything. They are the voguish equivalents of *nice.*

Slang is the surest way of dating written prose. A writer who would talk about *pitching woo* would be as absurd as an oldster in a zoot suit trying to pass as a hipster. Time takes its toll upon words. Passages of Carl Sandburg's *The People, Yes* (1937), which tries to record American speech and sayings of the 1930s, now seem as old hat as *old hat*. Slang is not bad because it is ineffectual; it is bad in writing because its effectuality is short-lived. We can scarcely imagine what *camp* will be by the time this book reaches print.

Other lingos

From a strictly utilitarian point of view, slang and other kinds of "in-talk," designated by such terms as *localisms, argot, cant, shoptalk, jargon,* and *patois,* are impractical in writing simply because they are not widely communicative. Very often, their purpose is to exclude outsiders. The speech of the group is a badge of belonging. Anyone who does not know the lingo cannot communicate. For instance, the phrases of underworld lingos shift rapidly to keep them confidential.

Here again is one of the essential differences between talking and writing. Unless writing is purposely designed for a restricted group of intimates, it needs to adopt a language that is generally recognized and approved by a wide audience of native American speakers. Good common sense will go further in helping a writer decide what words he should use and not use than a stack of dictionaries, which either fall far behind the times in labeling varieties of usage or renege at recording them at all.

Technical terms

Unlike popular words that have to make their way if they are going to be accepted into the corpus of standard English, technical terms generally have automatic entrance, despite the fact that they may be as exclusive in meaning as regional words. Technical terms, therefore, also represent a type of jargon, but the language of general usage very often includes less precise equivalents, which ordinary people use to avoid sounding like doctors, lawyers, and professors talking to one another. The popular names of flowers, diseases, chemicals, and parts of the anatomy permit nontechnicians to communicate with one another in an easy way about technical matters.

An accumulation of technical terms can produce a heavy, un-intelligible prose that disturbs even the specialists at times. Some industries have set up what they call a "fog index," a means of calculating how dense prose is by an analysis of its diction and sentences. About 1940 the notorious fogginess of government documents prompted a Texan, Maury Maverick, to coin the word *gobbledygook,* which now enjoys widespread application because the government certainly has no monopoly upon inflated and involved diction, as this professor's gobbledygook will testify:

> In general, the pedagogic strategy proposed in this project for implementing the programming principles of progressive differentiation and integrative reconciliation involves the use of appropriately relevant and inclusive organizers that are maximally stable and discriminable from related conceptual systems in the learner's cognitive structure.

Maury Maverick ended an article he wrote for the *New York Times Magazine* (May 21, 1944) by quoting a passage from the Bible. I repeat his quotation here, extending it to include another verse:

> For if the trumpet give an uncertain sound, who shall prepare himself to the battle?
> So likewise ye, except ye utter by the tongue words easy to be understood, how shall it be known what is spoken? for ye shall speak into the air.
>
> I Cor. 14:8–9

VARIETIES OF USAGE

The writer needs to concern himself chiefly with two varieties of usage, standard and nonstandard. Within each of these broad categories, there are degrees of appropriateness determined largely by the purpose of the writer, by the occasion, and by the audience. Standard English ranges from the highly formal language of official documents to the casual style of the informal essay. The category of nonstandard English ranges from the quaint phrases of a local dialect to the gross obscenities of pornography. Most people observe a kind of self-imposed etiquette of language by keeping the varieties as unmixed as possible, simply because mixtures of language are incongruous, even at times humorous or shocking. As we might expect, some individuals are more scrupulous observers of language etiquette than others, and their attitudes may very well create inhibitions in others. To some purists, illiteracies, localisms, obscenities, and slang are not primarily linguistic offenses; they are social blunders.

Because educated speech is a mark of prestige, we have to recognize that it often acts as a divider between those who have mastered it and those who have not, often between those who have been born into it and those who have not. The story of Shaw's *Pygmalion* has now been sufficiently popularized by *My Fair Lady* to serve as a familiar illustration that proper words in proper places earn social respect. Fortunately, language barriers can be surmounted through reading and education.

But the controversial question finally remains whether standardized usage is wholly desirable. It should be recognized that dialects of language are clear marks of cultural, racial, and regional identity and, therefore, sources of pride to their users. Standard usage does tend to regularize language and obscure identifiable characteristics, but not at the complete expense of personal language habits. Written language necessarily obliterates pronunciation differences; we cannot tell whether *greasy* is written by a Northerner or a Southerner, although pronunciation would probably make the distinction. But written language cannot completely erase the clues that vocabulary and usage give to age, sex, occupation, and cultural origins. We can make a bugbear of standard usage and act as if it destroys individuality and identity, or we can emphasize that it actually serves as a common bond of understanding among many different people and, if mastered, permits them freer movement within the structure of our society. In brief, it is possible for an individual to vary his dialect or usage just as easily as he might shift from English to Spanish if he were a master of both languages.

One might observe further that the kind of segregation that grows out of language differences has not necessarily been perpetuated by the educated elite as a mark of their intellectual aristocracy. Many cultivated speakers are lax in their usages, in fact, deliberately so as a kind of reverse snobbery. Yet their position is different from that of people who find flexibility impossible. The educated often have the assurance that their habits of standard English are deeply rooted. They use it when they choose; they deviate from it by design. To them varieties of usage are adjustable. To the uneducated, however, these divisions seem much more rigid. They idealize the notion of educated speech, thinking of it as impossibly remote.

Despite the social implications of language—and many people get belatedly concerned about them when they achieve professional status—no purpose is served by stressing "upper-level" usage and "lower-level" usage. Differences of language are not basically matters of levels. Nonstandard language is serviceable, forceful, and pungent. It is not to be scorned. Its services are merely limited. A student returning to school after service in the Navy expressed his awareness of these limitations:

> "Fo'cs'le French" is not a formal, school-type language, but an informal, earthy tongue, with wet feet and grimy hands, punctuated with skinned shins and cracked knuckles. It is a language to tell stories with, work with, and play with, if you stay among your own kind. Away from the waterfront, it isn't worth a tinker's damn on a cold Friday night—and therein lies my problem.

In this case, the young man overestimated his problem. In these few sentences he reveals a feeling for language that would certainly ease any adjustments he had to make in matters of usage.

Consistency of usage

Because varieties of usage overlap, a writer has considerable give-and-take in the words he can use without interfering with the general tone of his remarks. Fortunately, the language includes a mass of words that are used with appropriateness in both writing and speaking, that cannot be designated either standard or nonstandard because they are common to both varieties. For this reason, a writer is not actually bogged down by having to assess the nature of each word he uses. He has to be concerned chiefly with those that are simply incompatible with one another. Note this sentence:

> The coach uses encomiums wisely to draw the best from his team.

The use of *encomiums* in this sentence is accurate enough in meaning, but the writer has no sense of the context that it suits. To be sure, *encomium* doesn't suit the language of pep talks in the locker room.

By contrast, note what effect a skilled writer gains by a shift in usage:

> We have always had a curious feeling that though we crucified Christ on a stick, he somehow managed to get hold of the right end of it, and that if we were better men we might try his plan.
>
> George Bernard Shaw

Here, Shaw succeeds in shocking the reader by letting a colloquial expression twist a sacred subject. He has upset the reader's expectations.

A reader is also likely to be distracted by the obvious inconsistency between the thought and usage of the following passage:

> In southern California, where we now reside, there is an air of informalness. Everyone is in a hurry to reach his goal or destination and does not care for his neighbor's progress.

These sentences need informal California usage. The writer makes them stuffy by using phrases that sound like translations out of a Latin textbook.

The following passage also reverses its usage, but in a different way:

> This idea of an atmosphere of learning, which may be more properly stated as a feeling, is something that is hard to pin down—a feeling that can be created by the institution, backed up by the administration, assisted by the students and approved by the community. Yet if a prof doesn't care about teaching, why should we study? Before you know it, it's time for exams and we are not ready. Sounds crazy, maybe so, but it can happen unless students know where they stand.

After sentence 1, which is informal but not casual, the writer forgets the audience he has been addressing and begins a chummy dialogue. The change produces two levels of usage that are hardly compatible with one another.

ECONOMY OF LANGUAGE

In the *Nichomachean Ethics,* Aristotle says that the cultivation of the moral virtues is a practical matter of finding a mean between two extremes of conduct, both of which are undesirable. In a different context, we can think of economy of language as a virtuous mean between the extremes of profuseness on the one hand and penury on the other— both are vices in the use of language. We cannot excuse verbiage by saying that excess words are harmless. On the contrary, they are damaging to prose for two reasons: (1) they are doing no work *for* the sentence, and (2) they are actually working *against* it by obscuring the meaning. Test this sentence:

> Byronic romanticism was noted for its exhibitionism, its hatred for hypocrisy and sham as limitations preventing man from attaining the ideal and its dramatization of personal feelings, moods, and impulses.

The opposite extreme of penury can hardly be illustrated by a single sentence. It is an overall effect of barrenness or starkness growing out of the writer's inadequacy with language or his reluctance to open up enough to express himself fully.

Economy of language is known chiefly by its extremes. When a writer is economical, the number of words he uses is unobtrusive because all of them seem purposefully chosen. The meaning is full and clear. The writer has accomplished his purpose without resorting to excesses.

Wordiness: deadwood

Economy of language can be enforced by simply deciding which words are doing no work, either for the meaning or for the effect, and then striking them out or revising slightly. All the sentences below contain deadwood, although the revision indicated is not the only possible one. The context may set up a rhythmic pattern so that a sentence that has been shorn to the barest minimum may not be satisfactory when it is read with other sentences:

Sentence: The type of people represented by Napoleon exists even today.

Revision: People like Napoleon still exist.

Sentence: Large yards are also very handy for many things. They are a wonderful place to entertain guests and a safe place for children to play.

Revision: Large yards are wonderful places to entertain guests and safe places for children to play.

Sentence: Through this course I hope to obtain a background for further courses taken to result in my desired degree.

Revision: Through this course I hope to acquire background for other courses leading to the degree.

Better: Through this course I hope to acquire the background I will need for a degree.

Sentence: Although man has made great strides in the direction we call progress, he has not yet learned to love his neighbor.

Revision: Although man has made great progress, he has not yet learned to love his neighbor.

Sentence: This is my planned means of accomplishing my goal.

Revision: This is my plan for accomplishing my goal.

Better: This is how I plan to accomplish my goal.

Sentence: Love came with an understanding which was brought forth by knowledge about his past.

Revision: Love came with an understanding of his past.

Consistently, deadwood crops up in sentences that involve roundabout expressions rather than direct ones. As a result, the meaning suffers, and the prose loses its punch.

Redundancy

Redundancy may grow out of the attempt to be overly precise. On the other hand, it may also indicate an unawareness of the precise meanings of words. It usually amounts to saying twice what can be said more effectively once. The following phrases taken from student papers are all redundant:

> specifications for a play of tragedy
> basic fundamentals
> modern world of today
> different states of condition
> a certain understanding in mind
> the reason why
> Vernon he thought

Verbiage is so very common in the language that we have at least four words to describe the tendency: *redundant, repetitious, tautological,* and *pleonastic.* All of them imply uneconomical uses of language.

BLUNDERS: MALAPROPISMS

Blunders, which often result in malapropisms or strange new coinages, are symptoms of word blindness. Of course, they are almost always funny, but the irony is that the writer is usually dead serious. Note a few sentences:

> The girl blames the boy for her immortality because he pushed her out into the streets.

> We see Khrushchev sitting rejectedly on an army cot in the middle of a dingy room.

> Eliot is a playwright who writes for the intellectual rather than the mediocracy.

Mediocracy is clever enough to be an intentional coinage, but other words are clearly boners: *splendaciously, expediness, malhappening, disgrumpled, masticulated* (for *masticated*). Examples of this kind are not rarities; they occur frequently in unedited writing.

IDIOMS

Our word *idiomatic* is one of the clearest acknowledgments of the Intuitive dimension of language. We know intuitively when words come off right. In simple terms, *unidiomatic* means that an expression does not sound like English as we are familiar with it. *Idiomatic* refers both to set phrases that we characteristically use and to new arrangements of words that sound natural.

In the first category of conventional phrases are those that give lIttle trouble to native speakers. *To carry on* (to celebrate), *to carry off* (to bluff), *to carry over* (to postpone), *to carry through* (to finish), and *to be carried away* (to be enraptured) are all idioms, although each of these may be used literally in a different sense. The free choice of particles is often far more troublesome. Note what effect unidiomatic use has upon the following sentences:

The leader blamed the faults of the government to his predecessor.

[Preferred: *blamed* the faults of the government *on*]

His loyalty was typical to many people's under totalitarian rule.

[Preferred: *of*]

The protagonist had great insight toward the problems of society.

[Preferred: *into*]

Squealer, the pacifier in *Animal Farm,* exhibits genuine interest and concern of the animal's misfortunes.

[Preferred: interest *in* and concern *for*]

Although these sentences demonstrate obvious misuses, almost every writer has his moments of doubt about particles. Unfortunately, collegiate dictionaries are not always helpful because it would be impossible to list all the possible choices. (See Frederick T. Wood, *English Prepositional Idioms* [New York: St Martin's Press, 1967].)

The following sentences illustrate other kinds of unidiomatic expressions:

Harley stayed status-quo just as the others.

He is trying to decide what size college is the wise choice.

[Possible source: "What size shoe do you wear?"]

The book doesn't follow similarity with that information impressed upon me in my early school years.

Clearly, the student who wrote the last sentence has a more serious problem than the other two because he obviously finds the language of standard written English a completely foreign idiom.

ARRANGEMENT OF WORDS: RHETORICAL CONSIDERATIONS

As a student masters words at the utilitarian level—accumulating an adequate number of them, learning their meanings precisely, and being able to use them correctly, appropriately, economically, and idiomatically —he is at the same time concerned with their arrangement for the best possible effect upon the reader. Apart from grammatical considerations, that is, the structural patterns of sentences, the writer is free to arrange words as he sees fit. What I hope to show in the sections that follow are the effects, both good and bad, that grow out of arranging words.

Ambiguity

When Hemingway chose the title *A Farewell to Arms,* he undoubtedly intended the ambiguity, and it is a richer title for it. In other usages, however, ambiguity that invites uncertainty and stumbling is an unhappy accident. Note this sentence:

The cat claws, the horse rears, and the goose pecks.

Orally, the sentence is unambiguous. In written form, "the cat claws" needs to be moved further along in the series so that, once the pattern of noun and verb is established, the reader will interpret *claws* as a verb instead of a noun.

Other ambiguities must be remedied by a new choice of words:

Vain men break rules for their own advantage. This is illustrated by those who lie on their income tax forms.

My mother had a nose like a beagle; she could smell a drink you had the day before and thought that one drink made one drunk.

DeVanter's second wife was on the other side of the fence.

In some instances, punctuation solves the problem easily by eliminating the misreading:

Where I was hunting the deer were cautiously moving away from the scent that had already been set up by a previous party.

[Punctuated]
Where I was hunting, the deer were cautiously moving away from the scent that had already been set up by a previous party.

Polysyllabic cacophony

Fortunately, all the common words of the language are short. The rare ones tend to be long and Latinate. Big words are not bad because they are big. They are bad only if they seem ostentatious in the company of informal words or combine with other big words to create a discord of sound that interferes completely with the meaning. All of this is well put by a student who parodies his own style by describing his weakness as "the maladroit utilization of a plethora of speciously applied words for the simple pedantic thrill of it, when several less ostentatious but more discriminately selected ones would serve quite admirably."

Other sound effects

Since the eye perceives sound as well as the ear, the writer cannot ignore the effects he creates by the arrangement of words. Phrases like *Judging Joyce* or *an air of arrogance* cause the reader as much trouble as they cause the speaker. Yet all combinations that create sound effects are not to be condemned categorically. Many of them are not only pleasant, but useful as devices that tie the prose together. For instance, the echo of sound in this sentence reinforces the meaning:

Kurtz, if he chooses, is free to exercise the appalling self-knowledge that he finds appealing.

Or the repetition in this one:

Well-being is generally considered satisfying, but Harrington's well-being in the crystal palace is less than satisfying.

In fact, if we analyze memorable phrases—the kind that make the dictionaries of famous sayings—we will find that rather consistently they are combinations of words that fall "trippingly on the tongue." Here are three, each of a different variety:

The health of nations is more important than the wealth of nations. [Balance and rhyme]

Will Durant

Fondly do we hope, fervently do we pray, that this mighty scourge of war may speedily pass away. [Balance and alliteration]

Abraham Lincoln

Some books are to be tasted, others to be swallowed, and some few to be chewed and digested. [Parallelism]

Francis Bacon

What the writer of expository prose has to be wary of is not sound itself, but floods of sounds that deluge meaning.

Strategy of arrangement

Until we have experimented with arrangements, we do not realize all the possible effects that can be gained by variations. For instance, we may be inclined to think of a series in terms of the mathematical formulas that are often given in handbooks to illustrate punctuation: *a, b,* and *c* (stories, poems, and plays); *a, b, c* (intelligent, quiet, dispassionate); *a* and *b* and *c* (cars and trucks and buses). These three arrangements only begin to explore the possibilities of a series of words, which may undergo infinite variations to break the monotony of mere listing. Note this catalogue of flowers:

> The daisies are blooming, the roses, the zinnias, the pansies and marigold, salvia, daylily, calendula and columbine, the geranium and the cornflower, dandelion and delphinium, peony, poppy, the lanky snapdragons and the stately cannas.
>
> Student

Here we have an intricate arrangement of names varied with skill, sometimes singular, sometimes plural, sometimes preceded by an adjective, sometimes not, sometimes following rapidly in sequence, sometimes slowed by *and,* sometimes pointed by alliteration, and always metrically pleasing. The asymmetrical arrangement of the words conveys to the reader something about the garden itself. The sentence is considerably more imaginative than a straight listing:

> The flowers are blooming—the daisies, roses, zinnias, pansies, marigold, salvia, daylilies, calendulas, columbine, geraniums, cornflowers, dandelions, delphinium, peonies, poppies, snapdragons, and cannas.

The two sentences clearly illustrate the difference between statement that is literal and statement that is literary.

PRECISION AND PLAY: ARTISTIC CONSIDERATIONS

When a writer sacrifices all the pleasure of words in the interests of efficient communication, he has seriously jeopardized the readability of his prose. All precision and no play make reading a dull chore. What the artistic dimension of writing implies is that there are many excellencies beyond clear meaning and the most obvious arrangement of words. There is the irreplaceable word, the unique combination, the imaginative touch. Like most decisions about writing, efforts in this direction are questions of appropriateness. Are the words suitable to the writer's purpose and audience? If they are not, they indicate a lack of taste or misjudgment on the part of the writer.

All the following sections discuss the kinds of words and phrases that a writer freely chooses, not as a matter of absolute necessity, but as a matter of his own tastes and inclinations.

Exact quotation

The justification for exact quotation depends in part upon the artistic element of language. Most written material can be paraphrased and re-stated effectively. Occasionally, however, an author has phrased his remarks with such felicity or marked them so clearly with his own personality that to substitute words is to lose completely an unusual effect. For instance, to paraphrase the opening of Loren Eiseley's "The Fire Apes" is to lose its suspense and subtlety:

> I was the only man in the world who saw him do it. Everybody else was hurrying.

And to paraphrase would be to lose the remarkable condensation of the well-known opening of Bacon's essay "Of Truth".

> "What is truth?" said jesting Pilate, and would not stay for an answer.

Quotation should aim to preserve and popularize the best of the language. A writer exploits quotation when his main purpose is to pad his own prose and when he does it indiscriminately.

That quotation also has a utilitarian function should not be ignored, however. It demonstrates; it provides documentary proof. If we are arguing a point, we may need to quote from the record, whether the prose is good or bad. If we are discussing exotic usage, we need to illustrate with samples from actual writing. Quotation, in such instances, is evidence, not particularly a reflection of the tastes of the writer.

Inventions of language

One of the real indications of our basic conservatism about language is the reluctance with which many writers want to depart from the tired and trite. They fail to see that in those expressions that occur to them predictably they have a chance to be inventive, not to repeat them formulaically. A newspaper writer, pointing out that Arthur Sorenson apparently adopted many of the speaking mannerisms of President Kennedy, gets mileage from a worn expression by writing, "Sorenson is a good argument that familiarity breeds similarity." A report published by the Commission on English of the College Entrance Examination Board, attempting to make the point that utility cannot be the sole criterion for selecting studies in the English program, concludes a paragraph with the warning, "Humanists are ill advised to put all their eggs in the basket of utility." These are statements with an unexpected twist that revitalize the meaning of hackneyed expressions.

Word play is delightful if it is done discreetly and moderately. Flamboyant types will even venture to pun, despite an almost prudish censure of this kind of dallying in our time. Marshall McLuhan manages it pleasantly in *Understanding Media:*

> Moholy-Nagy notes how, to Europeans, America seems to be the land of abstractions, where numbers have taken on an existence of their own in phrases like "57 Varieties," "the 5 and 10," or "7 Up" and "behind the 8-ball." It figures.

Eccentric prose is attention-getting, although the effect may not always work to the writer's advantage. However, we can expect the offbeat in language, as well as in music, dance, and fashion:

> I get some fatsimile slapped down finally. It's then I really move it's good and I gurgle, and as some others propagand again and again, it's pretty pleasant.

Despite the jazzy tone of this sentence, it is not private jargon. Anyone can read it and understand. The writer plays with sounds and words, perhaps self-consciously, with a Joycean deliberateness. Whether one likes it or not is a matter of taste. But it is prose that cannot very well be ignored completely.

Word play obviously doesn't have a place in basically utilitarian and serious writing, but in any informal prose it may be a rich source of humor and delight.

Archaisms

Archaisms, past their day of usefulness for serious communication, are good for doing what they usually do—for causing amusement. Because they are anachronisms in a contemporary setting, like a doorman dressed like Benjamin Franklin in front of a modern hotel, they are funny, and often funny in a pontifical way. The following student sentences were all written as straight lines:

If a child were disrespectful in the *olden* days, he was punished.

It was *fraught* with excitement.

He himself was the greatest obstacle to his *amative* success.

If the special attributes of past generations *were bestowed upon* those born today, how would we cope with them?

These writers seem to be unaware that with the changing language words fall from active use, although usages of the past continue to be preserved in the reprints of literary works.

Foreign phrases

The attitude of some writers toward foreign phrases is simply chauvinistic, although they do not hesitate to use words like *via, verbatim, non sequitur,* and *et cetera* that have earned their citizenship in the language by long service and have now had the italics, the badge of foreignness, removed. Constant dabbling in foreign terms, of course, can be effete and showy. But in some instances their use is indispensable and inescapable. At times they are the most economical expressions to use because the English language seems not to have provided satisfactory equivalents for them. Any word or phrase in this category is probably well on its way toward being adopted, like *tour de force, torte, esprit de corps,* and *sine qua non.* When these words are fully assimilated, they will retain their flavor of foreignness, but in this respect they will not differ from a good number of words already absorbed: *garage, chauffeur, genre,* and *ennui.*

Figurative language

Figurative language is perhaps the most controversial part of the broad optional category that we are discussing. Some practitioners simply draw hard and fast lines and relegate figurative language to the resort areas of literature and demand straight talk for the urban districts of everyday prose. Such division implies fundamentally that figurative language is frothy and decorative. The fact is that figurative language is usually strong and practical because, like all concrete language, it sends its roots down into familiar experiences. In most instances, a figure of speech attempts to transfer our associations with the familiar and concrete to something unknown and abstract. We seldom compare the particular with the abstract. For instance:

He talked soothingly, like peace settling confusion.

Even the implied personifications of *peace* and *confusion* in this simile do not make the comparison a forceful one. Contrast the effect that another writer gets from the personification implied by the verb of this sentence:

Small shacks cling precariously on the slope behind the large houses.

Or consider what the verbs of these sentences do:

Bulldozers gulped entire front yards.

Sidewalks hump a little to accommodate their roots.

The last three sentences happen to be descriptive passages excerpted from expository prose. They demonstrate that factual writing is not a function completely segregated from narration and description. Passages of this kind are often brief, but they demand picturesque, vigorous, figurative language.

Figurative expression represents a natural way of thinking, for we characteristically accommodate our thoughts to the reader by this means. A simple analogy may have extended associations. For instance:

Somewhere I lost hold of the ring of success.

The reference in this sentence is simple but meaningful, possibly even puzzling to someone who has not grabbed for a ring on a merry-go-round.

The compactness of figurative language makes it not only a vivid form of expression but economical as well. Consider to what extent a whole attitude toward life is contained in the following question:

> What do I care about the other fellow's vest sprinkled with *fleur-de-lys* when my own is bright red with brass buttons?

Extending the implications of this particular comparison would only detract from the imaginative suggestion that grows out of its brevity. In many instances, however, writers use extended analogies for purposes of illustration. Analogies tend to clarify rather than to persuade because anyone can dismiss an argument based upon analogy by simply indicating that the differences between two things being compared are greater than the similarities. But analogy is compelling, and if the audience is not given to close scrutiny of the comparison, it may even serve to convince.

Analogy pushed too far, however, defeats itself, as this example illustrates:

> A cheater can be compared to a meandering river, lazily rolling around hills and through valleys, but always taking the path of least resistance. This course may very well suit a river, but a man has a goal. Can he be sure that the easy way, the path of least resistance, is the way to get through life successfully? The river has no goal toward which to strive. It can do anything it wants. There is no reason for it to get anywhere or for it to stagnate. The cheater who, like the river, chooses the easy way may not reach his destination.

In this instance, the metaphor works in a fairly effective way up until the end of the first sentence. All the key associations are contained in *meandering, lazily,* and *least resistance.* After that point, the analogy fails, not just because it is pushed beyond the point of usefulness, but because the facts seem genuinely contrary to nature. Rivers may not have goals in the sense that men have objectives, but rivers do have destinations, and they move toward them in a persistent, even though meandering, course.

Unlike rivers, analogies cannot meander. The writer has to stick to the course that he sets for himself. Note what happens in this short sentence:

> The octopus Red China uses each successive victim as a springboard to get a little closer to the next one.

And the mixture of figures in this one:

> Her flirtatious eyes can lure you to hover at her feet, where she will hit you over the head with the heartbreak of disappointment.

These blunders should not discourage a writer from trying a figure or two; they should, however, caution him about obvious difficulties that arise when he loses full control of his language. Most students are not highly experimental with language. They prefer to plod along on safe ground and leave the soaring to poets. I am reminded, however, of the classical emblem of inspiration, Pegasus, the winged horse. He seems such an unlikely creature for his role, but once in flight, we are told, he is inexhaustible. Some students, once encouraged to try figurative language, soar with a new pleasure in writing.

WORD TOLERANCE

In referring to language as a discipline and writing as a craft, we sometimes lose our awareness that the use of words is a most human function. Words are personally meaningful. Words objectify our inner thoughts and feelings. We are able to choose words and arrange them as no one else can. Above all else, as writers, we have the freedom to choose and to err. Our greatest writers are not great in every word in every sentence on every page. In this most human act of writing, tolerance is in order—tolerance for the choices we would not make, tolerance for the inevitable imperfections that arise in everyone's writing, including our own. Tolerance is not a compromise with quality, only a recognition of human differences and a hope. If we respect an individual's right to choose freely and to arrange imaginatively—and to err—we may eventually share his highest achievement in writing.

SUGGESTIONS FOR DISCUSSION

1. George Orwell wrote, "In prose, the worst thing one can do with words is to surrender to them." What does this mean as advice to a writer?

2. Comment upon the choice and arrangement of words in the following student sentences. Begin with a personal response (Clear? Confusing? Effective?); then, in terms of the discussion in this chapter, diagnose what the problem is and supply a remedy.

   A. We sell millions of dollars' worth of lead pencils each year. We have many words for soul. Yet we are in danger of pulling a white sheet over the essence of our being and losing that part of us that can be reborn.

   B. I wrap myself comfortably in woven fibers which are fabricated in a test tube, live in a spacious edifice with enough floor space to sleep seventy-eight men, eat food that was grown two years ago two thousand miles away, and dash away my green years trying to save enough to stretch out a longer retirement which will probably be condensed because of my dashing.

   C. Where a friendly atmosphere is desired, I often imagine myself talking to my reader over a friendly glass of cold beer.

   D. It disturbs me when my own home is messy, be it surrounding my exterior self or within my brain.

   E. Often, if a sequence of thoughts has gorged a circular convolution in my brain, it will help to write down this particular pattern on paper so as to gain distance from the thoughts and thereby look at them following out the logical implications and then organizing the possible conclusions.

   F. In a discussion of the aspects of writing, I believe, for instructional purposes, that techniques can be applied by all, though handled individually, who seek to tread the written path, while creativity must be an individual consideration coming from within each person.

   G. The final quality I would like to assess to good writing may be deduced from the above paragraph.

H. Somehow, I came up with the idea of putting my facts into a fiction setting, having an elderly gentleman who fought the Civil War over with anyone who was willing to fight explain his passion for the South's cause of his teen-age grand-daughter who thought he was a little bit screwed.

I. My elective hours the first four years were spent in amputation of my unneeded appendages. In dancing classes like folk, tap, and modern I was really at my height of discordant moronity.

J. At the outset of an assignment I generally rationalize into putting off the agonizing start of a paper for most of the interim between its assigning and its due date.

3. Attempt to describe the diction of the following passages; that is, from what stock of words in the language has the author drawn? What is the effect? What words and idioms mark some of the passages as clearly pre-twentieth century? What arrangements seem strange to the modern ear?

A.   But the iniquity of oblivion blindly scattereth her poppy, and deals with the memory of men without distinction to merit of per- petuity. Who can but pity the founder of the pyramids? Herostratus lives that burnt the temple of Diana, he is almost lost that built it. Time hath spared the epitaph of Adrian's horse, confounded that of himself. In vain we compute our felicities by the advantage of our good names, since bad have equal durations, and Thersites is like to live as long as Agamemnon. Who knows whether the best of men be known, or whether there be not more remarkable persons forgot than any that stand remembered in the known account of time? Without the favor of the everlasting register, the first man had been as unknown as the last, and Methuselah's long life had been his only chronicle.

Sir Thomas Browne from
Hydriotaphia (1686)

B.   A question was once, somehow or other, started between Collins and me, of the propriety of educating the female sex in learning, and their abilities for study. He was of opinion that it was improper, and that they were naturally unequal to it. I took the contrary side, perhaps a little for dispute's sake. He was naturally more eloquent, had a ready plenty of words; and sometimes, as

I thought, bore me down more by his fluency than by the strength of his reasons. As we parted without settling the point, and were not to see one another again for some time, I sat down to put my arguments in writing, which I copied fair and sent to him. He answered, and I replied. Three or four letters of a side had passed, when my father happened to find my papers and read them. Without entering into the discussion, he took occasion to talk to me about the manner of my writing; observed that, though I had the advantage of my antagonist in correct spelling and pointing (which I ow'd to the printing-house), I fell far short in elegance of expression, in method and in perspicuity, of which he convinced me by several instances. I saw the justice of his remarks, and thence grew more attentive to the manner in writing, and determined to endeavor at improvement.

> Benjamin Franklin from
> *The Autobiography* (this
> portion written in 1771)

C.   As far then as Mr. Wordsworth in his preface contended, and most ably contended, for a reformation in our poetic diction, as far as he has evinced the truth of passion, and the *dramatic* propriety of those figures and metaphors in the original poets, which, stripped of their justifying reasons, and converted into mere artifices of connection or ornament, constitute the characteristic falsity in the poetic style of the moderns; and as far as he has, with equal acuteness and clearness, pointed out the process by which this change was effected, and the resemblances between that state into which the reader's mind is thrown by the pleasureable confusion of thought from an unaccustomed train of words and images; and that state which is induced by the natural language of empassioned feeling; he undertook a useful task, and deserves all praise, both for the attempt and for the execution. The provocations to this remonstrance in behalf of truth and nature were still of perpetual recurrence before and after the publication of this preface. I cannot likewise but add, that the comparison of such poems of merit, as have been given to the public within the last ten or twelve years, with the majority of those produced previously to the appearance of that preface, leave no doubt on my mind that Mr. Wordsworth is fully justified in believing his efforts to have been by no means ineffectual.

> Samuel Taylor Coleridge from
> *Biographia Literaria* (1817)

D.   Martin's ever-present highball glass reinforces the general impression that he appears on-camera half gassed. But, as his bartender and his best friends know, Dean Martin is no more an out-of-control toper than Jack Benny is a 39-year-old tightwad. Dino on-camera affects a skinful for the same reason that Jack affects the skinflint. Martin's matchless comic timing, the testimony of his neighbors on Beverly Hills' Mountain Drive, his easy coping with a fast-moving life, all suggest a man who uses booze rather than letting it use him. He shoots enough golf to stay in the low 70s, enough films to make the top ten grossing actors every year. He sells more single records than any other crooner, stood 55 places ahead of Friend Frank Sinatra in 1965. Dean also earns about as much money as Sinatra—$1,000,000 a year—and nearly as much as before the 1956 bust-up with Jerry Lewis that was supposed to send him back to the mill in Steubenville, Ohio. Dean Martin drinks moderately. But he can't help quipping, "I keep a case of Moderately in my dressing room."

Time, March 11, 1966

4. Try to come to some conclusions about the relationships that exist between the audience and the words a writer uses. Does the audience determine the selection, or do the words determine the audience? What would be involved in writing a popularized version of a complex subject?

ASSIGNMENTS

1. Analyze the language of an advertisement in a popular magazine. How many verifiable facts are given? How many attention-getting words are used? How are feelings involved? What audience is appealed to? What values?
2. Make a list of words, similar in sound, that you are aware you often confuse with one another.

6

Feeling

Intellect is known to be connected with emotion, and is generally suspected of spoiling or chilling it—at least when emotion is not accused of warping Intellect.

Jacques Barzun

riting is feeling as well as thinking. The two are inseparably connected: ideas stir emotional responses; feelings endure by attaching themselves to thoughts. Without the link, both often fade away quickly. Yet by acting as if one corrupts the pure state of the other, we draw hard lines of distinction between cold rationality and warm feeling and regularly try to keep them apart. Notice the resistance that many students give to what they consider the unfeeling analysis of poetry. To them, poetry is a special thermal region not to be penetrated by the iciness of thought. On the other hand, intellectual snobs scorn the commonness of feeling. They imply that we are all capable of feeling—feeling sharply and intensely—but say it is quite another matter to claim that everyone is equally capable of thinking sharply and intensely. In his essay "Thinking as a Hobby," William Golding speaks of feeling as "grade-three thinking." Although he recognizes that his third category is clearly different from the pursuit of truth (grade one) and detection of contradiction (grade two), he claims that feeling is about as close to thinking as nine-tenths of the population will ever get.

Although not many of us are likely to accept Golding's arbitrary categories, we cannot easily dismiss his overall claim that feeling is a more prevalent and popular inclination than reflection. But the immediate question in this book is not whether man is both a thinking and feeling being—the answer is all too obvious. The question is rather whether the writer, particularly the writer of expository prose, is also entitled to be a thinking and feeling being or must attempt to negate feeling entirely in order to be a completely impersonal spokesman.

In Chapter 7, we discuss one major style of writing, commonly called the Plain Style, which is clearly characterized by its impersonality and lack of emotion. Here, however, we concern ourselves with other modes of expository writing that involve feelings. The issue, therefore, is not whether a writer should express feeling, but how he can and should when he wants to do so.

EMOTIONAL VALUES: MODERATION AND SUITABILITY

To generalize about feeling is itself difficult because, in speaking of it, we are in an area of complete subjectivity. Only the individual knows fully how he feels. Yet the understanding we have of our own feelings may be misinterpreted when we try to express those feelings, particularly in writing. An outsider—a reader—may react to our expressions of inner feelings without necessarily perceiving them as we do. He may misread our intentions. What we intend as honest criticism he may interpret as envy. What we think of as temperate expression he may read as intemperate. In a theme, for instance, a student may express indignation about courses he is required to take for his degree, expecting support in proportion to the intensity of his own feelings. The instructor may be unmoved, or even alienated, because he thinks the emotion is excessive, only an expression of shortsighted self-interest that ignores the theoretical basis of the requirements. This is not to say that the student may not have a justifiable complaint, but the problem is not likely to be solved on the basis of feelings. In fact, intense feelings usually get in the way of disinterested discussion and rational solutions.

Even though we might cite example after example, both personal and public, where feelings complicate the issues, it is not good enough to act as if we are merely victims of our natures and can do nothing. As writers, we can at least be aware of a few typical responses to feeling (if one is bold enough to generalize about typical responses, as diverse as they actually are).

First of all, most of us recognize a spectrum of feelings, with apathy at one extreme and effusion at the other. Either extreme we do not tolerate very well or very long, even though someone might argue that the current popularity of works featuring high-pitched scenes of hostility, violence, suffering, and dissipation marks a change in taste. But, as we noted in Chapter 5, excessive tone tends to dull sensibility, not excite it. In general, we get bored with indifference; we are easily surfeited by excess. Between the extremes are all degrees of lively concern—signs that the writer is sincere and indications that his feelings have not blinded his insights.

In the second place, besides the premium we place upon moderation, we tend to defer to some sense of suitability (*propriety* is probably a more exact term, but it sounds a bit old-fashioned and stiff in this context); that is, some expressions of emotion seem to be inappropriate or disproportionate to the cause. A student's distaste for obscenities in contemporary novels does not justify a tirade against realism in literature or a diatribe against the corruption of society in general. He is certainly entitled to object on the grounds that his sensibilities are offended, but he is not likely to win sympathy for his cause by magnifying the problem or offending someone else's sensibilities by extreme language of another kind. Every grievance is not an emetic.

The whole notion of suitability no doubt has some basis in the conduct we ordinarily observe. From experience, we expect high excitement in political conventions, grief in disaster, sentiment in love, and we comment on the unexpected. Even though as outsiders we see only the appearance of things and never know all of the reasons for unusual expressions of emotion, we react nevertheless in terms of probability, in terms of the customary response. It is one of the relatively predictable things about audience reaction.

SUBJECTIVITY AND OBJECTIVITY: PERSON AND POINT OF VIEW

Once when the members of a writing class were asked to state what each one thought he needed to know in order to become a better writer, a young man expressed his problem simply: "I've never yet found out how much of myself I should put into papers of different types." As with many other questions about writing, the answer to this dilemma is equivocal. I suspect, however, that this student's doubt arose from a conflict between his desire to include some of his feelings and his impression that any kind of self-indulgence would be frowned upon in so-called objective writing. Even though the most objective prose is written in third person, we should observe that all third-person writing is not necessarily objective. Note these sentences by John Stuart Mill:

> The greatest orator, save one, of antiquity, has left it on record that he always studied his adversary's case with as great, if not with still greater, intensity than even his own. What Cicero practised as the means of forensic success requires to be imitated by all who study any subject in order to arrive at the truth. He who knows only his own side of the case knows little of that. His reasons may be good, and no one may have been able to refute them. But if he is equally unable to refute the reasons on the opposite side, if he does not so much as know what they are, he has no ground for preferring either opinion. The rational position for him would be

suspension of judgement, and unless he contents himself with that, he is either led by authority, or adopts, like the generality of the world, the side to which he feels most inclination.

On Liberty

In this passage, Mill merely assumes the mask of impersonality that the third person gives. The statements are made as if they were fact, not opinion, and thus they gain the authority of fact. But the passage includes value judgments, opinions, and advice. Its subjectivity is inescapable. In other instances, however, writers clearly differentiate between fact and opinion by moving easily from third person to first or use first person plural (as this book does) to invite identity or imply a common interest. Science and mathematics texts often use *we* to refer to the scientific community; a physics text reads, "We arrived at Snell's law and the relation of n_{12} to the speeds by theoretical analysis of our previous results."

A look at professional writing reveals that subjectivity and objectivity are not as scrupulously segregated as one would like to claim for purposes of simple explanation. Are not all objects perceived? Are not all facts selected by the writer? Is not any selection to a certain degree an interpretation? Cannot a statement of fact evoke feeling? We are almost forced to conclude that different kinds of writing reflect only degrees of subjectivity and that *objectivity* is a useful but relative term that we know only by its opposite, just as heat by definition is the absence of cold. If we consider subjectivity as the measure to which we are prisoners of ourselves, then objectivity has something to do with our capacity to escape, to broaden our limited view, to give credence to other perceptions. Objectivity is a point of view that attempts to weigh outside evidence without letting personal biases and feelings override logical conclusions. When topics invite self-expression (What is the prevailing mood of Frost's "Acquainted with the Night"? Giving appropriate illustrations, argue for or against Galsworthy's statement, "Public opinion's always in advance of the law"), the writer's job is then to reveal his opinions, his feelings, his idiosyncrasies. In other instances, however, when the subject matter concerns objects and circumstances that place the individual in the role of observer (Review British attitudes toward the American colonies from 1765 to 1775. Give evidence in the plays of Ibsen from 1879 to 1884 of a shifting attitude toward the social reformer), then involving the self may be only a hindrance to the full investigation of the facts. After doing research, an ardent feminist no doubt finds it difficult to give an impersonal explanation of what appears to be misogyny in Milton. Or a present-day Rosicrucian no doubt finds himself emotionally predisposed to agree with the theory that Bacon wrote Shakespeare's plays. The stronger the individual's commitments and feelings are, the more difficult it is for him to approach any subject objectively.

If a student begins with little knowledge and no predispositions, then he too must be wary about intruding himself upon the discussion as if he were an expert. As a beginner, he is of course entitled to state his inclinations or to evaluate the arguments, but, even then, his opinions may add little significance to the discussion, particularly if he has not investigated the subject thoroughly. A writer's intrusion upon a factual discussion is almost always a matter of appropriateness and tact. The student who writes "Shakespeare agrees with me when he says . . ." inadvertently steals the scene from the main performer. If his line reads "I agree with Shakespeare when he says . . . ," then no one will object. Thus the whole question of a writer's place hinges upon the perspective a reader has of the writer in relation to his subject. Any student who is puzzled about how much of himself to put into his prose needs to study more his own reactions to the role that other writers assume in their prose. He may then learn that the tone of the writer's voice influences the reader's sense of the writer's presence.

THE WRITER'S VOICE: TONE

The human speaking voice is an extremely flexible instrument, capable of achieving all kinds of effects: we can growl, laugh, whisper, speak audibly, yell, and sing. We can even disguise our own voices by imitating others. Yet, despite all these variations, we usually think that we have a natural voice. It is the voice we use when we are not being overly conscious of ourselves. Or to use an analogy: we almost always recognize in the projected voice of a ventriloquist a false note, a kind of unvarying monotone that suggests that it is not able to exploit the full range of human expression. When the ventriloquist speaks in his own voice, we learn that he has resonance, that he can modulate and intensify his voice. In short, his own voice projects feeling with conviction.

Even though the voice of a writer is not audible in his prose, it is usually perceptible, unless, as we have previously noted, he chooses to write a Plain Style that deliberately attempts to neutralize the tones and variations of voice. The term *voice* is a convenient one for talking about a good number of matters in composition. We can say, first of all, that some writers, particularly inexperienced ones, are not even aware of the mannerisms they assume. Paradoxically, we are not the best judges of our own intonations, either in speaking or in writing. We are always in need of a sympathetic critic.

Therefore, with full awareness that to be deaf to one's own voice is the easiest thing in the world, I would like to describe a few voices that I hear in Freshman papers, particularly at the beginning of the year, when the writer is especially audience-conscious; that is, he wants to impress his professor. The first voice is the voice of the "scholar":

> In our continual quest for self-assurance and personal exoneration from our frequent mistakes, and in order to maintain ourselves in good standing, both morally and socially in the eyes of our fellow men, we have become habitual practitioners of the act of creating plausible explanations or excuses for our acts, beliefs, and desires, usually without realizing that these are not our real motives for the acts performed. This complex function of our reasoning processes is known as rationalization.

This student seems to assume that an educated man is one who packs as many big words as possible into involved sentences. Although we can certainly find plenty of examples of inflated prose in the scholarly journals, the frequency of big words is not necessarily a mark of erudition. The scholar who is secure in his knowledge does not need to impress his audience with the extent of his vocabulary. Students frequently try to. If big words are well used, fine. If they are not, then they are like the facades of Hollywood sets, impressive but with nothing behind them.

A second voice is the "salesman's" voice:

The content of a course is less important than the approach and the goal. Keep students thinking! Alive! Performance is what is wanted!

This writer thinks that persuasion in writing is proportionate to the number of exclamation points in a sentence. The prose is high-pressured. But notice also how, after the first sentence, the remaining phrases take on the overtones of speaking. The writer changes from third person to second person and addresses his audience directly. The change marks a shift in voice as well as in person. Note a similar kind of shift in the following passage:

From personal experience I know that there are many different groups of kids who go around together. There are good groups, and there are groups that consist of vandals and prospective drop-outs. You usually conform to the ideas of the group you go around with. By getting some of these would-be vandals into a better group of kids you could also help the teenage problem.

This is a buddy-buddy voice, not only because the writer chooses slangy terms like *go around* and *kids* but also because he writes the way he talks and shifts his point of view thoughtlessly. In the second sentence, *you* seems to address teenagers because it comments on teenage tendencies. In the third sentence, *you* presumably addresses adults who can do something about the problem. But we can't be sure of these references because the prose is imprecise.

The next voice is that of the blunderer:

Jane Eyre could easily represent the modern independent woman. Outwardly, Jane offers very little. She is neatly but quaintly dressed—a poor, inexperienced governess with plain features. Her treasure is on the inside, where it wouldn't be noticed at first glance.

This writer is serious, but because he blunders with words and falls into unintentional ambiguities, he produces a comic voice that he does not mean to.

Another voice is the voice of Pollyanna:

Bill is a teen-ager who is industrious and, I believe, desirous of a meaningful life. He is making every effort to obtain as much

education as his finances and ability will allow. Three quarters of
the year he pursues an education in music. The summer months
find him working swing shift in a quarry and giving piano lessons
in his off-hours. This he does to augment his parents' limited
financial aid. Thereby, he is also learning the joy of earning a
dollar for a job well done. His reverence for his spiritual heritage
sees him in church on Sunday morning playing the organ, giving the
regular organist a well-earned rest. Other free time one may see
him relaxing at the beach, fraternizing with a buddy or taking his
best girl to the Saturday night hop. There is every indication that
Bill is trustworthy, dependable, considerate and responsible for his
actions. With these assets, his contribution to society should be
praiseworthy, and for himself a life rich in happiness and rewarding
satisfaction should be earned.

This is a paragraph in which the writer's own feeling cloys the prose.
She describes Bill as if he were a superscout, not as a versatile young
man who seems to assume his responsibilities and have fun too. The
passage lacks honesty.

All the voices we have noted thus far are bothersome in some
particular way, and they therefore distract the reader. One further
example should emphasize by contrast what a voice can do when it
is well used (the following passage was actually written by a student in
a remedial group):

In a week or two, with any luck at all, I and three or four
friends will climb to the top of a mountain. Then we will ski down
through powder snow as good as any in the world. The mountains
will tower around us in a chiaroscuro of black trees against white
snow. But best of all will be the feeling of being alone, or almost
alone on a mountain. As I come out of the trees and round the
point of a ridge, I will stop to wonder at the magnificence of the
peaks and the valleys below. I will say to myself, "I hope that I
never have to leave this place." At the bottom, as I sip my beer,
I will think of other places I might live: Switzerland, San Francisco,
New Orleans, Paris, the Riviera, Alaska; and I will conclude that
here, in southeastern Idaho, is the best place in the world to live.

The voice in this passage is natural and pleasant, although that is
not to say that the writer would use this same voice if he were telling
the same thing in person. In fact, the diction of this paragraph is not
colloquial, but the sentences have an easy informality. The writer is not

telling us what happened. He removes himself from the scene. He pretends to tell us what will happen and what he will think in the future. In spite of this device of projecting the past into the future, the paragraph is unpretentious. When the writer gives his final judgment of southeastern Idaho as "the best place in the world to live," his tone is wholly convincing and sincere.

An interesting sidelight is that the student who wrote this paragraph was not asked to write about an experience. He was asked to write a short paragraph upon the advantages or disadvantages of living in a particular place. His approach of course is completely subjective. He does not resort to fact; he does not tell us that the snow in Idaho is superior to the snow in Switzerland. He persuades us on the basis of feeling. He simply lets us know how exhilarating it is to be in Idaho.

Even though we change our writing voice just as we do our speaking voice, the question arises whether it is possible for writers to think about voice without inherently falling into paralyzing self-consciousness and obvious affectation. The answer is simply that the writer needs to be no more aware of voice while he is writing than the speaker is of the sound of his voice while he is speaking. We are sometimes formal, sometimes casual, sometimes heated, sometimes pleading, and our words and tone seem to follow suit once we have decided how we want to behave. The same is true in writing. But the writer has an advantage over the speaker in being able to let the prose cool off. At that point, he can go back to it with an air of detachment and an analytical view to see if the voice he has presented is logically consistent and convincing. The prose of the homespun philosopher, for instance, doesn't mix very well with the prose of the man of affairs:

> Progress and change are indeed inevitable in a society with a rapidly growing population. It takes a heap of doing to preserve a community's character, tradition, and living space while admitting growth and change.

Of course, no writer ever maintains one tone in a composition. What results is usually a series of appropriately related voices. I have tried to demonstrate obvious incongruities. If a writer, however, wants to avoid forcing his own voice, he has to find out what someone else hears before he can be certain what his natural range of expression is.

THE GAUGE OF FEELING: OUR SENSE OF THE NORMATIVE

The term *voice* is convenient in talking about consistency of person and point of view in prose; it is also helpful in writing more precisely about feeling. When an instructor reads through student themes, in addition to considerations he may give to content and form and diction, he cannot avoid making judgments about the tone of the remarks, particularly those that impress him negatively as too pretentious, too cute, too commonplace, too crude, too patronizing, too blatant, too dogmatic, or too apologetic. These are not necessarily his isolated responses. It is possible that a dozen other readers would respond similarly. If there are general reactions of this kind, then we are not talking about an individual's private likes and dislikes. We are approaching the notion of some norm in all of us to which such feelings have reference. Sometimes we judge the tone of writing as excessive—too sensational, too hostile. Sometimes we judge it as deficient—too uninvolved, too ingratiating. One extreme tends toward flamboyance; the other, toward ineffectuality. But these extremes suggest a sense of the normative operating in most individuals, a kind of intuitive center of balance. Like their temperature, they are aware of it when it goes up or down. At other times, they are comfortable and receptive.

It is true, of course, that a single individual's sense of the normative does not correspond precisely to everyone else's, but there is enough overlap, and the extremes are usually well enough defined, that we have a way of predicting what responses a writer is likely to get when he tries to project feelings, particularly intense feelings. Ranting prophets characteristically protest that no one believes them. No one believed Cassandra. Jeremiah berated the indifference of his hearers. Philip Wylie, a kind of prophet of the 1940s, objected that no one paid any serious attention to him. Of course, these people often say things that upset the status quo, that invade our tranquility, that shatter the image we have of ourselves; and we protect ourselves by not listening. The writer who is consistently intemperate is likely to be disregarded, not because he is automatically a bad thinker or a bad writer, but because he overdoes. Pulling out all the stops produces a climax; keeping them out creates an annoyance that causes us to cover our ears.

It is also true that words indicating intense feelings may boomerang.

The writer who sets out to discredit someone else often discredits himself. He runs the risk of seeming a vitriolic person venting his rage on an innocent victim. Further, in many cases, where strong negative feelings are involved, we learn more about the writer than we do about his subject.

The publication in 1961 of *Webster's Third New International Dictionary of the English Language* prompted a rash of excited reviews. One of the most widely publicized has been Wilson Follett's article in *The Atlantic Monthly* (January, 1962), entitled "Sabotage in Springfield." One of its paragraphs reads:

> Examination cannot proceed far without revealing that Webster III, behind its front of passionless objectivity, is in truth a fighting document. And the enemy it is out to destroy is every obstinate vestige of linguistic punctilio, every surviving influence that makes for the upholding of standards, every criterion for distinguishing between better usages and worse. In other words, it has gone over bodily to the school that construes traditions as enslaving, the rudimentary principles of syntax as crippling, and taste as irrelevant. This revolution leaves it in the anomalous position of loudly glorifying its own ancestry—which is indeed glorious—while tacitly sabotaging the principles and ideals that brought the preceding Merriam-Webster to its unchallengeable pre-eminence. The Third New International is at once a resounding tribute of lip service to the Second and a wholesale repudiation of it—a sweeping act of apology, contrition, and reform.

Without doubt, this kind of writing is attention-getting; there is not a dull sentence in it. But to what extent do we accept Follett's impassioned comments as an accurate estimate of the dictionary? What is the purpose? Is it a rallying cry or a review? One thing is certain: we learn that Mr. Follett is agitated about the new dictionary, and his feelings in turn upset the equilibrium of a good many readers.

The extent to which a reader finds Mr. Follett's remarks either stimulating or irritating depends in part upon his own views about the dictionary and in part upon his tolerance for exaggeration. Readers respond differently, because the sense of the normative is not an absolute uniform factor—a fixed pitch in everyone. It is for the most part an affinity for moderation, but what moderation is to one individual is not moderation to another. The variances, however, are not so great that we are at a loss to know what is likely to be objectionable. In most expository prose, we are accustomed to an essentially moderate tone of feeling, with generous allowances for flamboyance and eccentricity. The writer who offends his reader usually grates on his sensibilities or arouses his temper by distortions of tone. To become more clearly aware of what the limits of tolerance are (assuming a writer wants to please rather than antagonize), he needs to start first with his own reactions in order to recognize what degrees of feeling offend him. More clearly aware of his own range of tolerance, he is likely to gain confidence in his own ability to write tactfully and tastefully for others.

TELLING AND SHOWING

Projecting emotions accurately in prose is one of the most difficult things a writer can undertake. He is never more likely to be misunderstood than when he is trying to convey the true measure of his own feeling, that is, if he depends heavily upon abstractions rather than illustrations. The words we use for the emotions are almost all vague approximations. A man who loves mathematics loves it differently from the way he loves his dog or a passing spectacle or a woman. To say that he respects the subject, likes the dog, admires the spectacle, and adores the woman is to suggest distinctions of a kind, but not of intensity, duration, or particularity. The difficulty with such general words as *love* and *hate* is that they attempt to make factual statements *about* feelings, whereas the appeal to a reader's feelings must be made chiefly through his own senses and imagination. Thus, of all writers, poets are perhaps most successful in communicating particular feelings. This they do best when their images are sharp and their words concrete. The poem becomes an experience in itself. It acts as a mirror for the reader. When he sees himself or his own experience in a poem, he is able to respond.

A one-to-one, direct and literal translation of a writer's emotion is impossible. The writer is one person; the reader is another; and the two represent two different worlds of private experience. A writer may try to tell us forthrightly how much he detests tyranny—he may say that he loathes it, detests it, abjures it—but he may be more convincing if he shows us, if he narrates circumstances so that we begin to experience vicariously. Feeling is always a matter of personal involvement, and the writer must write something that involves the reader if he wants that reader to respond with feeling. In this respect, the novelist has an advantage over the essayist because he can create a fictional universe in which his characters move. The essayist must accomplish his purpose with compressed action and simplified detail, probably with only a brief anecdote. But the reader gets involved in the same way. Notice how in a short paragraph Alfred Kazin communicates the intensity of his own feeling:

> There was my secret ordeal: I could never say anything except in the most roundabout way; I was a stammerer. Although I knew all those new words from my private reading—I read walking in the street, to and from the Children's Library on Stone Avenue; on the fire escape and the roof; at every meal when they would let me; read even when I dressed in the morning, propping my book up against the drawers of the bureau as I pulled on my long black stockings—I could never seem to get the easiest words out with the right dispatch, and would often signal miserably from my desk that I did not know the answer rather than get up to stumble and fall and crash on every word. If, angry at always being put down as lazy or stupid, I did get up to speak, the black wooden floor would roll away under my feet, the teacher would frown at me in amazement, and in unbearable loneliness I would hear behind me the groans and laughter: *tuh-tuh-tuh-tuh.*
>
> *A Walker in the City*

When Kazin's next paragraph begins, "The word was my agony," we are ready to accept his generalization about the feeling, because what he finally tells us he has already shown, and he has depended heavily upon narration and description, upon concrete details, to achieve that end.

CONTROVERSIAL TOPICS

Equal to the problem of projecting feelings accurately is the problem of controlling the emotions that sensitive and controversial topics stir up. In 1966, John Lennon set off an emotional furor in the United States when he reportedly said that the Beatles were more popular than Jesus and added that Christianity was doomed to pass away. The remark was a firebrand in this country. In fact, actual bonfires were lighted in several cities, and people burned Beatle records and photographs. Newspapers announced a ban-the-Beatles movement. But in England, reportedly, the comments caused no stir. Said Lennon, "They were taken as a bit of loudmouth thing."

In retrospect, we see that the feelings that erupted were caused less by Lennon's choice of words (he used no obscene or abusive language) than by the general inference that this was an antireligious statement. Particular words are not always responsible for arousing emotions. Obviously, some words are emotive; that is, they tend to stir feeling. But in other instances, especially in the Lennon case, the affective quality of the words was not a strong factor. Lennon managed to stir up the strong feelings that are attached to firm religious beliefs by an implied argument: because the Beatles are more popular than Jesus— a sign of Christianity's loss of relevance—Christianity will pass away. Some of Lennon's defenders pointed out that the influence of Christianity among the young was undeniably shrinking. But the violence of the whole incident lay in the strategy—in this case, presumably a blunder— of linking together two dissimilar elements, putting Jesus and the Beatles into one context. The popular imagination could not tolerate the comparison. A good number of Christians considered the remark blasphemous. But unexpected comparisons are a favorite shock device.

The same argument, differently presented, need not be offensive. A similar statement by Colin Wilson may serve to illustrate. Wilson's comments represent straightforward written discourse, although some of his phrasing suggests that he wants to arouse feelings. For instance, the use of the word *brutally* in the opening sentence is an obvious signal:

> Let me be brutally explicit about my meaning: I believe our civilization is dying. I believe that, as a mass, we are losing the will to go on living, because the conditions under which we live rob us of individuality. We are dying of laziness and boredom, and failure to find a purpose to make it worthwhile going on. I also believe that religion is the cement that holds a civilization together, just as a man's individual purpose is the cement that stops him from going to pieces under the constant challenges involved in living. I believe that conditions nowadays are such that we have outlived the old religion. And yet nothing could save us from bursting into

pieces except a religion. The problem is to brood on the conditions under which a new religion might be hatched—to try to do some fruitful thinking, some constructive thinking, about the structure of our civilization and the needs that a new religion would have to meet.

"Where Do We Go from Here?"

There is actually very little that is shocking about Wilson's comments, not only because he represents a different image to the public (possibly his name carries no image) but because his remarks are rationally conceived, even though strongly felt. He makes clear that he is not antireligious at all. His words "Let me be brutally explicit" prepare the reader for a frank statement, but there is nothing brutal about the strategy. In fact, Wilson's broad generalizations about our civilization and all people as a mass tend to reduce the impact of his remarks. Yet the loss in shock value is no real loss unless the writer, like Lenny Bruce, thinks that "the only medicine that's good for you is iodine, because it burns." Perhaps it is better to gain a point than to lose an audience. Better yet to invent than to be ignored.

At a very early time, writers learned the art of criticism—the way to use the dagger instead of the broadside, the way to lure the reader before he knows he is being attacked, the way to make the reader laugh at his own weaknesses, the way to be oblique. A few examples will illustrate strategies that operate chiefly by indirection—kinds of medicine that work but do not always cause immediate pain.

In his "Argument against Abolishing Christianity," Jonathan Swift uses sustained irony to attack the hypocrisy of those who profess Christianity. With a tone of reasonableness, he answers arguments he invents for abolishing Christianity and then adds "a few inconveniences that may happen, if the gospel should be replaced." The entire essay might be considered a rebuttal of Deistic doctrine, which Swift saw as an outside threat to Christianity; it is more likely a running commentary by a loyal churchman upon the inside threat—the worldliness of nominal Christians. In the following passage, Swift assumes an ironic aloofness to the "outside critics":

It is again objected, as a very absurd, ridiculous custom, that a set of men should be suffered, much less employed and hired, to bawl one day in seven against the lawfulness of those methods most in use, toward the pursuit of greatness, riches, and pleasure, which are the constant practice of all men alive on the other six. But this objection is, I think, a little unworthy of so refined an age as ours.

Here under a mask of controlled feeling, Swift is severe. In this essay, he demonstrates that the critic can also be an artist.

Mark Twain, no less caustic than Swift, frequently employs a lighter vein of humor. In a short narrative called "Story of the Bad Little Boy," he burlesques Sunday school literature in order to probe the deeper problem of naïve religious belief:

> But the strangest thing that ever happened to Jim was the time he went boating on Sunday, and didn't get drowned, and that other time that he got caught out in the storm when he was fishing on Sunday, and didn't get struck by lightning. Why, you might look, and look, all through the Sunday-school books from now till next Christmas, and you would never come across anything like this. Oh no; you would find that all the bad boys who go boating on Sunday invariably get drowned; and all the bad boys who get caught out in storms when they are fishing on Sunday infallibly get struck by lightning. Boats with bad boys in them always upset on Sunday, and it always storms when bad boys go fishing on the Sabbath. How this Jim ever escaped is a mystery to me. . . .
>
> And he grew up and married, and raised a large family, and brained them all with an axe one night, and got wealthy by all manner of cheating and rascality; and now he is the infernalist wickedest scoundrel in his native village, and is universally respected, and belongs to the Legislature.
>
> So you can see there never was a bad James in the Sunday-school books that had such a streak of luck as this sinful Jim with the charmed life.
>
> *Californian*, December 23, 1865; 1867, 1875

By the time this brief story has ended, Twain has ridiculed not only Sunday school stories and the concept of morality on which they are based but the hypocrisy of a society that is superficial in its observances. Twain's strategy is to control explosive reactions by substituting pleasurable ones.

In a similar vein of hard criticism, Bernard Shaw attacks the popular tendency in Christian teaching to emasculate the figure of Jesus:

"Gentle Jesus, meek and mild" is a snivelling modern invention, with no warrant in the gospels. St. Matthew would as soon have thought of applying such adjectives to Judas Maccabeus as to Jesus; and even St. Luke, who makes Jesus polite and gracious, does not make him meek. The picture of him as an English curate of the farcical comedy type, too meek to fight a policeman, and everybody's butt, may be useful in the nursery to soften children; but that such a figure could ever have become a centre of the world's attention is too absurd for discussion: grown men and women may speak kindly of a harmless creature who utters amiable sentiments and is a helpless nincompoop when he is called on to defend them; but they will not follow him, nor do what he tells them, because they do not wish to share his defeat and disgrace.

"Preface on the Prospects of Christianity"

This passage tends to be shocking because it uses words and analogies unexpected in the context, producing an effect not wholly unlike the effect of the Lennon remark, although the circumstances are different. Shaw's reputation for flamboyance always permitted him liberties that other writers could not assume. Over a period of time, he acclimated his audience. Young people, now unfamiliar with the image that Shaw created in his ninety-odd years, are often outraged. But the audience that knew Shaw was familiar with his overstatement and learned not to accept everything he said or wrote in a literal sense. Even when he was devastating in his criticism, he seldom forgot his wit: "Do not do unto others as you would that they should do unto you. Their tastes may not be the same." Humor was his leaven.

The five examples given above, all criticizing Christian attitudes and practices, represent a considerable range of strategy. They should lead to several conclusions about trying to express feeling in writing. First, when strong feelings are involved, the writer's manner, his choice of language, the nature of his arguments, or the disposition of his audience may trigger unexpected and unintended reactions. Second, if a writer on a controversial topic wants to inform an audience rather than stir it to action, he needs to look to strategies that will channel feelings, not let them rampage. Third, unless he deliberately sets out to antagonize an audience for his own purposes, he should know that loaded words and farfetched comparisons will do little to serve his purpose. Even though feelings support argument, they are not a substitute for it.

SUGGESTIONS FOR DISCUSSION

1. Does the premium we place upon moderation in expressing feeling encourage ineffectual writing? In what way does moderation work to the advantage of the writer?

2. George Cuomo, himself a published novelist, writes in his book *Becoming a Better Reader:* "Pure exposition is free of emotion. But the literary artist tries to write with such fullness, such richness, such exactness that he produces in the reader a powerful emotional response." From this passage, what are we led to infer about expository writing as opposed to literature? Are those inferences valid?

3. Give examples of typical experiences outside of reading and writing in which our sense of the normative acts as an emotional gauge. Consider appeals for contributions, political speeches, calls to social action, protests, and evangelistic warnings. What effects do these have? Are there indications that our "normal emotional temperature" changes? What moves people to fear?

4. Refer to the passage by Mill on page 129. Which statements are facts, which interpretations of facts, which value judgments, which opinions and advice?

5. Demonstrate by reference to voice, tone, and diction that the third-person passage by Wilson Follett on page 137 is highly subjective.

ASSIGNMENTS

1. Read the following passages. Characterize the voice of each one. Then, applying your own sense of the normative, indicate whether you consider the expression of feeling balanced, excessive, or deficient.

   A. Our generation has seen the world thrown into turmoil by an oriental horde of emperor-worshippers, by a super-mad leader who would perpetuate his master race by his genocidal feats, and by an international cabal of conspirators who have forced the assimilation of captive nations into the cocoon of Communism.

   B. The individual who engages in this form of fraud is wasting his time and energy in a rather useless endeavor. It must indeed be a sad experience to realize that you do not have the knowledge and integrity that you profess to have. In short, you are a fraud! You must be ever vigilant not to expose your ignorance.

C. Without faith we would not depend on friends, we could not plan for tomorow, we would be unable to love one another, we would not believe that man has purpose. Life would be chaotic.

D. This huge magnificent city has interests for every individual. If a movie is desired, one has a number of different types of pictures to choose from. Any atmosphere that is desired may be sought out in this city. An ocean-shore atmosphere may be obtained at the piers. A romantic, dimly lighted night club may be found in the better part of the city. Even if a folksinger or fringy-type atmosphere is desired, the University Avenue is a great place to obtain this.

E. Nor shall we need the teachers of English to take our ambitious compositions into their warped and stingy minds and hand them back to us again classified into bad's, worse's, and worst's.

F. While man was learning how to create energy in the form of steam, electricity, and atomic energy, he was forgetting how to love his neighbor. He was too busy to notice that the little boy down the block was crying his heart out or that his brother was dying a slow death of starvation.

G. Graduation from high school in June 1941 brought to abortive cessation my formal education, and the ensuing many years of personal groping, misguided efforts, and emotional turmoil wrought profound changes in my life. An omnipotent, hidden conspiracy against the development of my intellectual potential formed as practical necessities governed my pursuits.

H. Honesty is a concept upheld by people who oppose deceitfulness. Honesty envelops truthfulness, lawfulness, genuineness, sincerity, correctness, fairness and frankness.

I. But—wild, man!—they hate the rock-group sock for twisting everything into *the* wildest amplified whang-whang-twangy style of . . . like, *beat* of the swinging sixties.

J. I feel that the faculty should be resolute in their efforts to stop cheating in the colleges. It might be necessary for the faculty to take the initiative and encourage the colleges to adopt a uniform system to deal with cheating. They should refuse to graduate students who are known to cheat.

K. The irate wife flung her husband's shoes. As they went flying over his head, splintering against the outside door, I thought he was fortunate not to be in them.

2. Examine ten separate essays that are essentially expository in nature. How many employ *I, you, we,* or *one* in the course of the discussion? How many are exclusively third-person accounts? To what extent do you find an intermixture of various personal pronouns?

7

Style

Indeed many people think that a style that does not attract
notice is not style. *W. Somerset Maugham*

S ir James Barrie, the British playwright, tells about a long discussion on style he once heard at an exclusive club in Piccadilly, where Thomas Hardy invited him for lunch. During the afternoon, Barrie says, Hardy made a few remarks, but no one seemed to pay much attention. Barrie recalls that at the time he thought to himself, "How interesting it is that the only man among you who does not know all about style and a good deal more, is the only man among you who has got style." Any beginning student who does not know whether he is a rhetorical dualist, a psychological monist, or an aesthetic monist (to use Louis Milic's classifications of style) can take comfort in Barrie's remark.

What is less comforting, however, is the fact that some kind of stylistic effect is unavoidable. Barrie seems to imply that writers have style or have no style. I am inclined to think that "no style" is only a euphemism for a bad style, for a writer cannot be styleless any more than a man can be without posture. Style is the writer's posture. In fact, a good many words we use to describe our impressions of physical posture also describe impressions of style: *dignified, stiff, casual, awkward,* even *obscene*. These words characterize attitudes of mind as well as attitudes of the body. And in style it may be difficult to determine whether the effect derives specifically from the matter or the manner. Style is a creative construction that builds from the thought, the form, the words, the feeling, and the strategies. It involves our skills, intellectual habits, and tastes. Even though at times we use the word to designate a particular quality of style—a writer's style of thought or his style with words—in most instances we use it to characterize a total effect, good or bad, either appropriate or inappropriate to the writer's purpose.

Thus many of the previous chapters have already discussed elements of style. It is the purpose of this chapter to add to the discussion of strategy and then to consider the appropriateness of the strategies considered to the major modes of style.

IMITATION AS DISCOVERY

One of the best ways to discover the full meaning of style is to try to write like someone else, particularly like someone from a different period.

What we can often do is to reproduce a representative vocabulary, typical sentence structure, and characteristic punctuation, but the remainder—the writer's stance, his temperament, his involvement—is all illusive and difficult to approximate. Nevertheless, if we want to do something about style, not just talk about it as a metaphysical abstraction, we need to find an approach. Imitation is one of the very best means to learn what style is all about and how it is an actuality, not a mirage seen by literary critics.

Since in our own time imitation has come to be associated with slavishness—and thus the opposite of all that is spontaneous, independent, instinctive, idiosyncratic, and inventive—it might be useful to talk for a brief space about other possible attitudes toward imitation and then to explain more specifically how it may be used as a learning device.

First of all, we should remind ourselves that imitation, in general, is one of the fundamental means of learning. It is basic in learning penmanship, speech, languages, dance, painting—in fact, in learning numerous skills and arts. To be sure, imitation is associated with the beginning stages, particularly with childhood, but as an impulse it persists no less strongly in adults than in children, often, unfortunately, as a pressure toward dull conformity. In writing, it can also be an exercise that leads to sameness and leveling, or it can be a study that leads to discovery and invention.

We must then recognize kinds and degrees of imitation in writing. Imitation may be conscious and exact (plagiarism represents its obvious abuse); or it may be unpremeditated and tenuous (we euphemistically refer to this kind of similarity as influence); or it can be an imaginative and creative reconstruction of a model. One of the valuable testimonies to the link between imitation and invention may be found in a speech by Sir Joshua Reynolds before the Royal Academy in 1774. He was speaking, of course, about painting:

> For my own part, I confess, I am not only very much disposed to maintain the absolute necessity of imitation in the first stages of the art; but am of opinion, that the study of other masters, which I here call imitation, may be extended throughout our whole lives, without any danger of the inconveniences with which it is charged, of enfeebling the mind, or preventing us from giving that original air which every work undoubtedly ought always to have.

I am on the contrary persuaded that by imitation only, variety, and even originality of invention, is produced. I will go further; even genius, at least what generally is so called, is the child of imitation. . . .

Invention is one of the great marks of genius; but if we consult experience, we shall find, that it is by being conversant with the inventions of others, that we learn to invent; as by reading the thoughts of others we learn to think.

Discourses on Art, VI

In recent times, a worthy poet like Theodore Roethke has written something equally emphatic on the subject:

Imitation, conscious imitation, is one of the great methods, perhaps *the* method of learning to write. The ancients, the Elizabethans, knew this, profited by it, and were not disturbed. As a son of Ben, Herrick more than once rewrote Jonson, who, in turn, drew heavily on the classics. And so on. The poems are not less good for this: the final triumph is what the language does, not what the poet can do, or display.

"How to Write like Somebody Else" from
On the Poet and His Craft

If a painter and a poet think that imitation does not stultify, then a student of writing, particularly one who wants to know what he can do to work on his style, needs to consider this possibility.

Kinds of discovery

Usually the best thing to do in imitating is to start with a particularly striking passage from an essay or a story, for if we can come to some conclusion why the prose is striking and actually get to the source of the effect by looking at the grammatical and rhetorical patterns, we can begin to learn how a writer functions. If, after analysis, we go one step further to force ourselves—and often it is a hard job—to write an adaptation of the same passage in our own brand of current, idiomatic American English, we can discover firsthand whether we are able to approximate what the original writer attempted to do. We may find that we can't. We may find that we can, but that the manner is incompatible with our own. We may even find that the effort opens up new directions for our own writing.

For instance, someone might start with this widely quoted sentence from Bacon's essay "Of Studies":

> Reading maketh a full man; conference a ready man; and writing an exact man.

The barren analytical facts about this sentence are these: within the one sentence, there are actually three short sentences, arranged in a series like *a, b,* and *c. Man* is the common denominator in each part; however, the word always falls in an unstressed position. Each of the segments also mentions an activity (*Reading, conference, writing*) and a result (*maketh a full man, a ready man,* and *an exact man*). The grammatical pattern in each of the parts is regular (subject, verb, object), although the verb in the last two clauses is omitted.

Here is a twentieth-century version of the same sentence:

> Courtship makes a hopeful woman; marriage a happy woman; motherhood a fulfilled woman.

The imitation demonstrates that it is possible to translate the admirable qualities of the original to the modern idiom—its quotability, its rhythm and balance, its epigrammatic quality, its simple diction. Although the sentence pattern in the imitation is slightly altered from an *a, b,* and *c* series to an *a, b, c,* the change throws stronger emphasis upon the third part. The subtle alliteration of *hopeful woman* and *happy woman* further strengthens the sentence. An imitation of this kind indicates, therefore, that Bacon's effect is not unique. He simply hit upon a happy example of parallel structure, and a student can do something equally as good on his own if he discovers the importance of form and strategy in writing and if he becomes aware of his own capabilities to work in ways that are similar.

There are an infinite number of subtleties to discover from fiction as well as nonfiction. A sentence from Hemingway's "In Another Country," for instance, shows Hemingway using a series of three short sentences in a way completely different from Bacon:

> There was much game hanging outside the shops, and the snow powdered in the fur of the foxes and the wind blew their tails.

This is also three-pronged, this time in an *a* and *b* and *c* arrangement, but the effect has changed. The formal, tight effect of Bacon's sentence has disappeared. True, this one is descriptive, while Bacon's is didactic, but the epigrammatic quality has evaporated in the absence of the neatly balanced series. Hemingway uses asymmetrical parts, each patterning in a different way: (*a*) *there*-construction, (*b*) subject + intransitive verb, (*c*) subject + transitive verb + object. This radical departure from the balance that most writers maintain when they write coordinated sentences tells us something about Hemingway as a stylist.

A close look at an imitation reveals even more about the intricacy of the Hemingway sentence—this attempt, for example:

> There were many children playing on the beach, and the sand clung to their bodies, and the wind scattered their sand castles.

We notice in particular that the imitator cannot duplicate the middle clause of Hemingway's sentence, particularly the intransitive use of *powdered*. But, even though he cannot reproduce the exact structural features, he catches the spirit of the original by trying to create an imaginative quality that is implicit in Hemingway's conception. Obviously, the structure is not doing all of the work.

The more demanding an imitation is, often the more revealing the discovery. Here is an ambitious sentence:

> After hiking for some time, the boys walking near the bank of a stream noticed, through the branches of the thinning trees, a small cabin built of logs and surrounded by lush vegetation of a highly unusual nature which through the lattice work of the shadows appeared to be viney and alive serpents slithering from the darkness of the brush—morning glories, perhaps—growing to the roof of the cabin and distinguishable from it by the white of the blossoms like tiny specks of light on an asphalt drive.

The original from Faulkner's *The Hamlet* reads:

> A little while before sundown the men lounging about the gallery of the store saw, coming up the road from the south, a covered

wagon drawn by mules and followed by a considerable string of obviously alive objects which in the leveling sun resembled vari-sized and colored tatters torn at random from large billboards—circus posters, say—attached to the rear of the wagon and inherent with its own separate and collective motion, like the tail of a kite.

Anyone who attempts a sentence of this kind is bound to learn something about Faulkner's heavily textured sentences, but he is also likely to discover something wholly practical about writing in general, namely, that a sentence can be dilated without sacrificing its clarity if it is built upon multiple levels that continue to add more and more precise details. The kernel of Faulkner's sentence reads: The men saw a covered wagon. All the rest is modification.

The essential discovery

Discovery comes in the doing. And, in the doing, every imitator ultimately may come to a personal realization important to his own development as a writer. He first finds out quickly that exact imitations of the kind illustrated above, good ones in the spirit of the originals, are extremely difficult to write. He senses that imitation is not a natural way of composing, and he is right. In the process of imitating, a writer has to reverse the normal process; he has to begin with form and style and then find subject matter to fit. If he applies a grandiose style to a trivial subject—Milton's sentences to household hints—he ends up with a mockery of the style. If he applies a light style to a grand subject—Thurber's manner to the description of a disaster—he has something equally incongruous. Thus imitation makes clear, if the point is not already self-evident, that thought and feeling are the natural starting points of writing, form follows, style emerges.

SENTENCE STRATEGY: VARIETY IN STYLE

Most writers aim for an interesting and identifiable style that conceals the strategy that lies behind it. Of course, the intuitive operates strongly in choosing the ways a writer will express himself. The person who thinks expansively finds a natural friend in the dash, the parenthetical expression, and cataloguing. The person who thinks pointedly favors the semicolon, balanced structures, and economical diction. The student of writing, however, needs to learn that sentences have considerable flexibility; he needs to have resources that will enable him to make sentences bear the full burden of his thought and impressions, no matter how complex they may be.

Some of the following sections discuss familiar means of sentence variation; others attempt to demonstrate further possibilities of sentence sophistication. The comments are brief, leaving the burden of explanation to the examples themselves.

Compounding and subordinating

Compounding and subordinating are conventional means of varying simple-sentence structure and avoiding the childish effect that successive, short sentences give: "She grew old. She was happy. She died recently." A close relationship between clauses may be indicated by joining them with appropriate connectives (*but, so, then*); by altering one of the clauses with a subordinating conjunction (*although, because, when*) or a relative pronoun (*who, which, that*); by transforming one of the clauses into one of a variety of phrase structures; or by condensing the clause into a cluster of words such as an appositive. For instance:

[Two associated sentences, relationship undefined]

1. He followed the directions carelessly. He ended up far from his destination.

[Coordination: equal weight]

2. He followed the directions carelessly, and he ended up far from his destination.

[Causal relationship stressed]

3. He followed the directions carelessly; therefore he ended up far from his destination.

[Movable connective]

4. He followed the directions carelessly; he ended up far from his destination, therefore.

[Causal relationship: use of subordination]	5. Because he followed the directions carelessly, he ended up far from his destination.
[Relative clause]	6. The one who followed the directions carelessly ended up far from his destination.
[Subordination: use of participle]	7. Following the directions carelessly, he ended up far from his destination.
[Subordination reversed]	8. He followed the directions carelessly so that he ended up far from his destination.
[Reversal, with use of participle]	9. He followed the directions carelessly, ending up far from his destination.

All the sentences indicated above are possible variations, although some of them read better than others. Perhaps the most important point to be made, however, is that the clause or phrase in the subordinate position does not necessarily represent a lesser idea or lose priority because it is subordinated. In sentence 9, for instance, the phrase seems to gain emphasis because it occupies the climactic position in the sentence, even though it is subordinated. But in other instances one idea is clearly secondary in meaning, and reversing its position from the subordinate to the main clause distorts the logic:

	Since an institute program demands full-time involvement, a participant may not hold an outside job during the period of his enrollment.
[Confused logic with subordination reversed]	Since a participant may not hold an outside job during the period of his enrollment in the institute, the program demands full-time involvement.

The wide variety and frequent use of subordinate constructions means that in many sentences they are doing most of the communication, and the main clause may be only a kind of framework. In the following sentence by Sir Herbert Read, practically the substance of the entire sentence is incorporated in subordinate constructions:

> What we must finally recognize is the existence of two distinct modes of intelligence: one, which might be called the Cartesian intelligence since it began with Descartes, who was the first philosopher to divorce reasoning from a sensuous dependence on things (I *think,* therefore I am); and one which might be called the aesthetic intelligence since it maintains contact with the sensuous world at every stage of its reasoning (I *feel,* therefore I am: reality is a creation of my senses).
>
> "Art and Life"

The major justification for compounding and subordinating, apart from a writer's desire to vary his sentence construction, is to bring thoughts more closely together. But if closeness does not exist, then the parts cannot be arbitrarily forced together with a connective. The result is only a non sequitur. If the relationship between the parts is not self-evident or defined, the reader is left to wonder what the writer had in mind. Notice these sentences:

> Her sympathetic tendencies toward underdogs were probably brought about by her father, a doctor, who spent his life tending to the sick, and both father and daughter had a weakness for drink.
>
> In our society, workers make up a great majority of the people, but Boxer is sincere in his work.

The logic of the second example is particularly disturbing because *but* implies a contrast. The idea of one worker's sincere motivation, mentioned in the second clause, presupposes some statement about insincere motivation among many workers in the first clause. But the writer contrasts nothing.

The coordinating connectives (*and, but, or, for, nor,* and *yet*) ordinarily set up an expectation of parallel construction. Effective deviations, such as the asymmetry Hemingway uses in the opening sentence of "In Another Country" (page 152), become possible only in terms of our normal expectation of the symmetrical. Exceptions to anything are meaningless except in terms of standard practices.

Parallelism

The strictest forms of parallelism are uniform in phrasing and balanced in construction:

> Some people live this life in discouragement; some live it in glee; some live it in serenity.

From this point on, it is possible to maintain a basic parallelism in the sentence above but to upset its rigid uniformity and equilibrium by a series of variations:

[Variation of phrasing]	Some people live this life in discouragement; some live it in exalted glee; some live it in confidence and serenity.
[Ellipsis]	Some people live this life in discouragement; some in exalted glee; some in confidence and serenity.
[Shifting the balanced structure]	Some people live this life in discouragement; some in exalted glee; the sanest, at least the adjusted, in confidence and serenity.

Or, to illustrate another kind of off-balance in a compound sentence that still observes parallelism:

> The patient is resting comfortably, for whom medicine or religion will have to make an effort, or one or both may fail.

In spite of all kinds of subtle deviations signifying that writers do not need to observe parallelism in lockstep fashion, parallelism sets up such a strong anticipation in some sentences that a failure to follow the pattern, either in structure or phrasing, is clearly a fault. Sir

Arthur Quiller-Couch made the point obvious when he wrote, "To be, or the contrary?"

Note the kinds of expectations that are violated in the following sentences and the simple adjustments that restore parallelism and make them more readable:,

1. Toynbee believes that history is written in three stages: first, the ascertainment and recording of facts; second, the elucidation of these facts; and, third, the use of fiction in recording the facts.

[Revision]   Toynbee believes that history is written in three stages: first, ascertaining and recording facts; second, elucidating facts; and, third, using fiction to record the facts.

2. It took me twenty-two years before I discovered *Norma* and thirty-two for Katherine Anne Porter.

[Revision]   It took me twenty-two years to discover *Norma* and thirty-two to discover Katherine Anne Porter.

3. The harder the Chinese laborers work and the more they produce, the government takes much more and leaves them with the same bowl of rice.

[Revision]   The harder the Chinese laborers work and the more they produce, the more the government takes, leaving them with the same bowl of rice.

Texture

To speak of the texture of a sentence is to suggest something about its depth, not the depth of its thought, but the depth of its structure. Texture is a stylistic characteristic that shows the preference of some writers for multiple levels of particularity, of other writers for less density. Texturing often suggests a kind of improvisation, as if the writer were always adding words—more words in sequence—to make the thought more explicit. Note this sentence:

He would make the most fantastic threats to his class, in a tone so comically composed of gentleness and sternness, and the sternness so added as a spice to the gentleness, that no student could hear such strange warnings without trying harder, and yet trying for the mere joy of pleasing him.

By general standards, a fifty-two-word sentence is a long sentence. If the subject and verb of this sentence were widely separated, the reader would get lost. But the basic thought is contained in the first ten words; all of the rest is addition and elaboration. Texture of this order represents neither complication nor embellishment. It is a method of packing meaningful detail into the dimensions of a single sentence without resorting to the most obvious devices of coordination.

Description and narration lend themselves well to this kind of structure. Hemingway often uses it in his fiction and in passages such as the following from a report on the Spanish Civil War published in the *New York Times* (April 25, 1937):

> On the corner, twenty yards away, is a heap of rubble, smashed cement, and thrown-up dirt, a single dead man, his clothes dirty, and a great hole in the sidewalk from which the gas from a broken main is rising, looking like a heat mirage in the cold morning air.

If a sentence of this kind suggests that levels of particularity produce only loose, rambling sentences, notice how a scholar uses the same technique in expository prose with a decided effect of orderliness and balance:

> Other contemporary sources as well tease the scholar with matter-of-fact allusions to plays then very much alive: the chronicles of the two universities (where drama was not merely an entertainment but a device for teaching classical languages); the records of the court, which had command performances at frequent intervals; the many pamphlets of abuse which the Puritans published in their bitter campaign against the godless stage; and the records of the official licenser of the drama, the Lord Chamberlain.

> Richard D. Altick
> *The Scholar Adventurers*

The second part of Professor Altick's sentence itemizes chronicles, court records, pamphlets, and records of the licenser as the contemporary sources mentioned in the opening words, but within each section of the four-part series he adds comment, so that the finished sentence is not only richly textured but highly informative.

Cataloguing

Cataloguing represents a relatively simple way of expanding a sentence, but cataloguing is not as simple as writing down anything that comes to mind. An effective catalogue depends upon a selection of words and details that cumulatively seem to include almost everything possible, as Walt Whitman seemed to be able to do in both his poetry and prose:

> No great literature, nor any like style of behavior or oratory, or social intercourse or household arrangements, or public institutions, or the treatment by bosses of employ'd people, nor executive detail, or detail of the army and navy, nor spirit of legislation or courts, or police or tuition or architecture, or songs or amusements, can long elude the jealous and passionate instinct of American standards.
>
> Preface to 1855 edition of *Leaves of Grass*

At its best, the catalogue works imaginatively. A contemporary writer like Tom Wolfe uses the device to create his impression of teenagers at a dance, omitting most punctuation to add to the confused effect:

> Bangs manes bouffants beehives Beatle caps butter faces brush-on lashes decal eyes puffy sweaters French thrust bras flailing leather blue jeans stretch pants stretch jeans honeydew bottoms eclair shanks elf boots ballerinas Knight slippers, hundreds of them, these flaming little buds, bobbing and screaming, rocketing around inside the Academy of Music Theater underneath that vast old mouldering cherub dome up there—aren't they super-marvelous!
>
> "The Girl of the Year"

The sentence below, written by a student, uses a catalogue for purposes of illustration, the added levels sharpening the descriptive details but explaining the comment at the beginning of the sentence, which is then repeated as a kind of framework at the end:

Everything was unchanged, common and bad, the smell of asphalt, cooking grease, smoke, and the thin stifIng air of the alley, full of unhealthy growth, two orange halves fuzzy with green, garbage can ripening, and the potted tree sweating dog urine, the same as ever.

Another student suggests the rapid passage of time by means of a catalogue of short phrases:

Ranks pass: he is a private, then corporal, then sergeant, next year lieutenant, upward, and always shooting for the bright silver stars.

Tags

Tags are afterthoughts. Either they dangle feebly and disconnectedly at the end of a sentence, or they emphasize by using the final position to make editorial comment upon the thought in the main clause. A slight adjustment in the structure and phrasing may account for one effect or the other:

The worker stretches the cloth over a wooden or metal frame and washes the material to shrink it into a tight screen, which is important.

[Rephrased for emphasis] The worker stretches the cloth over a wooden or metal frame and washes the material to shrink it into a tight screen—an indispensable part of the process.

Comparing and contrasting

Comparing and contrasting are among the familiar devices of sentence development, sometimes accomplished simply by adding a phrase:

The athlete was imposing, powerful as a young stallion, poised, confident, lithe, and beautiful as a Grecian god.

Or the comparison may take the form of a metaphor incorporated into the texture of the sentence (note how in the following example sounds reinforce the parallelism indicated by the structure):

> For the contented, living is a plateau; for the discontented, a precipice.

Or, at other times, the comparison may be more complex and extended (note how in the following example Schlesinger picks up the simile at the end of sentence 1 to develop it in the phrasing of sentence 2):

> The grounds of our civilization, of our certitude, are breaking up under our feet, and familiar ideas and institutions vanish as we reach for them, like shadows in the falling dusk. Most of the world has reconciled itself to this half-light, to the reign of insecurity.
>
> Arthur M. Schlesinger, Jr.
> *The Vital Center*

All comparisons extend the meaning of a thought beyond its immediate context into another range of experience. Two worlds are brought to bear upon one another; and the figure of speech is the point of contact. Consider this sentence:

> Most people worship the god Materialism with their credit cards, not as orthodox worshipers, but as cultists.

Here the fanatical world of commerce and the fanatical world of cultism are brought into relation to one another; the credit card becomes a kind of new sacrament. The world of orthodox worship is excluded as unrepresentative of the zeal the writer wants to suggest. He contrasts by simply using the word *not.* At the same time that this writer has broadened the implications of his sentence, he has also deepened the texture and revealed an inventiveness that moves his prose beyond the commonplace.

Inverting sentence patterns

Inverting sentence structure strikes many readers as a perverting of the natural order of syntax: first things like subjects, they say, should come first; last things like objects should come last, following verbs. And, in truth, inverting is a strategy that attracts attention only because of our strong natural tendency to want to preserve the normal word order of a sentence, except of course in questions, where inverting the subject—Do we understand?—is routine.

But inversions are in most instances optional. The only true way to test their effect is to rephrase the sentence in its normal order and then try to determine what has been gained or lost:

> Hardened by war was Corporal Smith: he was violent, always too violent, surly, easily inclined to shoot now, challenge later.

> [Normal order   Corporal Smith was hardened by war: he was violent,
> restored]   always too violent, surly, easily inclined to shoot now, challenge later.

In the first sentence, does the writer want to place as much stress upon *hardened* as it gets? Is it the crucial word? Or is the writer chiefly interested in getting the *Corporal Smith: he* arrangement? Is the strategy too self-conscious and labored? The answers will, of course, vary with individuals. The writer chose to invert.

A further test of inverted structure is to examine the context in which the sentence appears to determine if the inverted pattern helps the meaning by means of emphasis or merely disrupts the rhythmic flow:

> It was customary among the ancient Greeks and Hebrews to select a human being each year as the sacrificial victim of the community. This scapegoat would bear upon his shoulders all the iniquities of his fellow townspeople. With his life would perish their sins, all evil spirits, and all omens of bad fortune. By his death they would gain good fortune and favorable crops.

Note that the writer does not choose to invert the subject and verb in the last sentence, even though the close parallelism of the two final sentences invites repetition of the device. His purpose seems to be to emphasize "their sins, all evil spirits, and all omens of bad fortune" by means of the inversion in that sentence.

Emphasizing

As we have already seen, variations of sentence structure often operate to shift emphasis, to place key words and phrases in strategic positions where the reader is not likely to ignore them. The strategies we have discussed thus far do not demand calculated, chesslike maneuvering of words; they very often spring freely from our own intuitive sense of climax or balance or repetition, that is, if from observation we have come to recognize that these are the natural ways of emphasizing both in speech and in writing. The following examples therefore represent a summary of those strategies we have already discussed, illustrating how we naturally combine strategies and how certain words (indicated by italics) gain special rhythmic emphasis by the special arrangement that the writer has chosen:

Repetition, interrupted movement, and balance

They are children—they are worldly wise, but they are *children.*

Parallelism and repetition: separation of the sentences

Here the animals would be safe from man, free from hunger, assured of equality. *Here* the strong would protect the weak.

In the second example, emphasis on the second *here* is reinforced by putting it in a separate sentence; a semicolon would blur the effect.

Contrast

Knowledge of love has not brought her madness, only *happiness.*

Inverted structure

The Prospector's blindness to beauty is so complete that he is willing to destroy all Paris to strike oil. The *Louvre* he would willingly *demolish.*

Cataloguing: climactic order

I have never had so many poor grades, on papers, on speeches, on tests, on *everything,* but always justified.

Extended analogy: periodic effect

> If you will take the longest stretch in the Mississippi River and travel up and down it, observing its markings carefully until you recognize every bend and snag and rapids and buoy marker and deep and shallow shoal by instinct, and can recognize them so readily that you can automatically discern what you are alongside of when you are put down at random in that river in the midst of an unbelievably heavy fog, you will then have a reasonable idea of the mastery of a cabby *who holds New York City in his mind.*

The periodic sentence characteristically holds the reader in suspense until the final words reveal the full meaning of the sentence.

Anticipatory "it" and "there" for periodic effect

> It is noteworthy that Evelyn Waugh and Jean Giraudoux both stress *the importance of simple joys.*

> There is one thing still to cling to—*love.*

In one sense, anticipatory phrases are always superfluous; they can be crossed out as deadwood. Yet they regularly appear in speech and writing, not only because they provide a kind of acceleration to the rhythm (note the pace of "It seems to me that . . .") but also because they loosen the prose by providing spaces between the main thoughts. Sentences that are too tightly packed easily exhaust the reader. Thus it is difficult to read too many Bacon essays at a stretch. The epigrammatic style is not unlike reading a book of famous quotations. In continuous discourse, the anticipatory phrase is a momentary relief. Every sentence cannot be a hammerblow of emphasis.

APPLYING THE STRATEGIES: SENTENCE LENGTH

All these strategies involve variations of basic sentence patterns or variations that combine two or more sentences into one. They permit the writer to condense as much meaning into one sentence as he wishes; they tend to produce highly textured sentences and therefore sentences rich in overtones of meaning. Almost all of them preserve the normal word order of the basic sentence patterns. They all tend to lengthen sentences.

The capacity to write a long sentence—a sentence that is itself more than a combination of short sentences strung together with *ands* —is no doubt one of the marks of a mature prose writer, journalistic prose notwithstanding. If we recall, primer sentences are short sentences, at first little more than subject and verb. More advanced sentences incorporate more complex structures. Maturity adds length, but adds without ignoring the value of the short sentence for special stylistic effect.

The short sentence, therefore, is a constant in prose style, not to be condemned categorically as childish, not to be outgrown. Unfortunately, many writers, even of college age, never get beyond the short sentence. Notice this passage written by a college Freshman:

> Harrington's essay is similar to Whyte's. They both deal with corporations. Harrington leads a very secluded life in his Crystal Palace. Inside the Palace, everyone conforms, while, outside, people express their thoughts. Harrington presents his corporations as ideal. The employees have everything they could want except freedom of expression. These people have conformed so completely that their minds no longer function. They have become no more than robots. They must be encouraged to strike out on their own.

Simply recording the number of words in each of these sentences will explain in part the immature effect they give: 6, 5, 10, 11, 6, 11, 12, 7, 10. Here we do not have sufficient variation of length to change the rhythmic pattern at all. Sentences begin and stop quickly. There is almost no subordination. There is no texture.

Writing both long and short sentences is perhaps the single most important principle of variation. Deprived of all other strategies, the writer no doubt could still produce varied prose by alternating long and short—obviously not long, short, long, short, long, but long and short as the thought and timing demand. But the fact is that no writer can very well extend the length of his sentences indefinitely without employing the strategies we have mentioned, without breaking the long sentence into segments that permit the reader to grasp the thought in chunks, not wholes (here we make the arbitrary assumption that the individual who reads more than 1,000 words per minute cannot very well concern himself with the qualities that style communicates).

In contrast with the student paragraph above, consider the following passage from Herbert Muller's *Issues of Freedom:*

> Although we may train Fido to behave as we see fit, and call him a good dog when he obeys or punish him when he does not, we do not consider him moral or immoral, still less reprove him for his affairs with other dogs. We assume that his behavior is governed by instinct and conditioned reflexes, not by conscious purposes of his own. The assumption that man is able to choose his purposes and to will his deeds is the premise of all moral judgment. It is an absolutely essential premise, and is in fact implicit in all social behavior. Whatever they believe, men feel and act as if they are more or less responsible for their deeds. They always feel that they deserve credit for their good deeds; if they often try to escape blame for their bad ones, they are still prone to feelings of guilt or remorse; and they advise, warn, threaten, or beg their fellows, always assuming that they may get others to change their minds. Yet the actuality of human freedom remains a live issue. It has been denied by many eminent men, on both religious and scientific grounds. And disbelief in it may also make a real difference in behavior.

In this paragraph, we can clearly perceive a maturity of thought and diction absent from the student paragraph, but we may not as readily realize in what way sentence length is also operating as a factor of maturity. The count of the words in these sentences indicates a considerably different pattern from the one we observed previously: 45, 19, 22, 15, 18, 52, 10, 14, 12. The two long sentences, the first and the sixth, are followed by a series of sentences of approximately the same length. The three short ones at the end clinch the thought and move the paragraph to a rapid conclusion. Reading other passages of Muller's book suggests that sentences of forty or fifty words represent just about his maximum. Most of his sentences, however, are considerably shorter.

One additional paragraph from a nineteenth-century essay will indicate further the relationship of sentence length to style, in this instance an effect that to twentieth-century readers, accustomed to newspaper prose, may seem ponderous:

It is a still more difficult consideration for our average men, that while all their teachers, from Solomon down to Benjamin Franklin and the ungodly Binney, have inculcated the same ideal of manners, caution, and respectability, those characters in history who have most notoriously flown in the face of such precepts are spoken of in hyperbolical terms of praise, and honoured with public monuments in the streets of our commercial centres. This is very bewildering to the moral sense. You have Joan of Arc, who left a humble but honest and reputable livelihood under the eyes of her parents, to go a-colonelling, in the company of rowdy soldiers, against the enemies of France; surely a melancholy example for one's daughters! And then you have Columbus, who may have pioneered America, but, when all is said, was a most imprudent navigator. His life is not the kind of thing one would like to put into the hands of young people; rather, one would do one's utmost to keep it from their knowledge, as a red flag of adventure and disintegrating influence in life. The time would fail me if I were to recite all the big names in history whose exploits are perfectly irrational and even shocking to the business mind. The incongruity is speaking; and I imagine it must engender among the mediocrities a very peculiar attitude towards the nobler and showier sides of national life. They will read of the Charge of Balaclava in much the same spirit as they assist at a performance of the *Lyons Mail.* Persons of substance take in the *Times* and sit composedly in pit or boxes according to the degree of their prosperity in business. As for the generals who go galloping up and down among bombshells in absurd cocked hats—as for the actors who raddle their faces and demean themselves for hire upon the stage—they must belong, thank God! to a different order of beings, whom we watch as we watch the clouds careering in the windy, bottomless inane, or read about like characters in ancient and rather fabulous annals. Our offspring would no more think of copying their behaviour, let us hope, than of doffing their clothes and painting themselves blue in consequence of certain admissions in the first chapter of their school history of England.

> Robert Louis Stevenson
> "Crabbed Age and Youth"

These sentences tally 71, 8, 41, 20, 42, 28, 26, 23, 23, 68, 37—evidence alone that Muller and Stevenson are two different kinds of writers who produce different stylistic effects on the basis of sentence length alone.

From these analyses, it should be apparent in what direction the student writer of the paragraph on page 166 needs to move. One thing he can do—one wholly practical, workable solution—is to try to build his sentences, not by padding them, but by combining them, by subordinating, and by applying sentence strategies that add meaningful detail and bring ideas more sharply into focus.

THE STRATEGY OF BEGINNING AND ENDING AN ESSAY

The most obvious thing one can say (but it should not be left unsaid) is that beginning and ending are important because they are first and last impressions. To think only of Introduction, Main Body, and Conclusion as the be-all and end-all of beginning and ending is to substitute a formula for personal strategy.

In the first place, not all writing requires a formal introduction, that is, if an introduction represents a declaration of intentions or a warming-up session before the essay actually begins. A skilled writer may literally begin in the middle of circumstances, fill in the beginning, and proceed to the end. If he explains first what he is going to do, he sacrifices his effect. The use of a formal introduction depends to a great extent upon the length of a work. What is in essence an introduction to a short essay may often be contained in the topic sentence of the first paragraph, such as:

My first reactions to Ed were consistently negative.

What more needs to be said as a beginning? All of the rest should be explanation, supported by evidence in the form of illustration.

Another student begins an analysis of a character in Chekhov's *The Three Sisters* by stating the thesis of his paper in an opening paragraph:

Paradoxically, the foolish old doctor Chebutykin is Chekhov's hero in *The Three Sisters.* It is he who finally realizes what life really is; it is he who discovers the truth about the ordinariness of life. Chekhov wrote: "All I wanted to do . . . was to say to people, 'Have a look at yourselves and see how bad and dreary your lives are!' " And Chebutykin sees.

After an excellent opening of this kind, one would expect the material that follows to relate what Chebutykin has seen to lead him to his conclusions. In this beginning, however, the writer gets off to a fast start. This introduction is itself doing work, moving the idea of the essay forward from the very first word. The prose has no useless surplus like this opening:

> To describe what I see in the cartoon I have before me, I would have to use a little discretion in my choice of words. To explain why, then, I will have to explain the picture. [At this point the description begins.]

Another student writing about the implications of a cartoon for the same assignment begins in this way:

> An official has just interrupted a television program to remind the people that they are lucky to be able to criticize government officials. Behind him is a desk where moments before an announcer had been on the air. Part of the desk has been shattered by cannonballs.

With an opening of this kind, we are given the relevant facts without the writer's apology or statement of intentions. This student seems to know what he is doing; the other student writing about the cartoon undermines our confidence by his cautious tone.

In addition to establishing the theme of an essay and setting its tone, an opening may actually forecast its organization:

> There is no doubt about it: the invention of the radio and the invention of television have acted as a leveling force in American society.

Three things are accomplished in this opening. The first words, possibly unnecessary if we want only facts, establish a tone of assurance and easy familiarity. The words that follow then announce the theme and forecast a twofold organization. Note that the writer does not speak of the invention of radio and television as one leveling force. His phrasing suggests that he will speak of the one and then of the other.

The stock ending, of course, is the one that begins "In conclusion" and proceeds to summarize what has already been said. Summaries may be appropriate to books and long term papers, but summaries attached to short student essays imply that the reader is not capable of remembering what has been discussed in the last 500 or 1,000 words. Summaries usually cause a short essay to fade away in a forgettable manner.

The writer's chief responsibility in ending is to give a sense of finality, that is, to convey to the reader that the topic has been adequately covered within the limits defined, that the arguments have been concluded, that the point of stopping, even though it may leave the reader in suspense, is intentional. The writer who introduces a new idea into his final sentence suggests that he has tagged on a last-minute thought, unless his phrasing indicates that he deliberately intends to open up a new topic to be discussed in another paper.

It is good if the writer himself recognizes when the end has come, that he has said what he has to say, that he must not bore the reader by dragging on interminably. Ending does not have to be a whimper or a bang; it can be suitable silence. All seems well that ends well.

THE MAJOR MODES: PLAIN, FAMILIAR, FORMAL

Individual styles sometimes turn out to be completely eccentric, unlike the writing of most other writers. Tom Wolfe calls his own style in *The Kandy-kolored Tangerine-flake Streamline Baby* "the wowie!" Reviewer Conrad Knickerbocker describes it as a "complex mixture of several vernaculars—teenage, jet set, academic and drugstore modern." Someone else might invent another set of terms to give his impression of the effect. In the final analysis, however, Tom Wolfe's style, unusual as it is, may be classified among the major modes; it illustrates a familiar manner of writing for a popular, fairly sophisticated audience.

The major modes are general classifications that embrace a wide variety of individual styles. Broad as the categories are, they nevertheless provide general guidelines for the writer. Of course, he is entitled to be as inventive in his style as he wants to be—that is his individual privilege; but he also has to consider whether his inventiveness is appropriate to his purpose and his audience—that is his social obligation. Even the rebel writer, who thinks that "social obligation" is a stuffy demand for regimentation, at least has to appreciate that proprieties make him what he is: he can be deviant only because most people observe regularities.

The plain style

The Plain Style makes the greatest demand for conformity upon the individual because, in essence, it asks the writer to be anybody, not himself alone. It is the kind of style that makes it possible for an encyclopedia to seem uniform in style, although its articles are written by hundreds of individuals. It has therefore been called the nameless style, the faceless style, the voiceless style, the neutral style—all of these to describe its basic impersonality and absence of feeling.

To designate this manner of writing as plain is not to condemn it (Schlesinger has coined the word *encyclopedestrian*), only to suggest that its plainness makes it suitable for the job of communicating facts. More than a thousand years ago, Aristotle wrote, "Nobody uses fine language when teaching geometry." The Plain Style is functional. It is the manner of workaday prose. We read it regularly in news reports, most of our textbooks, many business letters, technical reports, directions, minutes, examinations—any kind of writing that is primarily factual:

> The Pueblo Indians of the Southwest are one of the most widely known primitive peoples in Western civilization. They live in the midst of America, within easy reach of any transcontinental traveller. And they are living after the old native fashion. Their culture has not disintegrated like that of all the Indian communities outside of Arizona and New Mexico. Month by month and year by year, the old dances of the gods are danced in their stone villages, life follows essentially the old routines, and what they have taken from our civilization they have remodelled and subordinated to their own attitudes.
>
> Ruth Benedict
> *Patterns of Culture*

Note the clear simple sentences in this paragraph, the impersonal tone, and the almost absence of commentary.

The Plain Style also acts as a safety device for discussing controversial topics:

Across America today increasing pressures are exerted on schools to restrict the access of students to important and worthwhile books. In many communities attempts have been made to remove literary works from classrooms and school libraries. Certain modern writers, praised by recognized critics and well established in the curriculum, are suddenly charged with seditious sentiment or licentious intent. In familiar classics overt pornography is "discovered." The attacks extend even to books *about* writers. Recently a collection of biographies of great philosophers was condemned for including the life of Plato, who in his own writings, it was charged, "talked about free love and communal living and such."

From *The Student's Right to Read* published by the National Council of Teachers of English (1962)

Even though this statement discusses a sensitive topic, it attempts to do so in an emotionless, factual way. The statement was prepared by a committee and carries the endorsement of a national organization. Accordingly, the style is appropriately anonymous. The sentences are brief and simply developed. The words, even though they include a number of polysyllables, do not range beyond the working vocabulary of most adult readers (the Plain Style adjusts to all levels of education). The quotation marks around *discovered* in the fourth sentence convey some sense of irony, but otherwise the prose is deliberately objective. Above all, the statement is clear.

Since the chief purpose of the Plain Style is to inform, it needs to be clear, accurate, coherent, concrete, and correct, not qualities that it has to the exclusion of other kinds of writing, but the essential qualities by which it as a style is judged either good or bad. The Plain Style is writing that demands facility, not imagination. It avoids imbalances of tone that may divert the reader from the meaning. It shuns figures of speech and unusual words. It avoids contractions. It prefers condensation to addition as a principle of sentence strategy. At its best, the Plain Style is efficient; at its worst, it is drab and routine.

Familiar style

If the Plain Style is the commonsense style, the Familiar Style returns the writer to his five senses. He uses them intuitively to do more

than communicate fact alone; he communicates the meaning of involvement, the force of sound, the appeal of variety.

I use the word *familiar* to identify this broad classification because
almost all of the writing that falls under this category attempts to reveal
the writer's voice. Whether the writer speaks directly as "I" or assumes
another voice, he attempts to be on familiar terms with his reader, not
necessarily chummy, but sufficiently inviting and informal that the reader
is interested in him as well as his subject. E. B. White epitomizes the
Familiar Style in a light vein:

> There has been more talk about the weather around here
> this year than common, but there has been more weather to talk
> about. For about a month now we have had solid cold—firm, busi-
> ness-like cold that stalked in and took charge of the countryside
> as a brisk housewife might take charge of someone else's kitchen
> in an emergency. Clean, hard, purposeful cold, unyielding and
> unremitting. Some days have been clear and cold, others have
> been stormy and cold. We have had cold with snow and cold with-
> out snow, windy cold and quiet cold, rough cold and indulgent
> peace-loving cold. But always cold. The kitchen dooryard is littered
> with the cylinders of ice from frozen water buckets that have been
> thawed out in the morning with hot water. Storm windows weren't
> enough this winter—we resorted to the simplest and best insulating
> material available, the daily newspaper applied to north windows
> with thumbtacks. Mornings the thermometer would register ten or
> twelve below. By noon it would have zoomed up to zero. As the
> night shut in, along about four-thirty, it would start dropping again.
> Even in the tight barn, insulated with tons of hay, the slobber from
> the cow's nose stiffened in small icicles, and the vapor rose from
> the warm milk into the milker's face. If you took hold of a latch with
> ungloved hands, the iron seized you by the skin and held on.
>
> "Cold Weather"
> from *One Man's Meat*

Consistent with the casual tone, White's prose is remarkably flexible; it demonstrates that strategy can be applied with ease. White
catalogues, he compares, he plays with sounds, he interrupts, he writes
fragments, he alerts the senses, he amuses, but not at the expense of
informing. A weather report may be more factual, but White's prose is
more fascinating.

The passage from E. B. White, however, should not suggest that the Familiar Style is limited to a light, witty manner. The category is broad, including most persuasive writing, argument, expository narration and description, personal letters, advertising copy, most student themes that concern their own experiences, opinions, and analyses—in fact, almost any kind of expository prose in which the writer's stance is apparent.

Because he does not have to obliterate himself, a writer usually finds the Familiar Style a more comfortable and natural way to write than the Plain Style; but since he is involving himself, he has to be concerned with the image that his prose either intentionally or unintentionally projects by means of style. Stylistic features of writing in the familiar manner compensate for the dynamics of actual speech absent from writing: the speaker's physical posture, his gestures, his pitch, tone, and volume, his accent and timing. As a result, these writing strategies influence our response to the writer; we tend to react just as we might react to him in person. Two passages will illustrate, the first by Harvey Swados:

> The average automobile worker gets a little better than two dollars an hour. As such he is one of the best-paid factory workers in the country. After twenty years of militant struggle led by the union that I believe to be one of the finest and most democratic labor organizations in the United States, he is earning less than the starting salaries offered to inexperienced and often semiliterate college graduates without dependents. After compulsory deductions for taxes, social security, old-age insurance and union dues, and optional deductions for hospitalization and assorted charities, his pay check for forty hours of work is going to be closer to seventy than to eighty dollars a week. Does this make him middle-class as to income? Does it rate with the weekly take of a dentist, an accountant, a salesman, a draftsman, a journalist? Surely it would be more to the point to ask how a family man can get by in the Fifties on that kind of income. I know how he does it, and I should think the answers would be a little disconcerting to those who wax glib on the satisfactory status of the "formerly" underprivileged.
>
> *A Radical's America*

In this paragraph, Swados tells us certain things he believes and knows; he implies others. The questions he asks are undoubtedly addressed to middle-class dentists, accountants, salesmen, draftsmen, journalists, and others like them "who wax glib on the satisfactory status of the 'formerly' underprivileged." Swados is sardonic but not insulting. His intention is to bring about a sympathetic understanding of the laborer, not to press his readers to the point of antagonism. If he offends them, he cannot very well educate them, but he does not hesitate to shake their complacency.

The pairs of sentences in this paragraph reflect a changing strategy: two short factual sentences to begin with, two long sentences of fact to the contrary, arranged with an increasing intensity, two questions designed to clinch the point, because the implied answer must be "No," and two final sentences that prepare the reader for subsequent paragraphs that will give the disturbing answers to the third question that he has asked indirectly. Swados writes readable prose not only because he knows how to handle a sentence but also because he keeps the arguments, his own feelings, and our reactions in balance and control.

The second illustration is the opening section of a widely syndicated column written by Max Rafferty:

> An old, old story is told of a certain philosopher who in a dream one night was visited by Minerva, goddess of wisdom. In part repayment for a long life of dedication to philosophy, she offered him the answer to one question, with no strings attached.

> "Tell me, O goddess," cagily quoth the sage, "how I may find the one unfailing path of truth, justice and virtue?"

> "That's easy," quipped his Olympian visitant briskly. "Just define your terms."

> And with that she vanished in a flurry of ectoplasm, after the annoying manner of goddesses.

> I was reminded of old Min the other day when I received this letter from one of my less ecstatic correspondents.

> *Seattle Times* (June 25, 1967)

What is most apparent about this writing is that the author views his audience on a level beneath himself and makes a struggling effort to accommodate himself to that level—the Superintendent of Public Instruction in the state of California talking to all the people. The incongruous mixture of language is clearly intended as humor; it is a strange mixture of folksy and formal. The result is that the voice demands most of the reader's attention. The writer gets in the way of his material.

Since the Familiar Style both informs and pleases, it can be no less clear, coherent, concrete, and correct than the Plain Style, but added to these basic qualities it can also be as subtle, inventive, imaginative, and stimulating as the subject and purpose demand. At its best, it is witty, casual, persuasive; at its worst, cute, crude, ingratiating, labored.

Formal style

There is a tendency to think of the Formal Style only in terms of the impressive masterpieces of English prose, particularly those of the past—Milton's *Areopagitica,* Carlyle's *Sartor Resartus,* Mill's *On Liberty,* and one might continue to list works by Newman, Ruskin, Macaulay, Gibbon, Arnold, and Pater, but surprisingly few by Americans, Emerson and Daniel Webster excepted. Paine, Franklin, and Thoreau are exponents of the Familiar Style. Twentieth-century writers turn almost completely to the Plain and Familiar Styles except for the orators, particularly Winston Churchill and Franklin Roosevelt, and a writer like Toynbee.

The Formal Style in our own time has become almost exclusively an occasional or ceremonial mode. Even though it is associated with a grand tradition, including some of the most noble expressions of the English language, we need to remind ourselves that upon occasion we are all called upon to be writers of the Formal Style, modest as our efforts may be. Upon those occasions, usually solemn ones, we summon up as much dignity as we are capable of and employ a consciously polite, controlled expression that has come to be an acceptable mode of expression for serious occasions. We often use the Formal Style for ceremonial speeches, usually delivered from a written manuscript, formal personal letters, tributes, resolutions, and devotionals. Many essays, of course, are formal in tone, but mainly because the strategies that the writer uses create the impression of formality. These are written with great care and deliberateness. Rightness is primary.

The Formal Style is an anachronism in a prevailingly informal society. It perpetuates an aristocratic tradition of writing that respects preciseness, aptness, refinement, and flourishes of rhetorical and poetic imaginativeness. Our strongly democratic society still expects men of stature in serious moments to speak with well-bred elegance. Thus, presidential inaugural addresses consistently indulge the people's whim for polished, not plain talk. Here is a famous passage from John F. Kennedy's inaugural address, January 20, 1961:

> In your hands, my fellow citizens, more than mine, will rest the final success or failure of our course. Since this country was founded, each generation of Americans has been summoned to give testimony to its national loyalty. The graves of young Americans who answered the call to service surround the globe.
>
> Now the trumpet summons us again—not as a call to bear arms, though arms we need—not as a call to battle, though embattled we are—but a call to bear the burden of a long twilight struggle, year in and year out, "rejoicing in hope, patient in tribulation"—a struggle against the common enemies of man: tyranny, poverty, disease, and war itself.
>
> Can we forge against these enemies a grand and global alliance, North and South, East and West, that can assure a more fruitful life for all mankind? Will you join in that historic effort?
>
> In the long history of the world, only a few generations have been granted the role of defending freedom in its hour of maximum danger. I do not shrink from this responsibility—I welcome it. I do not believe that any of us would exchange places with any other people or any other generation. The energy, the faith, the devotion which we bring to this endeavor will light our country and all who serve it—and the glow from that fire can truly light the world.
>
> And so, my fellow Americans: ask not what your country can do for you—ask what you can do for your country.

And this kind of style occurs more frequently than once every four years. On June 23, 1967, for instance, Pope Paul VI issued an encyclical letter in all major modern languages that began with these words:

> Priestly celibacy has been guarded by the church for centuries as a brilliant jewel and retains its value undiminished even in our time when mentality and structures have undergone such profound changes.

The most striking feature of this sentence, of course, is the simile that adds a baroque quality to the prose.

Also during June of that year, upon the occasion of the crucial Arab-Israeli crisis, the President of the United States announced to the world:

> This is not a time for malice, but for magnanimity; not for propaganda, but for patience; not for vituperation, but for vision.

This sentence, like more memorable ones by Lincoln, derives its quotability from the strategies it uses: its balanced pattern, its contrasts, its alliteration.

During the very same month, again because of the Near East crisis, the historian Arnold Toynbee came into renewed prominence—a man whose style may be illustrated by a passage from an earlier essay on war:

> 'The military virtues' are virtues none the less for being jewels set in blood and iron; but the value lies in the jewels themselves and not in their horrible setting; and it is flying in the face of all experience to jump to the conclusion that the only place where we can ever hope to find these precious things is the slaughter-house where they have happened to make their first epiphany to human eyes. The diamond that is secreted in the clay does not remain there, but finds a fitter setting in the crown of a king; and when once the diamond-mine has yielded up its treasure it ceases to be anything but a death-trap for the miner who cannot now tear himself away from the scene of his habitual toil and his accidental trove. What is true of the dross in which the diamond has lain buried is likewise true of the ephemeral institution of War in which an eternal principle of goodness has glimmered darkly for a season, in the guise of 'the military virtues,' in order that it may shine out brightly hereafter in the perfect physical peace of the City of God. It is the divine virtue—unchanging in itself, but always changing its temporal abode—that casts the reflection of its own inner light upon each of its successive dwelling-places; and each of these dwelling-places assumes a derelict ugliness as soon as the temporarily indwelling spirit has ceased to lighten its darkness.
>
> "Militarism and the Military Virtues"

This is indeed twentieth-century baroque prose, perhaps too luxuriant for many tastes with its echoes of Biblical phrases and cadences, but nevertheless in the grand manner of English prose.

But the Formal Style does not always require grand proportions. The following student prose also represents the manner. It carries another kind of Biblical echo, not the moving splendor of Job, but the quiet simplicity of Genesis:

> I saw our brother in the field tending the young growth. And then I saw him tighten his jacket for the rain had come, and I saw that he was glad for the tiny plants.

This is a Formal Style that derives maximum suggestiveness by minimum means.

In yet another vein, with a manner worthy of the pen of Cyrano de Bergerac, Santayana writes another kind of Formal Style:

> The sentimental bandit is not always a highwayman or a burglar: sometimes he is a monarch or a general or the founder of a colony, or of a great business enterprise. Sometimes too he is a revolutionary leader, an enthusiastic humanitarian. He is not robbing and murdering for his own benefit; he is doing it for the greatness of his country or for the emancipation of the poor. He is cruel only in order to dry the people's tears, or those of a part of the people, or those which he himself has been shedding all his life long at the sight of human misery. Nothing could be nobler than the language and sentiments of such a romantic bandit. His every word is a eulogy of himself. He talks of his honor: tells you how unjustly fortune has treated him, and how wickedly his enemies have maligned him; how he has been driven unwillingly to defend himself; how he detests and despises the decrepit society of which he was a victim; although he may admit that his own victims personally were sometimes innocent. But invective and apology are not his only themes; he is even more eloquent in prophecy and self-glorification. The pure will of man, he says, is above all: if you have the gift of commanding you have the right, even the duty, to command; for the only duty of a free man is that which he imposes upon himself. But ah, what noble storms often agitate his free bosom! He will confess that in the midst of his hard cruel actions a strange wave of sensibility sometimes overwhelms him; suddenly he will cross himself or say the Lord's prayer or found a hospital or endow a college.

"The Sentimental Bandit"
from *Dominations and Powers*

Here one senses that, as the paragraph proceeds, Santayana more and more assumes a mock-heroic tone until he climaxes the effect with the exclamation, "But ah, what noble storms often agitate his free bosom!" He has given us an impression of chivalric eloquence with broad gesture.

The Formal Style continues to be a manner of distinction, of dignity, of ceremonial fitness. Of the three modes, it makes fullest use of the rhetorical and poetic resources of the language. In word, phrase, and tone, it deviates furthest from normative standards. At its worst, it is garish, pretentious, affected, bombastic; at its best, refined, imposing, dramatic, sublime.

THE MEASURE AND MAKING OF STYLE

We recognize the difference between gracious compliment and empty praise. The distinction is chiefly a stylistic effect. We expect an obituary to be written differently from a special tribute. The style of the one is impersonal; the style of the other is personal. We expect a student's interpretation of Marvell's "To His Coy Mistress" to sound like himself, not like T. S. Eliot. Pretentiousness is an abuse of style. We constantly use appropriateness of style as a factor in judging composition—the appropriateness of subject matter and style, of writer and style, of occasion and style. Even though the lines of distinction I have drawn between the major modes and the uses and abuses of style are not hard and fast, they are workable means of measuring the effects and the appropriateness of style.

In spite of its complexity, style is not just a matter of chance, hoping that something worthwhile will emerge. An appropriate style demands intuitive perception, sensing what is suitable. An effective style demands strategy, knowing what to do. An identifiable style demands concern, caring enough to be a writer who is known by his good works. Sensing, knowing, caring—these three, not chance, are the making of a good style.

SUGGESTIONS FOR DISCUSSION

1. Consider the following statements.

   A. Walter Scott and Pope's Homer were reading of my own selection, but my mother forced me, by steady long toil to learn long chapters of the Bible by heart; as well as to read it every syllable through, aloud, hard names and all, from Genesis to the Apocalypse, about once a year; and to that discipline—patient, accurate, and resolute —I owe, not only a knowledge of the book, which I find occasionally serviceable, but much of my general power of taking pains, and the best part of my taste in literature.

   John Ruskin

   B. One does not expect a modern writer to imitate Macaulay; but no student who has really *heard* his cadences will ever write a bad sentence.

   Charles Child Walcutt

   What do these two statements imply about the relationships between reading and writing?

2. The three theories of style mentioned on page 148 may be described briefly: (1) Rhetorical dualism—ideas and styles may be considered as separable; styles may be identified and used to dress ideas in different garbs. (2) Psychological monism—style is the man; therefore, ideas and style are one and the same. (3) Aesthetic monism— style is not isolable; ideas and style, just as content and form, are one.

   In terms of these classifications, discuss the implications of this student comment: "I would rather shock than inform, be beautiful than lucid, be stylish than cogent." What attitude toward style is implicit in this remark?

3. Evaluate the following passages as the beginning sentences of an essay. Are your responses positive or negative?

   A. Many of the people in the world today are discontent.

   B. People are similar to billiard balls, but each class is different in a different way.

   C. To begin with, I wish to qualify myself in regards to this topic. A definition of gentility depends upon an individual's own conception of it; therefore the following statements are merely expressions of my own opinions.

D. If I had only known then what I know now, I would have done things differently.

E. Americans are the victims of a "herd instinct," and they find security in numbers. They are lost in a maze of mathematics, in a frenzy of formulas, and in a vicious circle of cube-roots. Is it not normal that they should hide their fears and uncertainties behind a fail-safe curtain of numerals?

F. As illustrated in the novel *A Wreath for the Enemy,* the process of growing up is a complex one, involving contact with various types of people.

G. In Nathanael West's *The Day of the Locust,* a countless number of characters are represented.

H. American Negroes today are faced with two basic problems. First, there is the discrimination against the Negro by whites and, second, the discrimination against the Negro by other, more radical members of his own race. James Griffin, white man turned black, reveals his experiences with the Southern aspects of racial prejudice in *Black Like Me.*

I. Courage provides the theme, politics provides the situation for *Profiles in Courage* by John F. Kennedy.

J. Religion is always a hard topic to discuss to any great lengths, but Joseph Heller created two characters, John Yossarian and Chaplin A. T. Tappman, who always were able to get down to the discussion of God.

4. Analyze each of the following passages in terms of their style. Describe the individual style precisely in terms of voice, tone, diction, and sentence strategy. Then decide whether the prose represents essentially a plain, informal, or formal manner. Do you consider the passage a good or bad example of the mode it represents?

A.   Language influences the total psychological makeup of man. The influence of language categories upon behavior was demonstrated, for instance, when color-recognition tests were given to both Zuni and English speakers. The members of each group did better at recognizing colors for which their language had a specific designation. But the influence of the native language may be more pervasive than the naming of experiences. It is reported, for instance, that in an experiment where three staccato beats of equal intensity were presented to a Czech, a Pole, and a Frenchman, these were interpreted by them in accordance with the stress-pattern of their respective mother tongues. The Czech, whose language stresses the first syllable of the word, said the first beat was the strongest; the Frenchman, whose language has terminal stress, heard the last beat as loudest; while the Pole, in whose language the last syllable but one is stressed, chose the middle beat as the strongest.

John Lotz, "Linguistics:
Symbols Make Man"

B.   In the exposition of what I myself happen to believe, it is certainly not my purpose to argue or even to hint that this personal set of beliefs is either philosophically or emotionally admirable or that its adoption by anyone else is a consummation devoutly wished on my part. I suspect that what other men believe, though it be often objectionable to me, may stand them in quite as sound service as my own beliefs stand me, and that it may contribute equally to their self-esteem, happiness, bank accounts, worldly eminence and wives' low opinion of them. A man's beliefs, after all, save he be a professional practitioner of letters and hence a racketeer of words, a self-blackmailer and a Judas unto himself, are and should be his private, personal property, as safe from vulgar public scrutiny as his love-making or his underwear. There is something indelicate, even bounderish, in exposing one's most secret articles of faith, a fact appreciated by the relatively gentlemanly among the professional carpenters of letters mentioned, as may be witnessed by the obvious posturings, evasions and mendacities they indulge in when they engage, for hire, to contribute to the public prints. There is about the "beliefs" they expound on such occasions a considerable air of fraud; it is plain that, while they are ostensibly betraying their confidences, they are withholding much that is true of themselves and of their private philosophies, and much that, being true, would be altogether too embarrassing to set down in print. By way of subterfuge, they accordingly offer to the public a bold, forthright, cocksure and impudent front—but with their fingers carefully crossed behind their backs. If we may put any trust in the gossipy records, there never lived a bigger liar than Rousseau. And if I personally out of long association know anything of a number of writers who are in the habit of undressing their beliefs in public, you have my word for it that the ghost of Rousseau still walks.

George Jean Nathan, *Living Philosophies*

C.   It seems to me there are two aspects to women. There is the demure and the dauntless. Men have loved to dwell, in fiction at least, on the demure maiden whose inevitable reply is: Oh, yes, if you please, kind sir! The demure maiden, the demure spouse, the demure mother—this is still the ideal. A few maidens, mistresses and mothers *are* demure. A few pretend to be. But the vast majority are not. And they don't pretend to be. We don't expect a girl skilfully driving her car to be demure, we expect her to be dauntless. What good would demure and maidenly Members of Parliament be, inevitably responding: Oh, yes, if you please, kind sir!—Though of course there are masculine members of that kidney.—And a demure telephone girl? Or even a demure stenographer? Demureness, to be sure, is outwardly becoming, it is an outward mark of femininity, like bobbed hair. But it goes with inward dauntlessness. The girl who has got to make her way in life has got to be dauntless, and if she has a pretty, demure manner with it, then lucky girl. She kills two birds with two stones.

D. H. Lawrence, "Cocksure Women and Hensure Men"

D.   Yet our distress comes from no failure of substance. We are stricken by no plague of locusts. Compared with the perils which our forefathers conquered because they believed and were not afraid, we have still much to be thankful for. Nature still offers her bounty and human efforts have multiplied it. Plenty is at our doorstep, but a generous use of it languishes in the very sight of the supply.

Primarily, this is because the rulers of the exchange of mankind's goods have failed through their own stubbornness and their own incompetence, have admitted their failure and abdicated. Practices of the unscrupulous money changers stand indicted in the court of public opinion, rejected by the hearts and minds of men.

True, they have tried, but their efforts have been cast in the pattern of an outworn tradition. Faced by failure of credit, they have proposed only the lending of more money.

Stripped of the lure of profit by which to induce our people to follow their false leadership, they have resorted to exhortations, pleading tearfully for restored confidence. They know only the rules of a generation of self-seekers.

They have no vision, and when there is no vision the people perish.

The money changers have fled from their high seats in the temple of our civilization. We may now restore that temple to the ancient truths.

The measure of the restoration lies in the extent to which we apply social values more noble than mere monetary profit.

Happiness lies not in the mere possession of money; it lies in the joy of achievement, in the thrill of creative effort.

The joy and moral stimulation of work no longer must be forgotten in the mad chase of evanescent profits. These dark days will be worth all they cost us if they teach us that our true destiny is not to be ministered unto but to minister to ourselves and to our fellow-men.

> Franklin Delano Roosevelt
> First Inaugural Address, 1933

E.   Back in the days of dog-eat-dog—my first anecdote begins—there lived a playboy; whose father could easily have owned the original superskyscraper-de-luxe: a selfstyled Cathedral Of Commerce, endowed with every impetus to relaxation; not excluding ultraelevators which (on the laudable assumption that even machinery occasionally makes mistakes) were regularly tested. Testing an ultraelevator meant that its car was brought clean up, deprived of safety devices, and dropped. As the car hurtled downward, a column of air confined by the elevator shaft became more and more compressed; until (assuming that nothing untoward happened) it broke the car's fall completely—or so I was told by somebody who should know. At any rate, young Mr X was in the habit not only of attending these salubrious ceremonies, but of entering each about-to-be-dropped car, and of dropping with it as far and as long as the laws of a preEinsteinian universe permitted. Eventually, of course, somebody who shouldn't know telephoned a newspaper; which sent a reporter: who (after scarcely believing his senses) asked the transcender of Adam point-blank why he fell so often. Our playful protagonist shrugged his well-tailored shoulders—"for fun" he said simply; adding (in a strictly confidential undertone) "and it's wonderful for a hangover."

> e. e. cummings from Nonlecture Three
> i & selfdiscovery

ASSIGNMENTS

1. Choose five sentences from your reading that involve subordination. Reverse the subordination; that is, make the main clause subordinate and the subordinate clause independent. Does the revised sentence make sense? Has the meaning changed essentially?
2. Describe in as much detail as possible the strategies of the following sentences.

A. I am therefore in this point a professed disciple of Apollonius, a scholar of Socrates, I neglect phrases and labor wholly to inform my reader's understanding, not to please his ears; 'tis not my study or intent to compose neatly, which an orator requires, but to express myself readily and plainly as it happens. So that, as a river runs sometimes precipitate and swift, then dull and slow, now direct, then *per ambages,* now deep, then shallow, now muddy, then clear, now broad, then narrow, doth my style flow; now serious, then light, now comical, then satirical, now more elaborate, then remiss, as the present subject required or as at that time I was affected.

Robert Burton

B. These are the times that try men's souls.

Thomas Paine

C. Every morning the homeless puppy, as if trying to persuade me to adopt him, emerged from his hiding place with a sleepy yawn, skipped friskily to me, exuding all the charm he could muster, ran in circles around me, and bounded gaily onto the front porch, yelping all the while.

Student Sentence

D. A sex offense is not, of course, a serious attack on society, but it is a kind of physical assertion, a momentary wishing things were otherwise.

Student Sentence

E. The Guggenheim Museum is a formidable, ponderous, closed-in concrete structure of almost indescribable individuality; the main element, the art gallery, might be called an inverted ziggurat that tapers toward the bottom—not the Mesopotamian kind, which stood on a square base, but Bruegel's round version in his "Tower of Babel."

Lewis Mumford

F. New York is the concentrate of art and commerce and sport and religion and entertainment and finance, bringing to a single compact arena the gladiator, the evangelist, the promoter, the actor, the trader, and the merchant.

E. B. White

G. Negroes wanted to be treated like men: a perfectly straightforward statement, containing only seven words.

James Baldwin

H. But a university training is the great but ordinary end; it aims at raising the intellectual tone of society, at cultivating the public mind, at purifying the national taste, at supplying true principles to popular enthusiasm and fixed aims to popular aspiration, at giving enlargement and sobriety to the ideas of the age, at facilitating the exercise of political power, and refining the intercourse of private life.

John Henry Newman

I. Falsehood flies, and truth comes limping after it, so that when man comes to be undeceived it is too late; the jest is over, and the tale has had its effect; like a man who has thought of a good repartee when the discourse is changed or the company parted; or like a physician who has found out an infallible medicine after the patient is dead.

Jonathan Swift

J. The other day I was shoving some of my originals around on the floor (I do not draw on the floor; I was just shoving the originals around) and they fell, or perhaps I pushed them, into five separate and indistinct categories.

James Thurber

K. Lo-lee-ta: the tip of the tongue taking a trip of three steps down the palate to tap, at three, on the teeth.

Vladimir Nabokov

3. Choose ten sentences from a variety of sources (fiction, pre-twentieth-century nonfiction, and contemporary nonfiction) that seem worthy of imitation. Determine the structure and strategy of each sentence, and write a close imitation in current, idiomatic, American English, but invent rather than say anything downright awkward (cp. Orwell: "Break any of these rules sooner than say anything outright barbarous").

8

Mechanics

Asterisks and dots and strokes are hopeless. You can't
swear with those things. They won't read right....Read
aloud, as they are, they would turn the pirate story into:
> "*Three asterisks!*" *shouted the Pirate.*
> "*Four,*" *shouted the next.*
> "*I'll make it six,*" *yelled a third, adding a stroke and*
> *a colon.* Stephen Leacock

xcept in comic strips, we no longer need asterisks, dots, and strokes to swear, but we do need conventional marks of punctuation to say a good many other things. At times, if they are ignored or misused, they can do considerable damage. An omitted comma may win or lose a lawsuit; the substitution of a comma for a hyphen between *fruit* and *seeds* once cost the government several thousand dollars. But I use the term *mechanics* in this chapter to refer not to punctuation alone but also to italics, capitalization, spelling, and documentation.

One of the problems in discussing mechanics is that not very many people ever get excited about capitals, periods, and footnotes. Teachers may get excited, even nasty, because students use them incorrectly, but they seldom show passion or affection or curiosity or any kind of positive feeling about mechanics themselves. They accept them as characterless symbols, and we are left to pursue a loveless and humorless, but necessary, task.

I am grateful for a passage in one of Gertrude Stein's lectures, not because I agree with everything she says, but because she is the only person I have read who has written about mechanics with a true sense of feeling:

> There are some punctuations that are interesting and there are some punctuations that are not. Let us begin with the punctuations that are not. Of these the one but the first and the most the completely most uninteresting is the question mark. The question mark is alright when it is all alone when it is used as a brand on cattle or when it could be used in decoration but connected with writing it is completely entirely completely uninteresting. It is evident that if you ask a question you ask a question but anybody who can read at all knows when a question is a question as it is written in writing. Therefore I ask you therefore wherefore should one use it the question mark. Beside it does not in its form go with ordinary printing and so it pleases neither the eye nor the ear and it is therefore like a noun, just an unnecessary name of something. A question is a question, anybody can know that a question is a question and so why add to it the question mark when it is already there when the question is already there in the writing. Therefore I never could bring myself to use a question mark, I always found it positively revolting, and now very few do use it. Exclamation marks have the same difficulty and also quotation marks, they are unnecessary, they are ugly, they spoil the line of the writing or the printing and anyway what is the use, if you

do not know that a question is a question what is the use of its being a question. The same thing is true of an exclamation. And the same thing is true of a quotation. When I first began writing I found it simply impossible to use question marks and quotation marks and exclamation points and now anybody sees it that way. Perhaps some day they will see it some other way but now at any rate anybody can and does see it that way.

"Poetry and Grammar"

One of the things Gertrude Stein goes on to say is that when she first began writing she didn't really want to be concerned with marks of punctuation and capitals. All she wanted was to have the writing "go on." She finally learned that, even though she might want to push on, the reader needed a break. He was not physically up to her demands. And then she adds this comment:

Stopping sometime did not really keep one from going on, it was nothing that interfered, it was only something that happened, and as it happened as a perfectly natural happening, I did believe in periods and I used them. I really never stopped using them.

Particularly in "it was nothing that interfered," Gertrude Stein makes a crucial point that every student of writing ought to consider seriously. Mechanics do not interfere. They are not obstacles. Mechanics bother only those people who don't know what they signify—how they help the writer to say what he wants to say, how they help the reader to understand more accurately what the writer is trying to say, how they manage to say a few things on their own in their limited mechanical ways. Like talking dolls, marks of punctuation don't have many messages, but the ones they have they convey repeatedly and clearly. Once we get the message, the rest is simple.

PUNCTUATING

The period and the comma are the basic marks of punctuation. Between them, they do everything punctuation needs to do. All the others are refinements of them; the others do more specially or more emphatically what the period and the comma do. The period and the comma, therefore, are the utility marks. Because they usually operate in a relatively neutral fashion to facilitate clear and easy reading of the text, they are appropriate to all the major modes of style. Because the other marks have less generality, because they at times carry rather exclusive connotations (compare the exclamation point with the period, for instance), they tend to be used less frequently, unless a writer becomes sufficiently enamored of a mark that he uses it again and again as a stylistic characteristic. For instance, in an essay entitled "Artur Rodzinski and the Education of a Conductor" that appeared in *Saturday Review* (January 26, 1957), Robert Charles Marsh, within the space of seven paragraphs, approximately two pages of text, uses parentheses twelve times, not routinely, as the date inserted after the name of the periodical above, but rhetorically, as a means of making asides. In two of the instances, he is compelled to substitute square brackets for parentheses because he comments even as he quotes. These parentheses and brackets, serving as they do to insert the author's side comments, add a stylistic dimension that commas in this instance would not give.

A writer has a very limited view of the function of punctuation if he thinks of the marks only as blobs on the page to prevent misreading or as ornaments or as appropriate breathing spaces for reading aloud. Marks of punctuation can influence meaning, affect tone, reflect personality, determine structure, and facilitate inventiveness. In these senses, punctuation is necessary because it is an organic part of writing, not something added after the writing is finished. In fact, punctuation is no less integral to the writing process than any of the other elements we have discussed. Mechanical correctness is a part of effective writing. Incorrectness comments either upon the writer's ignorance of mechanics or upon his indifference toward them. Either is inexcusable.

The system of punctuation

Anyone who pursues punctuation formulaically—by the rules—or in piecemeal fashion, as if every usage were a crisis, is not likely to have a benevolent attitude. If, however, he is able to see a larger scheme, he may realize that the rules are more flexible than he thinks and that many of the marks are closely enough related that they can substitute for one another.

All the individual uses of the marks of punctuation have only five major functions: separating at the end of a thought, separating internally, introducing, enclosing, and indicating omission. Even these five functions may be reduced further to four or to three, but the smallest possible number does not necessarily provide the most workable system.

Once we have established the basic functions, we can see that some of the marks of punctuation perform only one or two functions; some perform four or five. Sometimes marks can be used interchangeably within a particular category, for instance, the colon and the dash to introduce. On the other hand, some marks have exclusive functions: no mark can substitute for the apostrophe to indicate possession. The basic functions are for the most part self-explanatory, but a few words about each of them will avoid any misconceptions.

Separating at the End of a Thought

The common terminal marks are the period, exclamation point, and question mark. If we also recognize how writers use marks of punctuation, not precisely how the handbooks say they ought to be used, we will find that the dash, colon, and ellipsis are occasionally used in the terminal position as well. The use of the word *terminal,* of course, signifies stopping, but, except for the period at the end of an essay or book, all stopping is only pausing to go on. Thus, so-called terminal marks are useful for separating the major units of thought within a paragraph or paragraphs within the total structure of a composition.

Separating Internally

The second category represents marks of punctuation that separate words or parts of words within a sentence. Because these marks separate what has already been joined, they may be thought of as linking as well as separating. The marks that serve this function include the comma, the semicolon, the colon, the dash, the hyphen, and the apostrophe.

The tendency of much contemporary writing, particularly in informal prose, is to dispense with as much punctuation as possible, consistent with clarity. Open punctuation, as it is called, rather literally gives prose a greater sense of openness and freedom. It is not to be confused with sloppiness that ignores standard usages altogether or with permissiveness that says anything goes. Even though the open style dispenses with much unnecessary punctuation, it also runs the risk of inviting ambiguity that the writer may not be aware of.

Close punctuation remains the conservative norm from which writers deviate. It is a style of internal punctuation that takes no chances. Legal and government documents, in particular, seek the most completely unambiguous meaning. They depend heavily upon the precise use of punctuation. Despite the dependability of the close style, it tends toward an overuse of punctuation and, in many instances, toward a chopped-up prose style.

Introducing

Introducing is, of course, another form of separating, but separating *initial* words or word groups from the rest of the sentence by means of the comma, colon, or dash. The only justification for a new category is to explain in part the substitution principle. For instance, a semicolon may substitute for a comma in its separating function, but not in its introducing function:

[Comma to introduce]   Among various handbooks on mechanics and typographical matters, *A Manual of Style* (University of Chicago Press) is one of the best.

[Substitution of semicolon impossible]   Among various handbooks on mechanics and typographical matters; *A Manual of Style* (University of Chicago Press) is one of the best.

Thus in terms of the basic functions we can speak of obvious misuse of marks of punctuation. Not everything goes.

Enclosing

Enclosing is also a form of separating, but like introducing it performs a sufficiently special function with its double use of punctuation —before and after the word group—that it cannot always be duplicated by other marks. For instance, the semicolon cannot substitute for the comma in its enclosing function, although, as we have noted, it can in its separating function. Commas, dashes, parentheses, square brackets, and quotation marks are enclosing marks of punctuation.

Indicating Omission

Indicating omission of letters in words or of words in the text is a basically servile function of punctuation. In various ways, the period, comma, dash, ellipsis, hyphen, and apostrophe serve this purpose.

If we then chart the marks of punctuation in their respective categories as in Table 2, we will begin to have a clearer notion of their range and utility.

Table 2

TO SEPARATE (TERMINAL)	TO SEPARATE (INTERNAL)	TO ENCLOSE	TO INTRODUCE	TO INDICATE OMISSION
period	period			period
exclamation point				
question mark				
	comma	commas	comma	comma
	semicolon			
colon [rare]	colon		colon	
dash [rare]	dash	dashes	dash	dash
ellipsis [rare]				ellipsis
	hyphen			hyphen
		parentheses		
		square brackets		
		quotation marks		
	apostrophe			apostrophe

The most noticeable feature of the chart is that the dash performs all the functions; it does not substitute for all marks in all their functions, but it substitutes for all of them in some of their functions. Here we have a commentary upon the dash as a mark of punctuation. It acts indiscriminately, and because it does, some writers use it promiscuously.

We will consider each mark of punctuation in terms of these functions. The uses listed below do not pretend to be exhaustive, but they are intended as useful guides to the common uses of punctuation. Familiar with these, a writer may begin to discover rhetorical uses on his own. All prohibitions have been omitted. Any writer learns these soon enough from his critics.

1 The period

The period is such an unpretentious mark of punctuation that we tend to overlook its strength. Because it gives a firm, unequivocal signal of ending, we do not even question whether the thought is a complete sentence or not. If we are reading aloud, we lower our pitch and let our voice fade.

Many writers act as if the period is outdated and overworked. They substitute commas, semicolons, dashes, and colons in various kinds of compound sentences, little realizing that at times the period is the most emphatic mark anybody can use.

The uses of the period are simple but important.

Separating at the End of a Thought

A. To end sentences or fragments, including single words, written as a complete thought.

Example   Love is as vital to a child as the air he breathes. Undoubtedly. Maybe even more so.

Separating Internally

B. To indicate segments of figures: $10.50, 4.2 percent, 72.66 centimeters.

C. To set off words or numbers as a typographical aid, as in outlining:

    I.

       A.

       B.

          1.

          2.

   II.

Indicating Omission

D. To indicate abbreviations: Ph.D., Mr., Jr.
[Open style omits the period in many abbreviations: CIO, AAUP,
US government.]

Special Notes

1. When the period substitutes for a question mark, the request
takes on the force of a directive, courteously phrased.
   Example Will you please act as coordinator of all activities in
              the day camp from June 15 to June 30.
2. When the period substitutes for an exclamation point, it carries
only the idea of termination, leaving the force of the exclamation
to the words and phrasing.
   Example What a fiasco that was.
3. Periods are always placed inside quotation marks.

2 Comma

Unlike the period, the comma conveys no sense of finality. It has a
quick passing quality that makes it an unobtrusive mark, unless it is
overused. Then it becomes obvious because it slices up the prose into
tiny segments that make reading difficult. When it is well used, it helps
the rhythm and clarifies meaning by marking off related words and appropriate pauses.

Some writers who have the notion that the comma is only a light-duty mark of punctuation substitute heavier marks like semicolons, colons, and dashes for emphatic effects. Even though the contrast works in many instances (it may even be necessary in some cases to prevent mis-reading), the comma is capable of a good bit of style as well as drudgery. Its uses are many, but not as diverse as the long lists in handbooks and dictionaries would suggest. Most of the uses merely reinforce the writer's own intuitive sense of what should be punctuated.

Separating Internally

A. To separate main clauses joined by *and, but, or, for, nor,* and *yet* or short sentences without a connective that follow one another closely and quickly.

Example 1   Dickens thinks that wonder, awe, daring, and fancy are the most important qualities a man can possess, for without them he cannot survive.

[Open style sometimes omits the comma before the coordinating conjunction, particularly in sentences joined by *and.* The conjunction *for,* however, may be easily confused with the preposition *for,* so that the comma is usually necessary.]

Example 2   He would agree, she would not.

[Compare the following: "In the process of attaining these objectives, the student will mature into an individual fully capable of finding his place in society and making an acceptable contribution to its welfare. When he has reached that stage, he has outgrown adolescence, that is maturity." The comma after *adolescence* is clearly a misuse, usually called a comma splice or comma fault. The context indicates that the writer needs a full break after *adolescence,* both to give the rhetorical effect he needs and to prevent misreading of "that is maturity" as a dependent clause.]

B. To separate words, phrases, or clauses in series (series begin with combinations of two).

Example 1   Mr. Gradgrind insists upon simple, uncompromising facts.

[Compare "He insisted upon simple scientific facts." In this sentence, because *simple* and *scientific* are not coordinate, the comma is omitted. *Scientific facts* has the force of a single unit; *simple* is the word modifying the unit. In the first sentence, *simple* and *uncompromising* are coordinate because one seems to have no priority over the other in modifying *facts*.]

Example 2   Whether I am in the subway, on the streets, or atop high buildings, I am reminded of the press of people in the city.

[Open style omits the final comma in the *a, b,* and/or *c* series, unless possible misreading results from the omission, as in "We visited Ray and Ethel, Bill and Carolyn and Marty."]

Example 3   Hedda kills herself because she can no longer bear "genteel poverty," because she cannot face the ugliness of childbirth, because she cannot submit to the ignominy of scandal.

C. To separate tags at the end of a sentence—either single words, phrases, or clauses—clearly not restricting the meaning of the main clause.

Example 1   He voted Democratic, undoubtedly.

[Open style might eliminate this comma, but the effect would be changed.]

Example 2   China looms as an uncertain menace in the background, ready to upset everything.

Example 3   The painting has a remarkably somber effect, even though it is done in bright colors.

D. To separate clusters of words representing different levels of generality (see "Texture," page 158).

Example   The professor was firm, never harsh, always cautious not to demolish a dullard.

E. To separate the parts of addresses, dates, and numbers: 4025 Winchester Road, Louisville, Kentucky; April 11, 1920; 100,000.

Enclosing

F. To enclose all kinds of interrupters of a nonrestrictive nature, including appositives, parenthetical remarks, contrasts, transitional words, and direct address. All of these occur medially, as opposed to introductory elements at the beginning or tags at the end.

Example 1   English, a Germanic language, developed a number of distinctive monosyllables because of the Germanic tendency to place heavy stress upon the initial syllable. [appositive]

Example 2   His conduct, I might add, was irreproachable. [parenthetical]

Example 3   The juggler used plates, not balls, to show how good he was. [contrast]

Example 4   A significant point, however, is the obvious intent of both sides to keep diplomatic doors open for discussion. [transitional]

Example 5   We appeal to you, dear friends, for your help. [direct address]

Example 6   "I heard the outbreak," he recalled, "but I did nothing." [split quotation]

Introducing

G. To separate any kind of word or word group in the initial position from the main clause.

Example 1   Moreover, it is possible to find the information in the daily newspaper.

Example 2   Near the end of the novel, the writer seems unable to sustain the reader's interest.
[Open style often eliminates the comma after introductory elements. A writer, however, has to be cautious of possible misreading: "By cheating a person could possibly prosper."]

Example 3   The announcer shrieked, "Here they are."

Indicating Omission

H. To indicate the omission of words, usually in parallel constructions.

Example   Progress to the young is a mark of discovery; to the old man, a mark of degeneration.

Special Notes

1. A writer who knows the difference between restrictive and nonrestrictive modifiers will be able to use the comma more confidently than someone who doesn't. The problem is mainly one of identification—the difference, for instance, between being able to identify one of three suspects as a thief and being able to supply details about a thief after he has already been identified.

   Example 1   The man who has the tattoo on his left wrist is the one I saw. [The *who*-clause is restrictive.]

   Example 2   The man on the right end [identification made], who did the shooting, is the one I recognize. [Nonrestrictive clause set off by commas.]

   Modifiers that identify and limit are restrictive. Those that add detail in a nonlimiting way are nonrestrictive. Even though nonrestrictive modifiers add information, they are not less important, only less crucial to a particular meaning. Nonrestrictive modifiers are separated or enclosed by commas.

2. Anyone who puts in a comma every time he pauses in speaking will end up with superfluous commas. The main components of sentence patterns are never separated by commas—the subject from the verb, the verb from the object or complement. Of course, commas may appear between the subject and verb or the verb and the object if they enclose words that may be interposed.

   Example   He swore, with the indignation of a man betrayed, that he would not return.

3. Commas, like periods, are always placed inside quotation marks.

3 Semicolon

If, by some quirk of fate, the semicolon were eliminated from our tradition and thoughts, it would not be necessary to reinvent it. We could get along very well without it. The chief reason is that it seems to have no absolutely exclusive function of its own. It reveals mongrel qualities; it is a mixture of comma and period, ironically named as kin to the colon. One early textbook calls it a dwarf period and a giant comma. Its adaptability as both marks causes some writers to misuse it consistently. Used most effectively, it is an emphatic mark of separation in long sentences containing heavy internal punctuation. In other instances, however, unless the writer shows inventiveness, the mark gives off an aura of stodginess. Ironically, students show a great affection for the semicolon.

Despite its ties with the period, the semicolon always appears internally as a separating mark.

Separating Internally

A. To separate main clauses, joined because of their close association in meaning.

Example 1   Representationalism in the theater depends upon illusion; it must seem like life, even though it isn't. [without a connective]

Example 2   He tried to provide for his family those things he thought were necessary; however, his thoughts were not his family's thoughts. [With connectives like *however, moreover, otherwise,* and *for example,* open style often drops the comma after the connective.]

Example 3   He tried to provide for his family those things he thought were necessary; but, because his ways of thinking were tied to a strict concept of utilitarianism, his thoughts were not his family's thoughts. [With connectives like *and, but, or, for, nor,* and *yet,* if one or both of the main clauses contain internal

punctuation, a semicolon is substituted for emphasis.]

B. To separate clusters of words and figures already containing
internal punctuation.

Example 1   Schnitzler's plays are often light works, but never
frivolous; often humorous, but never comic; often
dream-like, but never fanciful.

Example 2   Consider I Sam. 25:1–10; I Sam. 25:43–44; and II
Sam. 3:2–5.

Special Notes

1. Even though the semicolon serves as a heavy marker, particularly when confusion is likely to result from internal punctuation, it can substitute as a separator only in limited cases. It
may substitute for the comma, for instance, when it separates
elements of a series, but cannot substitute when it introduces,
encloses, or adds material at the end.

Example 1   If we collect as many points of view as possible,
soliciting personal letters, conducting mail surveys,
and interviewing; we may be able to come up with
solutions [misuse of the semicolon].

Example 2   Moses would go out among the other animals and
preach to them about Sugarcandy Mountain, a
land beyond the clouds where all animals go when
they die; a paradise for animals [misuse].

Example 3   "I could be wrong"; he replied [misuse].

2. The semicolon is always placed outside quotation marks and
parentheses unless it is substituting for a comma (see Bestor
paragraph, page 62).

4 Colon

Like many first-rate operas, highly respected but seldom performed,
the colon gets its share of praise and neglect. Its neglect in informal
writing may possibly spring from its close connection with the business
world, which abounds in salutations like "Dear Sir:" and expressions like

"Enclosed are the following materials:" (The use of the colon as a terminal mark is rare.) But because the colon, even in its most formal uses, sets up an anticipation of something to come, it has remarkable possibilities as a mark of punctuation. It looks forward; it looks toward the specific. It therefore encourages two qualities of good prose writing.

Separating Internally

A. To separate two parts of a sentence phrased so that the expectation set up in the first part is clearly met in the second.

Example 1   One strong belief is prevalent in America today: it is simply that Americans are better than anyone else.

Example 2   Rest without work can be as harmful as work without rest: it promotes indifference and mediocrity.

Example 3   There was one thing he liked more than anything else: bananas.

The semicolon might substitute in Examples 1 and 2, the dash or the comma in Example 3.

B. To separate references to act and scene, hour and minutes, chapter and verse, title and subtitle, place and publisher: *Othello* V:ii, 1–15; 2:45 P.M.; Gen. 2:5; *Understanding Media: The Extensions of Man;* New York: McGraw-Hill Book Company. [Acts and scenes are also separated by periods: *Othello* V.ii. 1–15.]

Introducing

C. To introduce quotations, especially as a means of avoiding the verb of saying, as in Example 1.

Example 1   We are concerned with the tone of his remarks as well as the literal meaning: [Followed by a quotation in sequence or set off in a separate paragraph.]

Example 2   Martin Buber observes: "The mythical has entered into this our field of vision by virtue of the truth of the myths."

D. To introduce any list of explanatory material that follows:

    Example   Space today holds the enticements that the West once held: undiscovered territory, adventure, and danger.

Indicating Omission

E. To indicate the omission of words in limited contexts.

    Example 1   Emily Dickinson slant-rhymes words like *comes: tombs, observe:love,* and *asleep:lip.* [The colon seems to stand for *and*.]

    Example 2   He read the illustration: 6:12::12:24. [The relationship that is symbolized can also be verbalized.]

Special Notes

1. Even though the colon in its own right most clearly anticipates, it takes on the summary function of the dash—a looking backward—when it is used in place of a dash.

    Example   *L'Assommoir, Sister Carrie, The Pit:* these illustrate Naturalism in the novel.

2. The colon is usually placed outside quotation marks, except in rare uses of the colon as a terminal mark.

5 Dash

The more informal writing becomes, the more dashes show up (or the opposite: the more dashes show up, the more informal writing becomes). The dash is a flexible mark that tends to loosen structure rather than tighten it. It is therefore useful for stream-of-consciousness effects and dialogue—writing that tries to reproduce the patterns of thought and speech.

Because the dash is adaptable to all the functions of punctuation, it becomes a dangerous mark—dangerous because it tempts some writers to use it when they are ignorant of stronger, more discriminating uses of other marks. Dash-men make the same garb do for all occasions.

Yet, for all its abuses, the dash does a few things particularly well, especially shifting the direction of a sentence abruptly or allowing the writer to pick up a word or an idea from the earlier part of his sentence in order to expand upon it. For these uses, the dash is quite indispensable.

Separating at the End of a Thought

A. To act as a loose substitute for the period or semicolon.

Example 1   "He lived long and prospered on account of his magnificent footwork—when they swung at him he was somewhere else."

Gerald W. Johnson
"Oh, for Mencken Now"

Example 2   " 'Breathe through your nose—your breath is warmer that way when it gets to your lungs.' "

Lois Phillips Hudson
"The Cold Wave"

Separating Internally

B. To anticipate a summary remark.

Example 1   The building quavered, cracked, shattered, and toppled—all in thirty seconds, as if it were nothing but play blocks.

Example 2   We went to London, Paris, Rome, and Athens—a distance of 10,000 miles in two weeks.

C. To indicate any kind of break in the thought for emphasis or intentional discontinuity.

Example 1   "The Indian armed forces did not shrivel away— as Gandhi would have hoped."

Homer A. Jack
"Mahatma Gandhi Ten Years After"

Example 2   Crowds of people mill about without recognizing one another—on the fairgrounds—crowds of people —on the buses—crowds of people—on the ferries.

Example 3   "Oh—Beth, you mean." [Compare "Oh, you mean Beth."]

D. To pick up a word or an idea temporarily suspended by the phrasing.

Example   Citizens and rulers of the powerful countries of the world have become aware of the fantastic power that is at their disposal—power that can be used to aid mankind or eliminate it.

Enclosing

E. To enclose parenthetical remarks, particularly in the form of complete sentences.

Example 1   An adult today—it doesn't matter if he is going to college or working—has to meet competition.

Example 2   "It was a noble instrument fit for a knight—or a king, like Solomon—but not for impersonating the bumble bee, bells, birds, or bulls."

Gregor Piatigorsky
"My Life, My Cello"

Indicating Omission

F. To indicate an incomplete utterance or omission of inclusive material: Mrs. Vander——
Matt. 3:3–5:16.

Special Notes

1. Printers distinguish between a short dash and a long dash, but in typed copy a dash is always represented by two unspaced hyphens.
2. Dashes are placed inside or outside quotation marks depending upon the context.

6 Parentheses

It may be a commentary upon the nature of writers (or at least upon their thinking) that mechanics include a variety of ways—commas, dashes, parentheses, and square brackets—for interjecting comment. Interpolations in parentheses may at times be purely formal and explanatory; at other times, familiar and confiding. But, one way or the other, they reveal things about the author to his audience: his willingness to translate a foreign phrase for them or let them flounder; his desire to be precise, to add a helpful comment, or to give directions; his wish to make known his own feelings by an aside. Parentheses embrace almost any kind of comment (this chapter draws to a close), wholly relevant or not.

Enclosing

A. To enclose information helpful to the reader or necessary for accuracy: CORE (Congress of Racial Equality); twenty dollars ($20.00).
B. To interpolate comments or asides.

Example   "I am aware now, away from the city for nearly two years, of how casually one accepts sudden death in New York—the killing of a woman crossing Herald Square, her skull crumpled by a truck (I saw that); a plane hitting the Empire State Building (I worked across the street); the forcing of someone off a crowded subway platform into the path of a train (I used to look at daily headlines describing that; they said the person jumped or fell, but how could anyone ever know?); the falling of a flower pot or a wooden beam from the heights of a building, to hit an old Negro man or kill a chauffeur in a Rolls-Royce (I read about these); and the countless daily acts of mayhem, so commonplace they never got into the newspapers."

Morris Freedman
"Wonderful Town?"

[Note how a combination of punctuation marks keeps this 136-word sentence in complete control.]

7 Square brackets

Square brackets are simply a special kind of parentheses. There is no way to keep a writer out of his own prose, even if he is quoting another writer's exact words. He cannot ethically change a quotation, but he can comment upon it as he is quoting. If he intrudes upon a direct quotation, however, he must be courteous enough to use square brackets to indicate that the quoted source does not include the interpolation. An interruption in square brackets may be a brief censorious *sic* (*thus:* thus it is in the original; I am not responsible), or it may be an ironic aside or any other kind of comment. Overuse of square brackets suggests something about a writer's egotism, his reluctance to let anyone else have his say, even in print.

Enclosing

A. To enclose any editorial interpolation, informational or ironic.

> Example 1   I like to place the primary accent on the third syllable of the word *apotheosis* [ap′ə-*the*′ə-sis].

> Example 2   Huntington Brown writes, ". . . we may say that impersonality [how appropriate] is the soul of the official style."

B. To enclose parentheses within parentheses.

> Example   Chaucer is sometimes described as a literary figure who is firmly a part of the Middle Ages (in England, a period from approximately the time of the Heptarchy [the division of England into seven parts in the Fifth Century] to the accession of Henry VII), but who anticipates the Renaissance, the period following 1485.

⅔ Ellipsis

Ellipsis is another means of ethically altering a direct quotation and clearly accounting for the change. The precise writer will use a series of three periods to indicate omitted words, four periods to indicate the omission of one or more complete sentences, a full line of periods to indicate the omission of one or more paragraphs. Asterisks sometimes substitute as fancy periods. Even though the ellipsis has a purely mechanical function, it is an important guide to a reader who may suspect that the writer has distorted a quotation by the omission of key words.

Indicating Omission

A. To indicate the omission of words, sentences, or paragraphs.

> Example 1   "The form of government in Persia up to the year 1906 was . . . similar to that of Turkey."
> *The Standard Dictionary of Facts*

Example 2   "It cannot be denied but that he who is made judge
to sit upon the birth or death of books, whether
they may be wafted into this world or not, had need
to be a man above the common measure . . . ."
            John Milton, *Areopagitica*
[The fourth dot in this instance is a period. Only
five words at the end have been omitted.]

Example 3   "There is not so variable a thing in nature as a
lady's headdress: within my own memory I have
known a rise and fall above thirty degrees. . . .
One may observe, that women in all ages have
taken more pains than men to adorn the outside of
their heads; and, indeed, I very much admire, that
those female architects, who raise such wonderful
structures out of ribbons, lace, and wire, have not
been recorded for their respective inventions."
            Joseph Addison from *The Spectator,* No. 98
[The ellipsis here represents the omission of four
sentences.]

⁊ Quotation marks

Quotation marks, as simple and obvious as their use seems, involve
a number of complications for the unsuspecting and unknowledgeable.
For instance, American publishers use double quotation marks, with
single marks for quotations within quotations. The British do just the
opposite. Both may choose not to use quotation marks at all, substituting
special indentation or typography for quoted material. In French, Spanish,
and German printing, the symbols for setting off quotations may look altogether different. Ordinarily, quotation marks are differentiated from
italics, but in a title, ordinarily italicized, which contains another title,
quotation marks substitute for italics to solve the dilemma of double-
italics (*A Study of James Joyce's "Ulysses"*).

But far more significant than the manipulation of quotation marks
in rather unusual situations is the obligation they place upon a writer
for unconditional accuracy. The marks guarantee that what has been
quoted is faithfully transcribed, unless the quotation has been altered

by means of ellipsis or square brackets, as we have already discussed. A most revealing demonstration is to ask twenty-five people merely to copy a few sentences from a text. The number of errors that typically show up intimate how subject we are to carelessness. The only thing to do is to check, to recheck if necessary, for accuracy. Guarantees that guarantee nothing are worthless.

Besides their chief function of setting off quoted material, quotation marks have a number of subsidiary uses, some of rather questionable reputation.

Enclosing

A. To enclose the exact words of a source or speaker.

> Example   Juliet says to Romeo, "What's in a name? That which we call a rose/By any other word would smell as sweet. . . ."
>
> [The slash is a mechanical device for indicating the end of a line of verse when the author does not wish to quote the lines in their usual form.]

B. To enclose the titles of short poems, paintings, articles, and parts of books.

> Example   Dylan Thomas' "Fern Hill" is frequently anthologized.
>
> [The division between short poems and long poems is undefined; why the titles of some paintings are italicized and some are put in quotation marks is vague. The only conclusion we can draw is that differences between quotation marks and italics cannot be sharply drawn.]

C. To enclose (almost as an act of apology) special coinages, slang, heavy irony, and bits of cleverness intended to be funny.

> Example 1   "The Sanskrit word *tat* (our 'that') is probably based on a child's first efforts at speech, when it points at something and says, 'Ta' or 'Da.' "
>
> Alan W. Watts, *The Way of Zen*
>
> [This sentence represents a legitimate use of quotation marks to enclose words and sounds.]
>
> Example 2   He said he wanted to get away from his "ball-and-chain."

[Uses of this kind are not forbidden. Everyone
understands what the intention is. The chief
problem is that this kind of qualification is a shiny
badge of the amateur.]

Special Note

Direct quotations may be worked into a sentence in the form of
indirect discourse, without the anticipation of a saying verb.

Example   If, according to Walter Kaufmann, it is true that "existen-
tialism is not a school of thought nor reducible to any
set of tenets," then we are obligated to study the chief
individual exponents.

10 Question mark

Anyone who has graded Freshman papers knows that the question
mark is very often forgotten. The question is there, but no mark. By force
of habit, the writer has used a period. The error may suggest carelessness, although it may also comment upon the superfluousness of the
question mark. Once the interrogation has been framed (Is he going),
the question mark adds nothing. Even in reading, a speaker anticipates
a question by a rising intonation, without benefit of the mark. When questions are phrased colloquially (You said he was going?), then the question mark clearly distinguishes between a statement and a question.

Ironically, the question mark has almost its greatest force as an
isolated symbol, used as it frequently is in cartoons to express doubt (?),
stronger doubt (??), complete puzzlement (???).

Separating at the End of a Thought

A. To mark the end of a question or a statement intended to be
read as a question.

Example   Are we going to tolerate discrimination in public
vehicles? In private clubs? In churches?

Special Notes

1. The question mark is sometimes used to express doubt or irony

by indicating the questionableness of a fact, but in such instances it does not function as a mark of punctuation, only as a
symbolic commentary.

Example 1   The impartial (?) witness asserted that the traffic
signal was red, not amber [an obvious and amateur-
ish usage].

Example 2   Walther von der Vogelweide (1170?–1230?), a German minnesinger, appears as a character in Wag-
ner's *Tannhäuser.*

2. The question mark is placed inside or outside quotation marks,
depending upon the context.

Example 1   We were assigned Gilbert Highet's "What Use Is
Poetry?"

Example 2   Have you read King's "Letter from Birmingham Jail"?

11 Exclamation point

The exclamation point, despite its intention to express surprise,
strong feeling, and drama, is a strikingly ineffectual mark of punctuation.
The very fact that the context often contains the feeling makes the exclamation point almost a superfluous mark. We may best think of it as an
intensifier, but using two or three exclamation points does not necessarily
have more effect than using one. Like the question mark, the exclamation
point seems to reach its full potential as an isolated symbol in cartoons
and comic strips that depend heavily upon contrivances to express strong
feelings in a limited space.

Separating at the End of a Thought

A. To indicate strong feelings, usually surprise, alarm, disbelief, or
special emphasis.

Example   "That is why those nuclear scientists passed on their
knowledge to Russia, not because they were 'spies'
but because that was their idea of how to keep
peace!"

Karl Shapiro
"Why Out-Russia Russia?"

The exclamation point is placed inside or outside the quotation marks, depending upon the context.

12 Hyphen

The potential of the hyphen is consistently underestimated. It is truly a word-making mark, a device that facilitates inventiveness. If the language provides no word accurate enough to suit a writer's purposes, he can coin one. The hyphen therefore serves temporary needs because many coinages will never be repeated, but it also gives full-time service in established forms like *ex-President, President-elect, self-employed,* and *mother-of-pearl.* Many words that were hyphenated yesterday are written as one today (*to-day* is itself an example). Thus the use of the hyphen varies from time to time. Dictionaries, although they necessarily lag behind current usage (see entries on *teenager* and *lovingkindness*), are at least one source of information about the hyphenated state of words.

Separating Internally

A. To indicate syllabication of words, particularly at the end of a typewritten line: scan-dal-ous.
B. To form compounds and special coinages: Afro-Asian, self-conscious, also-ran, ah-ah-ah-ah-tommy-gun effect.

Indicating Omission

C. To indicate an omitted prefix (-tion) or suffix (anti-).

13 Apostrophe

In fifty or seventy-five years, someone may be able to write a study of the decline and fall of the apostrophe. But since the fall has not yet occurred, careful writers continue their allegiance to a tradition that likes the kind of distinction that can be made between *horses, horse's,* and *horses',* all of which are audibly identical. "We watched the horses pace" is completely ambiguous if the writer intends *horses* to be a singular or plural possessive. "Michelangelos paintings are turbulent" is unambiguous, but "We observed the artists interest" is not. Omitting the apostrophe may get by in certain contexts, but in others the meaning may not get through. The possibility of error argues for the consistent use of the apostrophe.

Contractions are another angle of the problem. Even though it is impossible to misread *cant* (a word that has a meaning of its own) in a sentence like "I cant go," the appearance of a familiar word instead of *can't* is disconcerting. The same is true of *we'll* and *won't*, which become *well* and *wont* when the apostrophe is dropped. Bernard Shaw tried to effect some change in the use of the apostrophe by eliminating it from selected contracted forms. But his practice is puzzling. He consistently eliminates the apostrophe from *not*-contractions (*dont, wouldnt, mustnt*) and *is*-contractions (*heres, whats, lets*), but unexplainably writes *I'm, she's,* and *he'd,* but *youll* and *youre*. Shaw has not won many imitators. In fact, his efforts to reform punctuation have had little influence upon an entrenched tradition. But the impersonal forces of ignorance and carelessness wear it away.

Separating within a Sentence

A. To separate the plural markers of letters, numbers, and words used as words: *1*'s, 2's, *and* 's.

Indicating Omission

B. To indicate omitted letters in possessive forms (remnant of Middle English, which did not use the apostrophe): soul's (ME: soules), Venus'.

C. To indicate omitted letters in contractions: I'm, you're, he'd, Xerox'd.

Special Note

The most basic principle of forming the singular apostrophe is to add *'s,* with the option of omitting the *s* if the word ends in *s*. Thus,

Charles Dickens's novel

or

Charles Dickens' novel

The first step in forming the plural apostrophe is to write the plural form of the word: frame/frames, tax/taxes, woman/women, alumnus/ alumni. Then proceed to step two: if the word ends in *s,* add an apostrophe; if it doesn't end in *s,* add *'s.* Thus the possessive forms of the words above would appear as follows: frames', taxes', women's, alumni's.

14 Italicizing

Underscoring in written and typed copy may seem to be a form of punctuation, but it is actually a copy-editing device to indicate to the printer that particular words should be set in italics. In the sense that italics set off material for special attention, they may be said to have a separating or enclosing function similar to that of punctuation. Unless italics are used to indicate *emphasis,* they have no special rhetorical force. Even then, if they are *overused* for emphasis, they defeat their own purpose. The other uses are conventional.

A. To designate the titles of books, magazines, plays, musical works, movies, ships, and aircraft: *Nostromo, Time, Macbeth, La Boheme.*

B. To indicate foreign words and phrases: *joie de vivre, Weltschmerz.* [Foreign phrases that become thoroughly Anglicized are no longer italicized. Such abbreviations of foreign words as *etc., i.e.,* and *e.g.* are in a state of transition.]

C. To indicate a word used as a word.

Example   The plural of *cow* is *cows,* but the plural of *beef* is *beefs* or *beeves.*

D. To emphasize words or a complete sentence within the text.

Example   "Now, as a matter of fact, *to speak without thinking of the forms of language* is exactly what the boy should have done."

Charles C. Fries
The Teaching of the English Language

15 Capitalizing

Like periods and commas, capital letters are such a familiar part of manuscript form that deviations from the norm, either by omitting them when they are ordinarily expected or by adding them when they are not, become a rhetorical feature of style. Eccentricities of capitalization may be found in informal writing (chiefly by omitting), in grandiloquent writing (chiefly by adding), and in imaginative writing (by doing either), but seldom in the conservative Plain Style.

Eliminating capitals à la e. e. cummings has now become a conventional kind of nonconformity. Experimenting with typography, as Dos Passos does in *U.S.A.*, is ingenious, but ultimately more eye-catching than mind-engaging. A writer may attract attention by superficial devices, but he is not likely to sustain attention in that way. Every day in writing cannot be July 4.

Capitals are used:

A. To mark the first word of a sentence.

B. To designate that something has a name peculiarly its own, including the names of people, places, organizations, holidays, treaties, courses, books, special terms, et cetera: First Congregational Church, Magna Carta, Memorial Day, Introduction to English Literature, "The Notorious Jumping Frog of Calaveras County," the Life Force. Adjective forms derived from proper nouns are also capitalized: Algerian, Parisian, Byzantine. [The first word and all principal words of a title are capitalized. Articles (*a, an, the*) and conjunctions and prepositions of five or fewer letters are usually not capitalized.]

C. To dignify titles or references to the deity: Professor Padelford, His Excellency, God in His glory.

D. To personify.

Example   "And we are now men, and must accept in the highest ·
mind the same transcendent destiny; and not pinched
in a corner, not cowards fleeing before a revolution,
but redeemers and benefactors, pious aspirants to be
noble clay under the Almighty effort let us advance
on Chaos and the Dark."

Ralph Waldo Emerson
"Self-reliance"

Summary chart

1 Period

A. To end sentences or fragments
B. To separate figures
C. To serve as a typographical aid
D. To indicate abbreviations

2 Comma

A. To separate main clauses joined by *and, but, or, for, nor, yet*
B. To separate elements in series
C. To separate tags
D. To separate clusters of words indicating levels of generality
E. To separate parts of addresses, dates, numbers
F. To enclose nonrestrictive interrupters
G. To separate introductory elements
H. To indicate omission of words

3 Semicolon

A. To separate main clauses without connectives or with connectives like *however, moreover, otherwise*
B. To separate clusters of words containing internal punctuation

4 Colon

A. To separate two closely related parts of a sentence
B. To separate conventional references to parts of plays, time, the Bible, subtitles, and publishing information
C. To introduce quotations
D. To introduce lists of explanatory material
E. To indicate the omission of words

5 Dash

A. To substitute loosely for period or semicolon
B. To anticipate a summary remark
C. To indicate a break in thought
D. To pick up a suspended word or phrase
E. To enclose parenthetical remarks
F. To indicate an incomplete utterance

6 Parentheses

A. To enclose helpful information
B. To interpolate asides

7 Square brackets

A. To enclose an editorial interpolation, particularly in a quotation
B. To enclose parentheses within parentheses

8 Ellipsis

A. To indicate the omission of words

9 Quotation marks

A. To enclose quotations
B. To enclose titles of poems, paintings, and parts of books
C. To qualify meaning in a particular context

10 Question mark

A. To mark the end of a question or to express doubt or irony

11 Exclamation point

A. To indicate strong feeling

12 Hyphen

A. To indicate syllabication
B. To form compounds
C. To indicate an omitted prefix or suffix

13 Apostrophe

A. To mark plurals of letters, numbers, and words used as words
B. To indicate possessive form
C. To indicate contractions

14 Italics

A. To designate titles
B. To indicate foreign words and phrases
C. To indicate a word used as a word
D. To emphasize

15 Capitalization

A. To mark the first word of a sentence
B. To designate proper nouns
C. To dignify titles and reference to the deity
D. To personify

SPELLING

It is not my intention in this book to treat the problem of misspelling, only to comment briefly upon it as a factor in writing effectiveness. Misspelling at the college level is serious, not because it outweighs ideas, form, diction, and style in importance, but simply because it is an elementary matter that we associate with the early stages of learning English. Nothing creates an impression of illiteracy more quickly than gross misspelling. To make a categorical statement of this kind is not to ignore that many bright people have chronic spelling problems. But the fact of their misfortune does not condone misspelling or make it more palatable to readers. Nor do recognized variants justify inventing new ones.

Our normal expectation, at least in picking up any professional publication, is to be able to read it for meaning and effect, not to proof-read it for errors. If errors are numerous, we have reason to suspect the general quality of workmanship. An educated reader can no more over-look misspellings than he can ignore a squeaking chair. Both are annoying and distracting. Incorrect spelling therefore invites censure, although correct spelling deserves no special praise. A desire for correctness merely reflects an attitude that is basic to the whole area of mechanics: they must be thought of as working *for* the writing, not against it.

DOCUMENTING

I see no particular reason why anyone needs to work up an enthusiasm for documentation; all that is needed is an attitude of acceptance. Documentation is one of the prosaic tasks of scholarship. Its justification is that it works, that is, if it is not overdone. It is certainly overdone any time the footnotes take up more space than the text.

Footnotes and bibliography give information that people often want and need. For the sake of completeness and orderliness, the forms have been standardized, but not inflexibly, because they vary from discipline to discipline and occasionally within a discipline. For convenient reference, footnote and bibliographical forms are listed in Appendix C. Unless a student is an English major, the forms given are best followed as models, not memorized, because a history professor or a science professor will recommend different ones.

Rather consistently, students will come up with examples for which the manuals do not provide models. In such cases, the writer is free to invent his own form, providing information that usually makes a reference accessible to the reader. In general, however, most of the practices of documentation are standardized.

1. Footnote numbers in the text come at the end of the passage that is being cited. Footnotes should be included at the bottom of the

page on which the reference is made, unless all footnotes are grouped at the end of the essay or chapter or book.

2. The first reference to a source supplies full information according to the models below. For subsequent references, see secondary footnote references in Appendix C.

3. Footnotes may be numbered consecutively throughout an essay, or the numbering may begin again with "1" on each page. The former practice is more common.

4. Bibliographies are arranged in alphabetical order by the author's name. If several works by one author are listed, his name is not repeated; a line is drawn. It is often customary to separate books and periodicals.

SUGGESTIONS FOR DISCUSSION

1. If we consider indentation (paragraphing) as a mark of punctuation, what functions does it share with other marks of punctuation?

2. After doing one or two of the assignments given below, what conclusions can you draw about the use or misuse of punctuation? Specifically, what is misuse?

3. Explain what "the rhetorical use of punctuation" means. To what extent is it personal?

ASSIGNMENTS

1. All the following sentences can be punctuated differently, possibly more conventionally, by adding, omitting, or substituting marks of punctuation. Repunctuate the sentences. Then determine whether you have altered the effect that the writer has produced.

A. He has changed the Know Nothings' emphasis: instead of wanting to exclude the immigrant, he wishes to take him in and to propose a common ideal of disinterested public service.

Edmund Wilson

B. In South Africa, the English, it is said, are against the Afrikaner; both are against the Jews; all three are opposed to the Indians; while all four conspire against the native black.

Gordon W. Allport

C. When Picasso decides to disregard the laws of perspective, that means that he has passed through and beyond a certain technique—unlike the Egyptian painter, who has never acquired it.

Arthur Koestler

D. Since the grandchildren will face stiffer competition in terms of formal educational credentials, this penny-pinching view (sometimes abetted by local commerce and industry) simply kicks away a ladder to mobility which the new generation needs if it is to keep step with the rising educational and living standards of the country as a whole.

David Riesman

E. Persecuted by the Reds because he was a bourgeois; by the Whites because he was Trotsky's father, and deserted by his son, he was left to sink or swim in the Russian deluge, and swam on steadfastly to the end.

Winston Churchill

F. We crossed the street together, some of the girls in bright evening gowns and some in tweeds, Louis Aragon slim and dignified in a dinner jacket, Laurence bareheaded and wearing a raincoat which he never removed in the course of the hot starlit night, myself coatless, dressed in a workman's blue shirt, worn trousers and rope-soled shoes.

Malcolm Cowley

G. It offers them not rebellion but vicarious satisfaction, and therefore it is a kind of narcotic bolshevism as distinguished from the stimulant bolshevism that Lenin preached.

Walter Lippmann

H. The public instinctively, or let us say by a sentiment as deep as consciousness and probably deeper, rejects the hypothesis that to witness a fictional representation on the screen is to be tempted or stimulated to action.

Bernard De Voto

I. It is not unreal; where it confronts you, you really perceive it, you don't dream or imagine that you do.

Susanne K. Langer

J. He climbs trees with his fins and pursues insects; he snaps worms like a robin on the tide flats; he sees as land things see, and above all he dodges and evades with a curious popeyed insolence more suggestive of the land than of the sea.

Loren Eiseley

2. Many passages of nineteenth-century prose reflect practices of punctuation different from current practices. Below are three paragraphs by nineteenth-century writers with all punctuation (except apostrophes) and most capital letters removed. Repunctuate the paragraphs, not as you think Macaulay, Hazlitt, or Ruskin would have punctuated them, but as you would if you were writing their sentences. The original versions are given in Appendix B. Compare the changes in meaning and effect. To what conclusions about punctuation does an exercise of this kind lead you? Is it possible to reproduce someone else's punctuation exactly?

A. while he was thus irregularly educating himself his family was sinking into hopeless poverty old Michael Johnson was much better qualified to pore upon books and to talk about them than to trade in them his business declined his debts increased it was with difficulty that the daily expenses of his household were defrayed it was out of his power to support his son at either university but a wealthy neighbour offered assistance and in reliance on promises which proved to be of very little value Samuel was entered at Pembroke College Oxford when the young scholar presented himself to the rulers of that society they were amazed not more by his ungainly figure and eccentric manners than by the quantity of extensive and curious information which he had picked up during many months of desultory but not unprofitable study on the first day of his residence he surprised his teachers by quoting Macrobius and one of the most learned among them declared that he had never known a freshman of equal attainments.

B. the great leading distinction between writing and speaking is
that more time is allowed for the one than the other and hence
different faculties are required for and different objects attained
by each he is properly the best speaker who can collect together
the greatest number of apposite ideas at a moment's warning
he is properly the best writer who can give utterance to the
greatest quantity of valuable knowledge in the course of his
whole life the chief requisite for the one then appears to be
quickness and facility of perception for the other patience of
soul and a power increasing with the difficulties it has to master
he cannot be denied to be an expert speaker a lively companion
who is never at a loss for something to say on every occasion
or subject that offers he by the same rule will make a respectable writer who by dint of study can find out any thing good
to say upon any one point that has not been touched upon before or who by asking for time can give the most complete and
comprehensive view of any question the one must be done off
hand at a single blow the other can only be done by a repetition
of blows by having time to think and do better in speaking less
is required of you if you only do it at once with grace and spirit
in writing you stipulate for all that you are capable of but you
have the choice of your own time and subject you do not expect from the manufacturer the same dispatch in executing an
order that you do from the shopkeeper or warehouseman the
difference of *quicker* and *slower* however is not all that is merely
a difference of comparison in doing the same thing but the
writer and speaker have to do things essentially different besides habit and greater or less facility there is also a certain
reach of capacity a certain depth or shallowness grossness or
refinement of intellect which marks out the distinction between
those whose chief ambition is to shine by producing an immediate effect or who are thrown back by a natural bias on the
severer researches of thought and study.

C. all these pleasures then and all these virtues I repeat you nationally despise you have indeed men among you who do not
by whose work by whose strength by whose life by whose death

you live and never thank them your wealth your amusement your pride would all be alike impossible but for those whom you scorn or forget the policeman who is walking up and down the black lane all night to watch the guilt you have created there and may have his brains beaten out and be maimed for life at any moment and never be thanked the sailor wrestling with the sea's rage the quiet student poring over his book or his vial the common worker without praise and nearly without bread fulfiling his task as your horses drag your carts hopeless and spurned of all these are the men by whom England lives but they are not the nation they are only the body and nervous force of it acting still from old habit in a convulsive perseverance while the mind is gone our national wish and purpose are to be amused our national religion is the performance of church ceremonies and preaching of soporific truths or untruths to keep the mob quietly at work while we amuse ourselves and the necessity for this amusement is fastening on us as a feverous disease of parched throat and wandering eyes senseless dissolute and merciless.

A

Appendix

OUTLINING

The test of a good outline is the extent to which it reveals the substance and form of an essay in a relatively brief space. If the form of the outline is skeletal, the reader may be able to perceive the pattern of organization at a glance.

The examples below represent two types of outlining, the topic outline and the sentence outline. Both are outlines of chap. II of Herbert J. Muller's *Issues of Freedom: Paradoxes and Promises* (New York: Harper & Brothers, Publishers, 1960), pp. 21–37. Anything more extended than these forms would represent a paraphrase, not an outline.

These outlines show the orderly manner in which Muller has developed a difficult subject. The conclusion of the chapter is contained in two sentences of the final paragraph, not appended as a separate section as the outline might suggest.

TOPIC OUTLINE

THE NATURE OF MAN

Main Idea: Assumptions about man that one can demonstrate—that he is a social animal, a culture-building animal, and an animal with a distinctive capacity for individuality—lead to the conclusion that man has need for freedom of mind and spirit.

   I. The traditional, undemonstrable assumption about man: his dualistic nature

  II. The demonstrable assumptions about the nature of man on the basis of reliable knowledge in history and science

    A. Man as an animal: basic drives and appetites

    B. Man as a social animal

      1. Sociality the natural state of man

      2. Conformism and individualism both products of society

    C. Man as a culture-building animal: result of his capacity to reason

    D. Man as a self-conscious individual: concept of the individual as an end in himself

 III. The inter-relationship of the individual, society, and the issue of freedom

A. Individual differences responsible for progress in society
B. Man's ambivalent attitudes toward his own freedom
  1. Man's conflict between security and the demands of freedom
  2. Man's resentment of bondage
  3. Man's tendency to accept what he has experienced
Conclusion: Freedom is the way of life that allows man best to realize his potentialities and latent powers of choice.

SENTENCE OUTLINE

THE NATURE OF MAN

Main Idea: Assumptions about man that one can demonstrate—that he is a social animal, a culture-building animal, and an animal with a distinctive capacity for individuality—lead to the conclusion that man has need for freedom of mind and spirit.

I. The oldest concept of man as both flesh and spirit cannot be demonstrated.

II. On the basis of history and science, certain objective statements can be made about the nature of man.
  A. He is an animal with basic drives and appetites.
  B. He is a social animal.
    1. History confirms his natural sociality.
    2. Man's conformism and individualism are both social products.
  C. He is a culture-building animal because of his powers of mind.
  D. He is a self-conscious individual, demanding freedom, as a result of his culture.

III. The importance of the individual in society must not be ignored.
  A. Individual differences are responsible for whatever progress has been made in society.
  B. Man's attitude toward freedom in society is ambivalent.
    1. The majority of men may find the demands of freedom burdensome.

2. Even though men may not have a passion for freedom, they do resent bondage.

3. Men who have known freedom cling to it.

Conclusion: Freedom is the way of life that allows man best to realize his potentialities and latent powers of choice.

B

Appendix

PUNCTUATION IN NINETEENTH
CENTURY PROSE

See Assignment 2, pages 224–226.

A. While he was thus irregularly educating himself, his family was sinking into hopeless poverty. Old Michael Johnson was much better qualified to pore upon books, and to talk about them, than to trade in them. His business declined: his debts increased: it was with difficulty that the daily expenses of his household were defrayed. It was out of his power to support his son at either university; but a wealthy neighbour offered assistance; and, in reliance on promises which proved to be of very little value, Samuel was entered at Pembroke College, Oxford. When the young scholar presented himself to the rulers of that society, they were amazed not more by his ungainly figure and eccentric manners than by the quantity of extensive and curious information which he had picked up during many months of desultory, but not unprofitable study. On the first day of his residence he surprised his teachers by quoting Macrobius; and one of the most learned among them declared, that he had never known a freshman of equal attainments.

Thomas B. Macaulay from "Samuel Johnson"

B. The great leading distinction between writing and speaking is, that more time is allowed for the one than the other: and hence different faculties are required for, and different objects attained by, each. He is properly the best speaker who can collect together the greatest number of apposite ideas at a moment's warning: he is properly the best writer who can give utterance to the greatest quantity of valuable knowledge in the course of his whole life. The chief requisite for the one, then, appears to be quickness and facility of perception—for the other, patience of soul, and a power increasing with the difficulties it has to master. He cannot be denied to be an expert speaker, a lively companion, who is never at a loss for something to say on every occasion or subject that offers: he, by the same rule, will make a respectable writer, who, by dint of study, can find out any thing good to say upon any one point that has not been touched upon before, or who, by asking for time, can give the most complete and comprehensive view of any question. The one must be done off-hand, at a single blow: the other can only be done by a repetition of blows, by having time to think and do better. In speaking, less is required of you, if you only do it at once, with grace and spirit: in writing, you stipulate for all that you are capable of, but you have the choice of your own time and subject. You do not expect from the manufacturer the same dispatch in executing an order that you do from the shop-keeper or warehouseman. The difference of *quicker* and *slower,* however, is not all: that is merely a difference of comparison in doing the same thing. But the writer and speaker have to do things essentially different. Besides habit, and greater or less facility, there is also a certain reach of capacity, a certain depth or shallowness, grossness or refinement of intellect, which marks out the distinction between those whose chief ambition is to shine by producing an immediate effect, or who are thrown back, by a natural bias, on the severer researches of thought and study.

> William Hazlitt from "On the Difference
> between Writing and Speaking"

C. All these pleasures, then, and all these virtues, I repeat, you nationally despise. You have, indeed, men among you who do not; by whose work, by whose strength, by whose life, by whose death, you live, and never thank them. Your wealth, your amusement, your pride, would all be alike impossible, but for those whom you scorn or forget. The policeman, who is walking up and down the black lane all night to watch the guilt you have created there, and may have his brains beaten out, and be maimed for life, at any moment, and never be thanked; the sailor wrestling with the sea's rage; the quiet student poring over his book or his vial; the common worker, without praise, and nearly without bread, fulfilling his task as your horses drag your carts, hopeless, and spurned of all; these are the men by whom England lives; but they are not the nation; they are only the body and nervous force of it, acting still from old habit in a convulsive perseverance, while the mind is gone. Our National wish and purpose are to be amused; our National religion is the performance of church ceremonies, and preaching of soporific truths (or untruths) to keep the mob quietly at work, while we amuse ourselves; and the necessity for this amusement is fastening on us as a feverous disease of parched throat and wandering eyes—senseless, dissolute, merciless.

> John Ruskin from "Sesame and Lilies"

Appendix

FOOTNOTES &
BIBLIOGRAPHICAL FORMS

For convenience, footnote and bibliography forms are given for each reference. In most details, footnote forms follow *The MLA Style Sheet;* bibliography forms, The University of Chicago Press *A Manual of Style* (11th ed., 1949). For reference purposes, citations of various kinds have been labeled and arranged in alphabetical order.

Anonymous Article

Footnote: [1] "Devotional Poetry: Donne to Wesley," *TLS,* Dec. 24, 1938, p. 814.

Bibliography: "Devotional Poetry: Donne to Wesley." *Times Literary Supplement,* December 24, 1938, p. 814.

Anonymous Manual

Footnote: [2] *Getting Around in Your University Library* (Tucson, n.d.), p. 8.

Bibliography: Getting Around in Your University Library. Tucson, Arizona: University of Arizona Library, n.d.

Article

Footnote: [3] James Holly Hanford, "The Debate of Heart and Eye," *MLN,* XXVI (1911), 163.

[When the volume number is given, the symbol for page is dropped.]

Bibliography: Hanford, James Holly. "The Debate of Heart and Eye," *Modern Language Notes,* XXVI (1911), 161–65.

[Bibliographical reference gives inclusive page numbers of entire article. If a periodical has separate pagination for each issue, then the month must be given: (November, 1929).]

Article, in Collaboration

Footnote: [4] Warren Spahn, in collaboration with Bill Fay, "You Can Fool Some of the Hitters All of the Time," *Collier's,* CXXXVI (July 22, 1955), 64.

Bibliography: Spahn, Warren, in collaboration with Bill Fay. "You Can Fool Some of the Hitters All of the Time," *Collier's,* CXXXVI (July 22, 1955), 62–65.

Article, No Volume Number

Footnote: 5 "Realism at Bargaining Table," *Business Week,* November 26, 1955, p. 164.

[Bibliographical reference follows the same form, but furnishes the inclusive page numbers of the article. See footnote 3 and corresponding bibliographical entry.]

Article, Reprinted in an Edited Collection

Footnote: 6 Thomas Wheeler, "Milton's Twenty-Third Sonnet," in *Milton: Modern Essays in Criticism,* ed. Arthur E. Barker (New York, 1965), p. 138.

Bibliography: Wheeler, Thomas. "Milton's Twenty-Third Sonnet," in *Milton: Modern Essays in Criticism.* Edited by Arthur E. Barker. New York: Oxford University Press, 1965, pp. 136–41.

Authorship, Multiple (See footnote 17 and corresponding bibliographical entry)

Biblical Reference

Footnote: 7 Gen. 1:1.

[The Bible ordinarily is not listed in a bibliography unless the paper concerns various translations.]

Book

Footnote: 8 John Beresford, *Gossip of the Seventeenth and Eighteenth Centuries* (London, 1923), p. 14.

Bibliography: Beresford, John. *Gossip of the Seventeenth and Eighteenth Centuries.* London: Cobden-Sanderson, 1923.

Book, Edited (See also footnote 17 and corresponding bibliographical entry.)

Footnote: 9 *The Paradise of Dainty Devices 1576–1606,* ed. Hyder E. Rollins (Cambridge, 1927), p. 56.

Bibliography: Rollins, Hyder E. (ed.). *The Paradise of Dainty Devices 1576–1606.* Cambridge: Harvard University Press, 1927.

Book, Introduction to

Footnote: [10] Sidney Lee, Introduction to *Elizabethan Sonnets* (Westminster, 1904), I, xiii.

Bibliography: Elizabethan Sonnets. Edited with an introduction by Sidney Lee. Vol. I. Westminster: Archibald Constable and Co., Ltd., 1904.

[This is a two-volume work. The entry indicates that only vol. I was used by the author citing the work. If both volumes had been used, "2 vols." would appear in the bibliographical entry where "Vol. I." appears.]

Book, in a Series

Footnote: [11] Ruth Kelso, *The Doctrine of the English Gentleman in the Sixteenth Century,* University of Illinois Studies in Language and Literature, XIV (Urbana, 1929), p. 167.

Bibliography: Kelso, Ruth. *The Doctrine of the English Gentleman in the Sixteenth Century.* ("University of Illinois Studies in Language and Literature," Vol. XIV.) Urbana: University of Illinois Press, 1929.

Book, More Than One Volume

Footnote: [12] *Literary History of the United States,* eds. Robert E. Spiller *et al.* (3rd ed. rev.; New York, 1963), I, 353.

Bibliography: Spiller, Robert E., *et al.* (eds.). *Literary History of the United States.* 2 vols. 3rd edition revised. New York: The Macmillan Co., 1963.

[This entry indicates that both volumes were used. See bibliographical entry following footnote 10 for entry if only one volume is used.]

Book, Part of a (See also footnotes 6 and 10 and corresponding bibliographical entries)

Footnote: [13] F. W. Moorman, "Cavalier Lyrists," *The Cam-bridge History of English Literature,* eds. A. W. Ward and A. R. Waller (Cambridge, 1911), VII, 28.

Bibliography: Moorman, F. W. "Cavalier Lyrists," *The Cambridge History of English Literature.* Edited by A. W. Ward and A. R. Waller. Vol. VII. Cambridge: Cambridge University Press, 1911, pp. 1–29.

Book, Translated

Footnote: [14] Baldesar Castiglione, *The Book of the Courtier,* tr. Leonard E. Opdycke (New York, 1903), p. 14.

Bibliography: Castiglione, Baldesar. *The Book of the Courtier.* Translated by Leonard E. Opdycke. New York: Charles Scribner's Sons, 1903.

Documents

Because of the great variety of information in documents issued by the courts and legislatures, the best guide is to give as much information as may be necessary to identify the document properly and permit the reader to locate it if he wishes. The card catalogue will usually indicate essential information.

Footnote: [15] Trial Brief (Thomas Miller *et al.,* Plaintiffs, vs. Lake Washington School District, No. 414, Defendants), Superior Court of the State of Washington, King County, No. 674155, p. 3.

[The bibliographical entry would add the total page numbers: 22 pp.]

Drama

Footnote: [16] *Othello* III. iii. 157.

Bibliography: The *Complete Works of Shakespeare.* Edited by George Lyman Kittredge. Boston: Ginn and Co., 1936.

[If variant texts of a play exist, it is customary to indicate the edition in the first footnote reference and list it in the bibliography.]

Editorship, Multiple

Footnote: [17] Henry A. Pochmann and Gay Wilson Allen, eds., *Masters of American Literature* (New York, 1948), I, 512.

Bibliography: Pochmann, Henry A., and Gay Wilson Allen (eds.). *Masters of American Literature.* Vol. I. New York: The Macmillan Co., 1949.

[Compare footnotes 9 and 17. Footnote 9 would document a poem in Rollins's collection; footnote 17 would document a comment in prefatory remarks by the editors.

When authorship or editorship is multiple, it is customary to list the names in the order given on the title page, whether or not they are in alphabetical order. For more than three editors, see footnote 12 and corresponding bibliographical entry; for multiple authorship, drop the designation "eds."]

Encyclopedia

Footnote: [18] *The Reader's Encyclopaedia* (1948), III, 805.

[The bibliographical reference would add inclusive page numbers if the article covered more than one page. It is customary not to list editors and publishing information concerning fairly standard reference works.]

Encyclopedia, Special Edition

Footnote: [19] "Rome," *Encyclopaedia Britannica,* 11th ed., XXIII, 598.

Bibliography: "Rome," *Encyclopaedia Britannica* (11th ed.), XXIII, 584–684.

Newspaper

Footnote: [20] *New York Times,* July 2, 1967, Section 1, p. 12.

[The bibliographical entry is the same.]

Quotation Taken from Secondary Source

Footnote: [21] Francis Meres, *Palladis Tamia,* as quoted in G. B. Harrison, *Introducing Shakespeare* (New York, 1947), p. 2.

[Harrison would be listed in the bibliography only if other references were made to the book.]

Secondary Footnote References

Footnote: [22] Beresford, p. 16.
[Second reference to book cited in footnote 8.]

Footnote: [23] *Ibid.,* p. 18.
[*Ibid.* is used to refer to a reference immediately preceding, in this case to Beresford.]

Footnote: [24] Lee, *Elizabethan Sonnets,* I, xii.
[If two books by Lee have been used, each must be identified by a short title, not the author's name alone.]

Footnote: [25] *Ibid.,* II, 14.
[Same reference, different volume.]

Footnote: [26] Lee, *Shakespeare,* p. 16.
[The short title identifies a different book by Lee.]

Unpublished Material

Footnote: [27] Seymour Brick, "Eugene O'Neill: The Deterioration of a Dramatist" (Unpubl. Master's Thesis, Dept. of English, University of Arizona, 1935), p. 45.

Bibliography: Brick, Seymour. "Eugene O'Neill: The Deterioration of a Dramatist." Unpublished Master's Thesis, Department of English, University of Arizona, 1935.

SAMPLE BIBLIOGRAPHY

Hanford, James Holly. "The Debate of Heart and Eye," *Modern Language Notes,* XXVI (1911), 161–65.

Kelso, Ruth. *The Doctrine of the English Gentleman in the Sixteenth*

Century. ("University of Illinois Studies in Language and Literature," Vol. XIV.) Urbana: University of Illinois Press, 1929.
Lee, Sidney. Introduction to *Elizabethan Sonnets*. Vol. I. Westminster: Archibald Constable and Co., Ltd., 1904.
————. *A Life of William Shakespeare*. 6th ed. London: Smith, Elder and Co., 1908.
Merrill, Robert V. "Platonism in Petrarch's *Canzoniere*." *Modern Philology*, XXVII (November, 1929), 170–73.

ABBREVIATIONS COMMONLY USED IN NOTES

c., ca. (*circa*)	about
cf. *(confer)*	compare
chap., chaps.	chapter, chapters
cp.	compare
ed., eds.	edited by, editor, editors
et al. (*et alii*)	and others
f., ff.	and the following page(s) or line(s)
ibid. (*ibidem*)	in the same place
il.	illustrated
l., ll.	line, lines
loc. cit. (*loco citato*)	in the place cited
ms., mss.	manuscript, manuscripts
n.	note, footnote
n.d.	no date of publication
n.p.	no place of publication
n.s.	new series
op. cit. (*opere citato*)	in the work cited
p., pp.	page, pages
rev. ed.	revised edition
tr., trans.	translated by
vol., vols.	volume, volumes

Index

NAME & SOURCE

Student writers are not indexed.

Index

SUBJECT